THE WORD

Jewish Wisdom Through Time

THE
WORD

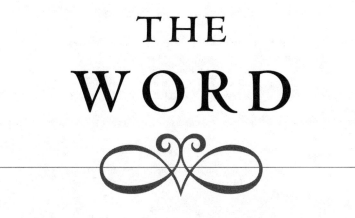

Jewish Wisdom Through Time

A SPIRITUAL SOURCEBOOK

Noah benShea

Villard
New York
1995

Library of Congress Cataloging-in-Publication Data

The Word : Jewish wisdom through time : a spiritual sourcebook /
[compiled] by Noah benShea
p. cm.
ISBN 0-679-42584-5
1. Jews—Quotations. 2. Judaism—Quotations, maxims, etc.
3. Spiritual life—Judaism—Quotations, maxims, etc. 4. Proverbs,
Jewish. I. benShea, Noah.
PN6095.J4W65 1995
296.1—dc20   95-5649

Manufactured in the United States of America on acid-free paper
9 8 7 6 5 4 3 2
First Edition
Book design by JoAnne Metsch

This Book Is Dedicated to
Jordan Arin and Adam Joseph

דור לדור

Hear the word . . .

—Isaiah 1:10

A WORD ON HOW TO USE
THE WORD

THE WORD IS WRITTEN FOR THOSE WHO KNOW A LITTLE AND WANT TO know more. It is also written for those who know a great deal and wish to discover more. This book is for religious scholars, seekers, rabbis, or families. It is for anyone who has a question or a problem, for any soul-searching comfort, practicalities, or a point of view that makes you laugh at what was once troubling you. *The Word* is for those on a path of spiritual renewal who wish to again touch a faith they were born into but have yet to embrace, or for any who embraced at one time a childhood faith and want to connect again with the wisdom behind that faith. It is a book for those who have lost touch, were never in touch, or rejected the embrace of Judaism as well as for those who are not Jewish but have always wondered: "What do Jews think?"

The Word is intended to serve the spirit while providing a reference source. The chapters and information have been organized so the material might be read from beginning to end, with the author's hope that embracing the work in this way is as transforming as it is edifying.

The book is also organized so the reader may, with some ease, begin anywhere and pursue a macro- or microsubject, discovering in brief quotes and stories what scriptural sources, great minds, and engaging wits have to say. However you travel through *The Word* you will soon discover thoughts from three thousand years ago alongside ideas from seven hundred years ago reconsidered by a Nobel Prize winner from thirty years ago. This layering of ideas through time also allows the reader to observe the maturation of an idea and to witness how growth is not always nurtured by agreement. Finally, the wisdom herein is from the sources themselves. It is an opportunity to lift the albeit often enlightened veil of those who would tell you what you ought to think about what others said.

In order that this book might function at supplemental levels and be of even greater service and strength for the reader, following the main text is an "Index of Biographical and Scriptural Descriptions," offering the reader's curiosity detailed information on any person or source quoted. This index is complemented by a "Time Chart of Jewish History and Surrounding Events, 2000 B.C.E.—Mid–Twentieth Century C.E.," so that with reference to any idea or person the reader may discover what other events, inside and outside of the Jewish realm, were going on in the world at that time. And all of this is supported by a "Selected Bibliography of Basic Texts and Further Spiritual Reading," affording direction on any subject or idea that attracts the reader's interest. Lastly, there is a general index offering the reader ready access to the broad range of *The Word*.

A WORD BEFORE
THE WORD

MY GRANDFATHER JACOB USED TO SAY THAT A MAN LEARNS AND learns and still dies a fool. Consequently, after a lifetime of reading and reflection, I still find it uncomfortable to come to you in this book posed as a scholar. Instead, I more simply arrive at these pages as a man who loves the learning and wisdom of his people. And as a poet.

Tied to this is my long-held conviction that poets are not so much people who write poetry as those who discover poetry in the world surrounding them. Such people pluck pieces of dialogue and incident as if they are pulling notes from midair, and in their rearranged placement allow us to hear the greater truth in the composition of experience.

It is in this process that I conceived of this book. My aim has been to uncover and recover the wisdom in the broad and profound minds of our people and our God. The journey of this effort has been as personal as it has been moving. It has taken my mind and my soul around the world and across time.

While researching this project, it was not unusual for me to find myself sitting in the predawn morning with a blanket on my lap attending my *minyan,* my prayer group, and serving as its recording secretary. Included in this circle, long hidden or ignored or studied only by the erudite, might be a seventeenth-century Hebrew cabbalist, a second-century martyred rabbi, a nineteenth-century British wit. As I gathered their words for these pages, I could feel ancient souls stir to life. My hope is that this connection becomes part of your experience, that once or twice you will take an obscure name whose mind moves you and find out more about this person, perhaps become more of a person yourself in the process.

The work in front of you is a mix of wit, pain, brilliance, and pathos, much of it stirred by humor. Too often the first thing people lose when they want to be taken seriously is their sense of humor, and though this book should be taken seriously, we are a people who understand that sometimes laughter is the best way to cry.

Criteria for material to be admitted to this collection were limited first by my ignorance, and although it is impossible for any work of this kind to be all-inclusive, I apologize to you for the absent giants I was too small to see. Additionally, my bias toward the talmudic teaching that "the highest wisdom is kindness" has clearly played its role in what was selected for inclusion.

Beyond this, in order for material to be considered, it had to fit into one of the following categories, for which I give examples:

Jewish source material: The Bible, the Talmud, the Zohar, the Midrash Rabbah, the Shulhan Aruk.

Jewish sages of learning: Hillel the Elder, Rabbi Akiba, Rashi, Maimonides, Ba'al Shem Tov, Nachman of Bratslav.

Sages of learning and wit who were Jewish: Benjamin Disraeli, Sigmund Freud, Heinrich Heine, Albert Einstein, Golda Meir, Marcel Proust, Hannah Arendt.

Wisdom wise, and sad, and funny from Jews over time: Yiddish proverbs, anonymous sayings in the culture, uncommon sense from the common person, stories that have been remembered when those who wrote them have been forgotten.

This book has deeply influenced my life. As a writer, it has meant that rather than sitting down each day to learn my mind, I have instead spent my days discovering the wisdom of others. And while I cannot say how *The Word* will infuence your life, I have no doubt it will enrich your life and perhaps even a few of the lives of those who follow us. At least that is my prayer.

In peace,

Noah benShea
Tammuz 5755

ACKNOWLEDGMENTS

OVER TIME THE FOLLOWING HAVE BEEN FRIENDS, COUNSELORS, TEACH-
ers. They have encouraged and guided me. Some of them are gone. All
of them are with me. I cannot tell you that their lives are more because
of me, but I know that my life would have been less without them.
Thank you.

Saul Alinsky, Jeffrey Kent Ayeroff, Esq., Rabbi Eliezer Berkovits, Sal-
lie Berkovits, Dr. Peter Birnstein, Mark Bloomfield, Steve Breuer,
Bruce Brickman, Esq., Carlos Castaneda, Rabbi Steve Cohen, Rabbi
William Cutter, Dr. Shamai Davidson, Rabbi Joseph Edelheidt, Dr.
Emile Fackenheim, Rabbi Harvey Fields, Rabbi Aaron Gelman, Dr.
Mordechai Gilboa, Alvin Gilens, Paul Goodman, Blu Greenberg, Henry
Greenberg, Rabbi Irving Greenberg, Lawrence Grobel, Aron Hirt-
Manheimer, Murray Horwitz, Arnold S. Jaffe, Esq., Evelyn Jacob Jaffe,
Marc Kaplan, Rabbi Bernie King, Ron Koslow, Esq., Sandy Koufax,
Rabbi Maurice Lamm, Shirley Lamm, Morris Langer, Leonard Lazarus,
Dr. David Leiber, Dr. Glenn Leichman, L. K. Levine, Dr. Samson
Levey, Rabbi Richard Levy, Tom Linton, Sybil Litman, Rabbi Yosef
Loschak, Dr. John McManmon, Dr. John Merkle, Dr. Jacob Neusner,
Frederick M. Nicholas, Esq., Rod O'Connor, Dion O'Donnel, Dr.
Stephen Passamaneck, Rabbi Jacob Patakofski, Rabbi Pinchas Pelhi, Dr.
Jacob Pomerantz, Chaim Potok, Diane Reverand, Rabbi Shlomo
Riskin, Rabbi Ephraim Rottenberg, Rabbi Baruch Rubanowitz, the
Rubanowitz family, Carolyn Sacks, Dr. Mordechai Sacks, Robert

Schaeffer, Eugene Schwartz, Joel Seigel, Brian Shapiro, Bruce Shapiro, Rabbi Milton Steinberg, Rabbi Adin Steinsaltz, Albert Sussman, Bob Toben, Rabbi Max Vorspan, Rabbi Joseph Wagner, Dr. Howard Weinberg, Rabbi Simcha Weinberg, Dr. Harold Weingarden, Joshua Weinman, Esq., Rabbi Melvin Weinman, Carl Weintraub, Jacob Weisberg, Esq., Dr. Trude Weiss-Rosmarin, Eddie Wiesblatt, Herman Wouk, Young Israel of Santa Barbara Minyan, Renée Zarlow, Rabbi Isaiah Zeldin, Arie Zimmerman, and Shlomo Zimmerman.

Thank you to Jack Roth, bookseller, a wise counsel and caring soul to myself and so many others. His rare knowledge has allowed me to locate obscure texts and material over the years and to prepare the attached bibliography, with the help of Dr. Marc Cohen.

Thank you to my mother and father, who have given me life and the courage to live it.

Thank you to the circle of caring at Villard Books/Random House, without whose effort *The Word* would not be.

Thank you to my brothers and their families and my family over distance, for family is sacred.

Thank you to my wife, Danyel benShea, of whom it can be said from the Book of Proverbs: "She opens her mouth with wisdom . . . and her husband praises her."

Thank you to my daughter, Jordan Arin, and my son, Adam Joseph, to whom this book is dedicated, for their loving patience with a father who in looking to the heavens often stumbles here on earth.

CONTENTS

PART TWELVE
IMAGINATION IS MORE IMPORTANT THAN KNOWLEDGE / 325

PART ONE

Hear O Israel,

the Lord Is Our God,

the Lord Is One

SINCE ABRAHAM BARGAINED WITH GOD IN AN ATTEMPT TO SAVE SODOM and Gomorrah, the alliance between God and the Jews has been one of dialogue. Although there are those who in the face of history might argue to the contrary, the prevailing belief among Jews is that if we will talk, God will listen.

A simple and necessary truth of life is that it requires hope. Beyond hope is faith, and curiously enough, from faith hope is often fashioned. Certainly it would have been impossible for the Jewish people to exist without their will to mine faith from hope. And any of us who have experienced the taming of our fears know faith to be a gift of the Divine.

In the Book of Genesis we read that the Divine shaped each act of creation. We also read that the Hand of God fashioned woman from man and man from the clay of the red earth. Our biosphere is covered with God's fingerprints; this nature is divine sculpture. Therefore, by observing the world around us, we may, by reflection, glimpse the Sculptor.

Much of the wisdom in the chapter that follows speaks of what cannot be spoken of directly. The words, in many cases, are from those who, like Jacob, have wrestled with God and God's significance, and in the process have been transformed into the children of Israel.

CHAPTER 1

God,

God and People

How would man exist if God did not need him . . . ?

—*Martin Buber*

A rabbi, wishing to instruct a small boy on God's omnipresence, said to the boy:

"Show me every place that God is, and I will give you a penny."

"Rabbi," answered the boy, with the insight of youth, "show me any place that God isn't, and I will give you two pennies."

—*Adapted from a Yiddish folk story*

Wherever a person's thoughts are, there they are. Let a person think holy thoughts, and he will be in a holy place.

—*Nachman of Bratslav*

In essence, all human beings are identical. We are all part of One; we are One.

—*Erich Fromm*

He is One—there is no second . . . without beginning, without end.

—*Adon Olam, Hebrew prayer*

Man must believe that while his [freedom] might have boundaries everywhere else, [freedom] is without boundary in Man's relationship with God.

—*Franz Rosenzweig*

God is not rich; all He does is take from one and give to the other.

—*Yiddish folk saying*

God is peace, His name is peace, and all is tied together in peace.

—*Zohar*

The true believer is in a high degree protected against the danger of certain neurotic afflictions; by accepting the universal neurosis he is spared the task of forming a personal neurosis.

—*Sigmund Freud*

The intellect . . . links us to God.

—*Maimonides*

Randomness scares people. Religion is a way to explain randomness.

—*Fran Lebowitz*

God is a father; luck is a stepfather.

—*Yiddish folk saying*

What God does is best—probably.

—*Yiddish folk saying*

God is subtle but He is not malicious.

—*Albert Einstein*

Fear is tangled with humility, and humility is tangled with grace.

—*Zohar*

Keep me as the apple of Your eye.

—*Bible, Psalms 17:8*

When you conduct yourselves like the children of God you are called God's children.

—Talmud

And God said unto Moses, I AM THAT I AM: and he said, Thus shalt you say unto the children of Israel, I AM hath sent me unto you.

—Bible, Exodus 3:14

The Lord is my shepherd, I shall not want.

—Bible, Psalms 23:1

Please God, help me to get up! I can fall down by myself.

—Yiddish folk saying

A man who is filled with himself has no room for God.

—Yiddish folk saying

If a people sincerely try . . . to do what they can, God will help them to achieve what they cannot.

—Bahya ben Joseph ibn Pakuda

Man rides, but God holds the reins.

—Yiddish folk saying

Life is God's novel so let him write it.

—Isaac Bashevis Singer

While I was young, when I burned with the love of God, I thought I would convert the whole world to God. But soon I realized that it would be more than enough to convert the people who lived in my town, and I made an effort for a long time, but was not successful. Then I realized that my agenda was still too ambitious, and I focused on the people in my household. But I could not convert them either. Finally I realized: I must work on myself, if I'm really going to have something to offer God. But I didn't even accomplish this.

—Hayyim Halberstram of Zans

... [What] makes us one is to honor the one God.

—*Philo*

Everything is one and nothing is separated from the Lord.

—*Moses Cordovero*

Hear O Israel, the Lord is our God, the Lord is one.

—*Bible, Deuteronomy 6:4*

It is all one path.

—*Zohar*

We understand only that He is, not His essence.

—*Maimonides*

Your word is a lamp unto my feet, and a light unto my path.

—*Bible, Psalms 119:105*

Man—of all ages and cultures—is confronted with the solution of one and the same question: the question of how to overcome separateness, how to achieve union, how to transcend one's own individual life and find at-onement.

—*Erich Fromm*

The striving to find a meaning in one's life is the primary motivational force in man. That is why I speak of a will to meaning in contrast to the . . . will to pleasure.

—*Viktor E. Frankl*

God gives Himself to men as powerful or perfect—it is for them to choose.

—*Simone Weil*

The more we comprehend the individual things, the more we understand God.

—*Baruch Spinoza*

The word of someone who wishes to speak with people without speaking to God cannot be fulfilled; and the word of someone who wishes to speak with God without speaking with people is never heard.

—*Martin Buber*

And I heard the voice of the Lord, saying: "Whom shall I send, and who will go for us?" Then I said: "Here am I; send me."

—*Bible, Isaiah 6:6*

Religion is the sum of scruples which limit the free exercise of our mind.

—*Solomon Reinach*

Monotheism means not only the positive search for unity but also, negatively, the refusal to set man in the throne of God.

—*Leon Roth*

Wherever a Jew goes, his God goes with him.

—*Tanhuma*

. . . He knows how we are formed; He is mindful that we are dust.

—*Bible, Psalms 103:14*

We are the clay, and You are our potter.

—*Bible, Isaiah 64:7*

Reason is God's diplomat.

—*Abraham ibn Ezra*

The reason for religion is not reason.

—*Noah benShea*

. . . in God the tragedy of man may find its transformation.

—*Rabbi Eliezer Berkovits*

Ye shall be as God, knowing good and evil.

—*Bible, Genesis 3:5*

Don't ask God for what you think is good; ask Him for what He thinks is good for you.

— *"The Chofetz Chaim"*

If a Jew breaks his leg, he thanks God he didn't break both legs; if he breaks both legs, he thanks God he didn't break his neck.

—*Yiddish folk saying*

A king asked a rabbi: "Why is God's name mentioned only in the first five Commandments and not in the last five?"

The rabbi responded: "Your statue is placed only in places which are clean and not where there is dirt. In this same way, God does not allow His Name to be placed in the Commandments that deal with thieves, adulterers, murderers, false witnesses, and those who covet their neighbor's goods."

—*Pesikta Rabbati*

A man said to Rabbi Gamaliel: "We do better than you because we can see the idol to which we pray."

And Rabbi Gamaliel answered: "You may see the idol, but it does not see you. We do not see God, but He sees us."

—*Midrash Shoher Tob*

I love them that love Me.

—*Bible, Proverbs 8:17*

God does not depend on being glorified by those who He created . . . But everything that has been created gives reason for its creation by honoring the Lord.

—*Judah Low*

God's voice at Sinai was heard in all languages.

—*Talmud*

God cannot be defined.

—*Joseph Albo*

If all the Jews who ever lived were to come together at one time they could not pronounce the name of God.

—*Adapted from the tradition*

I appeared to Abraham, to Isaac, and to Jacob as God Almighty, but by My name YHVH I did not make Me known to them.

—*Bible, Exodus 6:3*

Moses thought of the Deity as a Being Who has always been in existence, does currently exist, and will always exist in the future, and he [Moses] consequently called Him Jehovah, which in Hebrew stands for these three notions of time.

—*Baruch Spinoza*

But in addition know this, those of you who read this, that despite its worth beyond estimation, despite its elevated position, and despite the incredible beauty of its language, which sheds light on the universe and its mystery, those who are servants of God would be in error to believe that outside of the Bible there is nothing that would give people cause to believe in the Eternal.

Indeed, we are all bound by duty to know that many other proofs exist.

—*Sa'adia (Gaon) ben Joseph*

The important thing is not to stop questioning. Curiosity has its own reason for existing. One cannot help but be in awe when he contemplates the mysteries of eternity, of life, of the marvelous structure of reality. It is enough if one tries merely to comprehend a little of this mystery every day. Never lose a holy curiosity.

—*Albert Einstein*

I have set before you life and death, the blessing and the curse; therefore choose life.

—*Bible, Deuteronomy 30:19*

The majority of mankind are still in the stage of spiritual adolescence. They have outgrown the traditional ideology, but they have not yet acquired an ideology which . . . might help them achieve an affirmative and spiritual adjustment to life.

—*Mordecai M. Kaplan*

There is not one today who is not alienated or who does not contain within himself some small fraction of alienation.

. . . [As] Jews we must not give up anything, not renounce anything, but lead everything back to Judaism. From the periphery back to the center. . . .

. . . The center of the circle looks different from each point of the periphery. There are many ways that lead from the outside in. Nevertheless, the inside is oneness and harmony. Only the outset, only the point of departure, will be different for everyone.

—*Franz Rosenzweig*

I am the Lord your God, who brought you out of the land of Egypt, out of the house of bondage.

—*Bible, Exodus 20:2*

You shall be holy, for I, the Lord your God, am Holy.

—*Bible, Leviticus 19:2*

Every person should carry two cards at all times. . . . On one card should be written the words, "For my sake was the world created"; the other should say, "The Lord God formed man from the dust of the earth."

—*Hasidic folk saying*

Fear the Lord your God.

—*Bible, Deuteronomy 6:13*

There is a difference between fear of God and being afraid of Him.

—*Maurice Samuel*

God can teach us everything, except the fear of God.

—*Talmud*

God hides Himself from our minds, but shows Himself to our hearts.

—Zohar

To be pious to God is to be caring to men.

—Philo

Without a love of humankind there is no love of God.
—Sholem Asch

The Emperor Hadrian had just returned from conquering the world and called the men of his court to his side. "Now I demand that you consider me God."

On hearing this, one of the men said, "Please, great king, help me at my time of need."

"How can I help?" asked the emperor.

"I own a ship which is becalmed three miles from the shore, and it contains all I possess."

"Then I will send a fleet to rescue it," said the emperor.

"Why do you bother to do that?" asked the man. "Why don't you simply send a puff of wind?"

"And where am I to get the wind?" asked the emperor.

"If you do not know this," said the man, "how can you be God, who created the wind?"

—Tanhuma

The Lord shall be for you an everlasting light.
—Bible, Isaiah 60:19

CHAPTER 2

Ritual, Prayer, Sabbath

The central aspect of worship is the feeling of being at one with God.

—Ba'al Shem Tov

All religion is an attempt to express . . . what is essentially inexpressible.

—Leo Baeck

From the Jewish heritage, I have derived my world outlook, a God-centered interpretation of reality in the light of which man the individual is clothed with dignity, and the career of humanity with cosmic meaning and hope; a humane morality, elevated in its aspirations yet sensibly realistic; a system of rituals which interpenetrates my daily routines and invests them with poetry and intimations of the divine.

—Milton Steinberg

And the heaven and the earth were finished, and all the host of them. And on the seventh day God finished His work which He had made; and He rested on the seventh day. . . .

And God blessed the seventh day, and hallowed it; because in it He rested from all His work.

—Bible, Genesis 2:1–3

A follower of a rabbi used to plow with his cow, but as the man was a Jew, the cow became used to not working on the Sabbath.

Over time, the follower became poor and was forced to sell the cow to a non-Jew.

When the Sabbath came, the cow refused to work behind the plow. The man who bought the cow went to the previous owner and complained. The original owner spoke to the cow, saying: "You may work when your master works."

Understanding her role, the cow bent to the task and began pulling the plow. The non-Jew asked the cow what the previous owner had said.

On hearing the answer, the man said to himself: "If a beast without any wit wants to rest on the Sabbath, should I, a person of reason, do less?"

The man became a convert and was called Rabbi Hanina ben Turta [the Son of a Cow].

—*Midrash Asseret ha-Diberot*

Our life is like a tapestry. And by the tapestry's nature, it demands we work on it from the back. In a blind. The Sabbath is a reminder that one day in seven, or one hour in seven, or one minute in seven, we should step back and turn our tapestry over so we can see the larger pattern of who we are, the implication of our efforts, and the world wherein we work.

—*Noah benShea*

The meaning of the Sabbath is to celebrate time rather than space. Six days a week we live under the tyranny of things of space; on the Sabbath we try to become attuned to *holiness in time*. It is a day when we are called upon to share in what is eternal time, to turn from the results of creation to the mystery of creation; from the world of creation to the creation of the world.

—*Abraham Joshua Heschel*

We can worship Thee in holiness only as we serve our brothers in love.

—*Union Prayer Book*

If people practice cleansing and purification but dirty their mind while they clean their body; or if through their wealth they spend much money to build a place to pray; or if they offer gifts and sacrifices, or gild a shrine with rich artifacts, or give forests of wood and crafts, even worth more than gold and silver—let these people not be called any more religious.

For they have traveled far from the road of religion, confusing ritual for what is holy, and are attempting to bribe God who cannot be corrupted, and flatter Him who cannot be flattered.

God invites genuine prayer, and that is the service of the soul which is given bare with the simple sacrifice of truth, but from false prayer, the pretense of material wealth, He turns away.

—Philo

Those who say their prayers out loud so they may be heard are those of little faith.

—Talmud

Rab said: Whoever has the capacity to pray for a neighbor and does not is called a sinner.

—Talmud

No synagogue shall be demolished until a new synagogue is ready.

—Talmud

Notice quickly came to the king's officers and the soldiers in Jerusalem, the City of David, that those Jews who resisted the king's commands had gone into hiding in the wilderness. A large body of soldiers was quickly dispatched, discovered the rebels, and took up positions across from them. The soldiers prepared their attack for the Sabbath.

"You still have time," shouted the soldiers. "Leave your hiding places, do as the king says, and you will not be killed."

"We refuse," shouted the Jews. "We will not serve this king and we will not desecrate the Sabbath."

The attack was begun immediately, but the Israelites did not respond; they didn't throw rocks, nor block the doors to their caves.

. . . So the king's men made war on the Jews and massacred them all on the Sabbath including men, and women, and children. . . .

Mattathias and his comrades when they heard of this were
overcome with grief. Then they spoke to one another saying: "If all
of us do just as our brothers and sisters have done, if we refuse to
take up arms against [those who attack us] to protect our lives, our
laws, and our customs, they will soon remove us from the face of the
earth.

On that day it was decided that whoever came to attack the Jews,
even if it was on the Sabbath, the Jews would resist and fight, and die
rather than die as their brothers and sisters had done in the caves.

—I Maccabees 2:31–41

Customs are more powerful than laws.

—Talmud

It's good to fast . . . with a chicken leg and something to drink.

—Yiddish folk saying

The very absence of formal theology in Judaism is a virtue.

—Norman Bentwich

Give thanks unto God because we are able to give thanks.

—Talmud

God sees that the best place to pray is in the heart.

—Hasidic saying

The Sabbath . . . prevents us from reducing our life to the level of a
machine.

. . . If to labor is noble, of our own free will to pause in that labor
which may lead to success . . . may be nobler still.

—Claude G. Montefiore

Better to pray for yourself than to curse another.

—Yiddish folk saying

Rabbi said: "It is forbidden us to pray to God that He send death to
the wicked."

—Zohar Hadash

The Holy One lends a person an extra soul just before the Sabbath and retrieves it at the close of the Sabbath.
> —*Simeon ben Lakish, Talmud*

The best way to worship God is through silence and hope.
> —*Solomon ibn Gabirol*

A person who is angry is not fit to pray.
> —*Nachman of Bratslav*

Tears smash through the gates and doors of heaven.
> —*Zohar*

Look deeply and you will find a way to serve God in everything and in every work and in every place.
> —*Nachman of Bratslav*

Differences in ritual and in religious customs have always been practiced side by side in rabbinical Judaism.
> —*Abraham Kohn*

Prayer is a path where there is none. Ritual is prayer's vehicle.
> —*Noah benShea*

What is service of the heart?
This is prayer.
> —*Talmud*

The Sabbath is . . . the queen whose arrival transforms the humblest home into a palace.
> —*Judah Halevi*

The inner life-force of Judaism has always constructed itself by building on earlier foundations.
> —*Gustav Karpeles*

Absolutely unmixed attention is prayer.
> —*Simone Weil*

Even the Holy One, blessed be He, prays.

What does He pray?

"May it be My will that My mercy overcomes My anger, and that My mercy dominates all My attributes so that I may deal with My children mercifully."

—*Talmud*

All are equal before God in prayer.

—*Shemot Rabbah*

The submergence of self in the pursuit of an ideal, the readiness to spend oneself without measure, prodigally, almost ecstatically, for something intuitively apprehended as great and noble, spend oneself one knows not why—some of us like to believe that this is what religion means.

—*Benjamin N. Cardozo*

Only that person's prayer is answered who lifts his hands with his heart in them.

—*Talmud, Ta'anit*

The Sabbath is the day of peace between man and nature . . . By not working—by not participating in the process of natural and social change—man is free from the chains of nature and from the chains of time.

—*Erich Fromm*

Remember the sabbath day, to keep it holy.

—*Bible, Exodus 20:8*

The heart's cry to God is the highest form of prayer.

—*Zohar*

There is a time for long service and long sermons, and a time for short ones.

—*Mekilta Beshallah*

If it is written about God, who never grows tired, that He rested on the seventh day, how much more should we, humankind, take rest on the Sabbath from our weariness.

—Pesikta Rabbati

Rabbi Yudan said: "According to the custom of the world, the lord tells his servants: 'Work for me six days and one day shall be for yourselves.' God, however, says: 'Work for yourselves six days, and for Me one day.'"

—Pesikta Rabbati

Every idol requires sacrifices.

—Shemarya Levin

A man woke on the Sabbath and discovered a pot of gold under his bed.

Reaching for the gold, it moved away from him.

Frustrated, the man gave up his efforts and went to pray.

Upon arriving at the synagogue, the man turned and discovered that the pot of gold had been following him.

—Jewish folk tradition

Danger to life takes precedence over the sanctity of the Sabbath.

—Talmud

The Sabbath became the most capable patron saint of the Jewish people. . . . The ghetto Jew shed all the toil and trouble of his day-to-day life once the Sabbath lamp was lit. All insult and iniquity was thrown off. The love of God, which came back to him one day in seven on the Sabbath, returned to him also his honor and human dignity even in his lowly hut.

—Hermann Cohen

Once, during a terrible drought in Judea, word came to Rabbi Abbahu that there was a man whose prayers for rain never failed to deliver. The man's name in the vernacular was "Five Sins."

Rabbi Abbahu spent time with the man talking and trying to discover how he came by his strange name.

"My job," said the man, "is to work among the prostitutes. I clean the rooms, I carry containers to the bath, I make clients laugh with my jokes, and I make music with my flute."

"I don't understand," said the rabbi, "you must have done something very special that causes your prayers to be heard by God."

"Well," replied the man, "once, while I was cleaning the theater, I saw a woman standing to the side and crying terribly. I discovered that her husband was being held a prisoner. As the woman was poor, only by sacrificing her honor could she hope to ransom him. When I heard this, I sold everything I owned and gave her the money to save her husband."

When he heard this, Rabbi Abbahu declared: "You are truly a man who is fit to pray for us in this hour of our anguish."

—*Talmud*

There is no room for God in someone who is filled with himself.

—*Ba'al Shem Tov*

It has been said that the highest praise of God consists in the denial of Him by the atheist, who finds creation so perfect that he can dispense with a creator.

—*Marcel Proust*

When you pray to God, you do not need to delineate your needs, or point out how you should be saved, as if you were talking to a person. God knows better than you what is in your best interest.

—*Raphael Norzi*

Rab said: He whose mind is not quieted should not pray.

—*Talmud*

The Sabbath *is* a world revolution.

—*Franz Rosenzweig*

Rabbi Me'ir said: A person's words should always be few when speaking to God.

—*Talmud*

[Religious] custom when it decays degenerates into a kind of religious fashion.

—*Solomon Schechter*

We should not laugh at the person who becoming caught up in his prayer bends his body or moves about in strange ways.

Perhaps he moves in this manner to wave off unwelcome thoughts that would interrupt the prayer.

Would we find it funny if we saw a person drowning going through strange motions doing whatever was necessary to save his life?

—*Ba'al Shem Tov*

It is the nature of gold and silver that they are refined through the heat of fire.

If we, after we have prayed, do not feel that we have been refined and improved then maybe the reason is that we are made of a baser metal or our prayer was not filled with enough fire.

—*Rabbi Phineas Shapiro, the Koretzer Rebbe*

Hezekiah said to Isaiah:

. . . This tradition was taught to me by my forefather, King David: "Regardless if a sharpened sword is put on your neck, a person should not stop praying."

—*Talmud*

On the evening of the Sabbath, a good angel and an evil angel come home with a man on his way from the synagogue. If the man arrives home to discover the candles have been kindled, the table laid out before him, and the bed made, the good angel then declares, "May the next Sabbath be like this one!" and the evil angel is compelled to answer, "Amen." But if the conditions the man returns home to are found otherwise, the evil angel then says, "May the next Sabbath be like this one!"—and the good angel is forced to answer, "Amen."

—*Jose ben Judah, Talmud*

The Sabbath is as a mirror of the world to come.

—*Zohar*

Two great servants move through the ages: prayer and sacrifice.
—*Martin Buber*

It is good to give thanks unto the Lord.
—*Bible, Psalms 92:2*

Moses did not give the name of rest [Sabbath] to simple inactivity.
—*Philo*

Never undervalue the blessing of a common man.
—*Ishmael ben Elisha, Talmud*

Forcing someone to do something in religion is useless.
—*Solomon ibn Verga*

You shall rejoice before the Lord your God.
—*Bible, Deuteronomy 12:12*

Prayer without concentration is like a body without a soul.
—*Talmud*

Prayers are not heard from those who do not pray from peace.
—*Nachman of Bratslav*

To pray is not the same as to pray for.
—*Claude G. Montefiore*

From your mouth to God's ear.
—*Yiddish folk saying*

May the words of my mouth and the meditation of my heart be acceptable before Thee, O Lord.
—*Bible, Psalms 19:15*

The holiness of time sanctifies every moment of life. It makes us aware of the fact that every minute is pregnant with possibilities of divine significance.
—*Norman Lamm*

Jacob looked down at his path as if it were the current of a great river. As he stared into the flow he saw the seemingly unending line of moments given to him. Then, like a man marking a trail, he began to put his prayer between the moments, making the common profound by pausing.

Using prayer to tie knots in time, Jacob isolated the details that would pass before others as a stream of events.

In this way Jacob secured the moments in his life, returned their individuality, allowed the luster in each of them to be observed, and, appreciated and saved, transformed his moments into a string of pearls.

—Noah benShea

May the Lord bless you and keep you.

May the Lord cause His face to shine upon you, and be gracious to you.

May the Lord turn His face toward you, and grant you peace.

—Bible, Numbers 6:24–26

CHAPTER 3

Faith, Hope, Belief, Atheism, Free Will

All laughter had gone from him and all tears with it, and now only a deep untroubled gentleness was left, a wordless faith.

—Henry Roth

As for me, I declare my faith that our history is not meaningless, and that nihilism is a hallucination of sick men. God lives, and we are his people, chosen to live by his name, and his law until one day when the Lord will be one and his name one.

—Herman Wouk

Faith is clearer than sight.

—Menahem Mendel of Kotsk

The Ba'al Shem Tov said: "In the Talmud we read that, concerning understanding, Moses was given the key to forty-nine doors out of fifty. So we ask, since we, as human beings, always want to know more and more, how was it possible for Moses to pass through the fiftieth door?

"What happened was that when Moses came to the fiftieth door and found it locked to the mind of man, Moses replaced understanding with faith and began his meditation over again.

"In this way, every one of us should train our minds. We should learn and reflect to the best of our capacity, but when we reach a point where we are unable to make sense of life, we should supplant faith for understanding, and reflect again on what we do know."

—*Ba'al Shem Tov*

A father explained sadly to the Ba'al Shem Tov that his son had abandoned God. "What shall I do, Rabbi?"

And the Ba'al Shem Tov answered, "Love him more than ever."

—*Ba'al Shem Tov*

And He shall be for you a sanctuary.

—*Bible, Isaiah 8:14*

Everything is foreseen, yet freedom of choice is given.

—*Rabbi Akiba, Pirke Avot*

. . . Man is ultimately self-determining.

—*Viktor E. Frankl*

It has been taught: When a human being is created, on the day he comes into the world, simultaneously, all the days of his life are arranged above.

—*Zohar*

Happy are all they that wait for Him.

—*Bible, Isaiah 30:18*

Desire engenders belief: if we are not usually aware of this, it is because most belief-creating desires last as long as we do.

—*Marcel Proust*

A man should believe in God through faith, not because of miracles.

—*Nachman of Bratslav*

A soul that thinks it can say *no* to its destiny will find out that it isn't free but simply naked . . . without destiny.

—*Franz Rosenzweig*

I believe with complete faith that the Creator, Blessed is His Name, has created and is a guide to all creatures, and that He alone made, makes, and will make everything.

I believe with complete faith that the Creator, Blessed is His Name, is unique and His uniqueness is singular, and that only He is our God, Who was, Who is, and Who will always be.

—*Maimonides*

Before you can find God you must lose yourself.

—*Ba'al Shem Tov*

There are no atheists on turbulent airplanes.

—*Erica Jong*

Entering into the pure relationship does not involve ignoring everything but seeing everything in the You. . . . Whoever beholds the world in Him stands in His presence.

How would man exist if God did not need him. . . . You need God in order to be, and God needs you—for that is the meaning of life . . . The world is not a divine play, it is divine fate.

—*Martin Buber*

Fervent atheism is usually a screen for repressed religion.

—*Wilhelm Stekel*

With faith, there are no questions, and without faith there are no answers.

—*"The Chofetz Chaim"*

You shall find Him, if you search after Him with all your heart and with all your soul.

—*Bible, Deuteronomy 4:29*

If God gave us teeth, He will give us bread.

—*Yiddish folk saying*

Dear God, do not cause us to learn what we cannot endure.

—*Yiddish folk saying*

Return to Me . . . and I will return to you.

—*Bible, Zechariah 1:3*

Men plan and plan but God sits up in heaven and laughs.

—*Yiddish folk saying*

If you want to give God a good laugh, tell Him your plans.

—*Yiddish folk saying*

The Lord gave, and the Lord hath taken away; blessed be the name of the Lord.

—*Bible, Job 1:21*

But of the mystery of faith, it is written:
"Her ways are ways of delight,
all her paths are peace."

—*Rabbi El'azar, Zohar; Proverbs 3:17*

Where reason concludes, faith begins.

—*Nachman of Bratslav*

Call upon Me in the day of trouble.

—*Bible, Psalms 50:15*

God is our refuge and strength, a very present help in trouble.

—*Bible, Psalms 46:1*

God is responsible for having created a world in which man is free to make history.

—*Rabbi Eliezer Berkovits*

Tinnius Rufus asked, "Why didn't God make man just as He wanted him to be?"
Akiba answered, "Because it is man's duty to perfect himself."

—*Tanhuma*

Man is being born to believe. And if no Church comes forward with its title-deeds of truth . . . to guide him, he will find altars and idols in his own heart and his own imagination.

—*Benjamin Disraeli*

Every day people are straying away from the church and going back to God.

—Lenny Bruce

Faith means intense, usually confident, belief that is not based on evidence sufficient to command assent from every reasonable person.

—Walter Kaufmann

The essence of Judaism is conformity in our actions and freedom in our belief.

—Moses Mendelssohn

The picture of a despotic God who wants unrestricted power over men and their submission and humiliation was the projection of the middle class's own hostility and envy.

—Erich Fromm

Hope is a very unruly emotion.

—Gloria Steinem

Where there is no vision, the people perish.

—Bible, Proverbs 29:18

Each time he [the Messiah] hears Jews groan, he tries to break his chains . . .
But God has vowed not to release him till the Jews . . . tear the chains from their hands.

—Sholem Asch

To be a Jew is a destiny.

—Vicki Baum

Thus saith the Lord that made thee, and formed thee from the womb . . . Fear not.

—Bible, Isaiah 44:2

God is with me, I shall not fear.

—Adon Olam, Hebrew prayer

Fear ye not, neither be afraid.

—Bible, Isaiah 44:8

Thou shalt remember the Lord thy God.

—Bible, Deuteronomy 8:18

A man is driving his car too fast down a treacherous mountain pass. The car goes over the cliff, and the man barely survives by reaching out and grabbing a clump of bushes growing from the side of the mountain wall.

Dangling in space, the man pleads with God. "Please, help me. Rescue me. I will change forever. I will do anything. Please. Help me."

God calls out to the man. "You want my help?"

"Yes," says the man. "Anything. Anything!"

"I'll help you on one condition," says the voice of God.

"Anything."

"All right," says God. "Trust me and let go."

The man hears the message. Thinks about it for a minute. And then shouts: "Is there anybody out there who can help me?"

—Anonymous

Socrates was asked, "Why do we not see in you even the slightest apprehension?"

He answered, "Because I have never claimed ownership over anything that would give me sadness if I lost it."

The sage also said, "Everything needs a fence."

Then he was asked, "What is a 'fence'?"

And Socrates answered, "Trust."

"Well," questioned the others, "what is a 'fence of trust'?"

"The fence of trust," explained the sage, "is to fear nothing."

. . . Who are the most sagacious of people and those most filled with faith? Those who come to accept experiences as they arrive and depart.

—Solomon ibn Gabirol

Why the people of Israel stuck to their God all the more devotedly the worse they were treated by Him, that is a question we must leave open.

—Sigmund Freud

It is better to be a superstitious person of faith than to be a person who uses reason to lose faith.

—*Nachman of Bratslav*

. . . To love God always means a simultaneous happy and unhappy love. . . . He comes close, most close—and then backs away to the most distant distance. He is at once the most longed for, and the hardest to bear.

. . . The solution . . . like the solution of all the difficulties and antitheses of love, lies with the lover, with his strength to . . . bear . . . [and be] borne.

—*Franz Rosenzweig*

. . . The essence of Judaism: First, there is a God, indivisible, eternal, spiritual, most holy and perfect. Second, there is an immortal life and man is a son of eternity. Third, love thy fellow men without distinction of creed or race as thyself.

—*Max Lilenthal*

There must be a dimension beyond history in which all suffering finds its redemption through God. This is the essential faith of a Jew.

. . . This is no justification for the ways of providence but its acceptance. It is not a willingness to forgive the unheard cries of millions, but a trust that in God the tragedy of man may find its transformation.

—*Rabbi Eliezer Berkovits*

Through faith humankind experiences the meaning of the world; through action we give the world meaning.

—*Leo Baeck*

Once as Hillel the Elder was on his way home from a long journey, he heard screams coming from the city.

"I'm sure the screams are not coming from my house," said Hillel.

On Hillel's attitude, the Bible says: "He is not afraid of bad news; his heart is firm, he trusts in the Lord" [Psalms 112:7].

—*Talmud*

I make it a rule to believe only what I understand.

—*Benjamin Disraeli*

You cannot command belief.

—*Samuel David Luzzatto*

Be strong and God will give your heart courage.

—*Bible, Psalms 28:14*

In Judaism faith is . . . the capacity of the soul to perceive the abiding . . . in the transitory, the invisible in the visible.

—*Leo Baeck*

Faith sees beyond fate.

—*Noah benShea*

The Lord will not forsake His people.

—*Bible, I Samuel 12:22*

Coincidence is God's way of remaining anonymous.

—*Albert Einstein*

. . . I believe that a void stands where once we experienced God's presence; I do not think Judaism has lost its meaning or its power. I do not believe that a theistic God is necessary for Jewish religious life. . . . We no longer believe in the God who has the power to annul the tragic necessities of existence.

—*Richard L. Rubenstein*

God . . . give me the heart to fight—and lose.

—*Louis Untermeyer*

The Lord God will wipe away tears from all faces.

—*Bible, Isaiah 25:8*

Wait for your God continually.

—*Bible, Hosea 12:7*

Is anything too hard for the Lord?

—*Bible, Genesis 18:14*

And the Lord went before them by day in a pillar of a cloud, to lead them the way; and by night in a pillar of fire, to give them light; to go by day and night.

—*Bible, Exodus 13:21*

I believe in the sun even when it is not shining.
I believe in love even when not feeling it.
I believe in God even when He is silent.

—*Scratched on cellar walls*
by anonymous people hiding from Nazis

Human misery is too great for men to deal with without faith.

—*Heinrich Heine*

CHAPTER 4

Miracles, Revelations, Spiritualism, Mysticism, Messiah, Prophets, Rabbis, Tzaddikim

A tzaddik [righteous person] does not depart from this world until another tzaddik has come into it.

—*Talmud*

The Greek grasped the present moment, and was the artist; the Jew worshipped the timeless spirit, and was the prophet.

—*Isaac Mayer Wise*

A prophet is never a fool, and a fool is never a prophet.

—*Yiddish folk saying*

The Sages and Prophets did not hope for the arrival of the Messiah in order to rule over the world, or ruling over the unbelievers, or being held in high esteem by other peoples, or eating, drinking, and rejoicing.

The ambition of the Sages and Prophets was to be allowed the time and openness to focus their attention on the Torah and its wisdom, without others oppressing or bothering them, in the hope that they might be worthy of living in the World-To-Come.

. . . The single obligation around the world will be to be at One with the Lord. And people then will experience an unparalleled wisdom, understand what is now beyond understanding; they will achieve a full knowledge of the Creator as it is within the talents of human beings—for it is said, "The earth shall be full of the knowledge of the Lord, as the waters cover the sea" [Isaiah 11:9].

—Maimonides

If we were to treat every person we met as if he were the Messiah, then it wouldn't make any difference if he weren't.

—Yiddish folk tradition

. . . The laws of Nature are free of error, lacking nothing and needing nothing, and . . . miracles only seem to us as something original because of our ignorance.

—Baruch Spinoza

In every generation there are thirty-six sacred souls who are called *lamed-vovniks* [the numerical value of the Hebrew letters *lamed* and *vov* totals thirty-six]. These people are not public about their role, and in many cases are not even aware they have been chosen. Often their lives are steeped in sorrow and abuse. But it is only for the presence of these *lamed-vovniks* that God does not give up hope in mankind and destroy His creation.

—Jewish mystical tradition

[A rabbi] and Rabbi Hiyya came to a town where a blind sage lived.
After they visited the sage and took their leave, the wise man observed: "Because you came to see one who is seen but sees not, may you be worthy to visit the One who sees and is not seen."

—Talmud

How God rules the universe . . . is a complete mystery.

—Maimonides

A truly righteous person [a Hasid] is seldom found. Consequently it is very unlikely that two Hasidim would be found residing in the same community.
And if you found one Hasid in a community it would not be enough.
Why?
Because every community should have as inhabitants one and a half

Hasidim. As a result of this, each Hasid would see himself as the half, half of what he might be, and in his counterpart see the whole.

—*The Lubliner Rebbe*

Miracles sometimes occur, but one has to work terribly hard for them.

—*Chaim Weizmann*

One who has never been bewildered, who has never looked upon life and his own existence as phenomena which require answers and yet, paradoxically, for which the only answers are new questions, can hardly understand what religious experience is.

—*Erich Fromm*

It is imperative that men break away from the habit of identifying the spiritual with the supernatural.

—*Mordecai M. Kaplan*

It is all one mystery.

—*Rabbi Shim'on, Zohar*

A man came to his tzaddik and asked:
"How is it that the righteous put less effort into making others righteous than those who do evil spend on trying to convince others to do wrong?"
And the tzaddik answered:
"The righteous person walks in the light of God and therefore is not afraid to walk by himself. But the person who does evil moves in the darkness and knowing this wants others for company."

—*Hasidic folk tradition*

Man by nature is a mystic.

—*Abraham Isaac Kook*

Nothing is revealed while the person is still under the spell of the body.

—*Zohar*

Listen, you deaf ones! You blind ones, look up and see.
—*Bible, Isaiah 42:18*

The secret things belong to the Lord our God.
—*Bible, Deuteronomy 29:28*

Happy are they . . . who walk in the law of the Lord.
—*Bible, Psalms 119:1*

Each man is obligated to give new life to his own being by modeling his personality upon the image of the prophet; he must carry through his own self-creation . . . until he is worthy and fit to receive the divine overflow . . . each person is obliged to aspire to this rank . . . every man should make a supreme effort to scale the mountain of the Lord, until he reaches the pinnacle of the revelation of the Divine Presence.
—*Joseph B. Soloveitchik*

When there is a possibility of danger, do not depend upon a miracle.
—*Talmud*

God sends the remedy before the disease.
—*Yiddish folk saying*

Miracles do happen, but they rarely provide food.
—*Nahman ben Jacob, Talmud*

A miracle is our capacity to see the common in an uncommon way.
—*Noah benShea*

A miracle does not prove what is impossible; rather it is an affirmation of what is possible.
—*Maimonides*

Solitude is the highest level. Only in solitude can a person achieve . . . union with the eternal God. Consequently, a person must make an effort to be alone, for at least one hour each day, particularly in the evening, when all others are sleeping and everything is quiet. Solitude in the out of doors, in the forest or in the desert, is of the greatest importance.

—*Nachman of Bratslav*

The prophetic spirit is given to people only after they have moved themselves to receive it.

—*Zohar*

You declare it a miracle when God follows through on the will of your tzaddik; we declare it a miracle when it can be honestly said that the tzaddik carries out the will of God.

—*Leib Kagan*

A large part of the popularity and persuasiveness of psychology comes from its being a sublimated spiritualism: a secular, ostensibly scientific way of affirming the primacy of "spirit" over matter.

—*Susan Sontag*

Science without religion is lame; religion without science is blind.

—*Albert Einstein*

The miracle of rain is greater than the resurrection of the dead, for the resurrection is only for people, whereas rain is for animals as well; resurrection is only for Israelites, rain for other nations as well; resurrection is only for the righteous, while rain comes down upon the righteous and the wicked alike.

—*Talmud*

The rabbi is the teacher in Israel, no more and no less.

—*Isaac Mayer Wise*

Because a goat has a beard doesn't make him a rabbi.

—*Yiddish folk saying*

The prophet is established to oppose the king and offer even greater opposition to history.

—*Martin Buber*

The manner of achieving saintliness that is in order for someone whose work is the study of Torah is not the same as for the hardworking laborer, and neither of these is the same as for the person who is involved with business.

Each person must have an opportunity to see a manner that works for his work.

This is not to mean that there are different sorts of saintliness, because saintliness is always conditioned on what is pleasing to God.

What it does mean is that there are different kinds of people, so the ways of accomplishing saintliness are sure to vary.

The person who is forced to work at the most degrading and demeaning physical labor is just as capable of being a saint as the person who never retreats from his study of Torah.

—*Moses Luzzatto*

A youth arrived at the doorway of the Riziner Rebbe and wanted to be made a rabbi.

The Rebbe asked the youth what he did every day.

"I dress only in white. My only drink is water. I put nails in my shoes to give myself pain. Absent of clothes, I lie in the freezing snow. And I demand the man who takes care of the House of Study to whip me forty times every day."

While the young man spoke, a white horse came into the community's open space, took a drink of water, and then rolled on his back in the snow.

"I have listened to you," began the Rebbe, speaking with patience, "but look at that horse. He is white, and takes only water, and has nails in his shoes, and lies in the snow, and is whipped even more than forty times during a day. But even with all this, he remains nothing more than a horse."

—*The Riziner Rebbe*

A rabbi whom people don't want to force out of town isn't a rabbi, and a rabbi whom the community drives out of town isn't a man.

—*Israel Salanter Lipkin*

A follower of a certain tzaddik happened to hear rumors about the sage Rabbi Israel Meir ha-Cohen, the Radiner Rebbe. Curious to know more about this famed teacher, the follower approached one of the Radiner Rebbe's students and asked:

"Can you tell me if your tzaddik can honestly make miracles?"

The follower of the Radiner Rebbe answered:

"You think it is a miracle when God does what your Rebbe requests. We, on the other hand, feel it is a miracle when we can say in all honesty that our tzaddik conducts himself as God wills."

— *"The Chafetz Chaim" (the Radiner Rebbe)*

Would that all the Lord's people were prophets.

—*Bible, Numbers 11:29*

The Messiah lives in an incredibly beautiful palace in heaven but his hands are bound by gold chains.

"Why," you may ask, "is the Messiah bound by chains?"

"The reason is this," says a great rabbi. "If the Messiah was not wearing the gold chains, he might look down and, wanting to wait no longer, suddenly begin his work too soon, at the wrong moment."

—*Heinrich Heine (from the Talmud)*

. . . Jewish mysticism . . . enlarges man . . . so his action reaches the infinite, so that his ethical act also becomes a cosmic act.

—*Leo Baeck*

If you should find yourself holding on to a sapling and they tell you that the Messiah has just arrived, first finish planting the tree and then go out and meet the Messiah.

—*Avot de Rabbi Nathan*

The Jewish prophets were men of compassion. They would influence the idol worshippers to abandon their evil, for God stretches out His hand to both the evil and the righteous.

—*Rashi*

On the day the Temple was destroyed, the Messiah was born.

—*Abin Halevi, Jerusalem Talmud*

To atone is to be *at one* with God, to sink self into the not-self, to achieve a mystic unity with the source of being, wiping out all error and finding peace in self-submergence.

—*Isaac Goldberg*

The prophet and the martyr do not see the hooting throng. Their eyes are fixed on the eternities.

—*Benjamin N. Cardozo*

The prophets are God's interpreters.

—*Philo*

There is no sharp distinction in religious status between the rabbi and the layman in Judaism.

—*Rabbi Louis Finkelstein*

The rabbis said that the Messianic age of Israel cannot come suddenly, but will arrive gradually and slowly, in the same manner as the sun with measured pace rises in the dawning day.

—*Midrash Shoher Tob*

People should allow themselves the opportunity to really know what the unity of God means. To grasp a part of the nondivisible union is to grasp the whole.

. . . If I . . . fulfill just one commandment in and through the love of God, it is, in a manner, as I have [joined with the One and] satisfied them all.

—*Ba'al Shem Tov*

For even one righteous man, the world would have been created.

—*Eleazar ben Pedat, Talmud*

I will put My spirit in you, and you shall live.

—*Bible, Ezekiel 37:14*

CHAPTER 5

God's Commandments,
Good Deeds, Sin, Penance,
Repentance, Forgiveness, Soul

The Jew was not given the commandment to believe, but to search after the knowledge of God.

—*Moses Hess*

Live by the commandments; do not die by them.

—*Talmud*

It is only to the individual that a soul is given.

—*Albert Einstein*

Since I the LORD am your God, who brought you out of the land of Egypt, out of a state of slavery, you must have no other gods beside Me.

You must not carve an image for yourself in the shape of anything that is in the heavens above, or that is on the earth below, or that is in the waters under the earth. You shall not bow down to them or serve them. . . .

You must not draw on the name of the LORD your God for evil intent. . . .

Be careful to hold the sabbath day holy . . . Six days you are to labor and do all the work, but on the seventh day . . . you must not do any work at all, neither you, nor your son, nor your daughter . . . nor your ox, nor your ass, nor any of your cattle, nor the alien in your employ who lives in your community. . . .

Honor your father and mother . . . that you may live long and prosper. . . .

You must not commit murder.

You must not commit adultery.

You must not steal.

You must not lie against your neighbor.

You must not lust after your neighbor's wife, nor covet your neighbor's house . . . or anything at all that is your neighbor's.

—*Bible, Deuteronomy 5:6–21*

Out of consideration for human dignity you are not obligated to carry out a negative commandment in the Torah.

—*Rabina ben Huna, Talmud*

Thou shalt love thy neighbor as thyself.

—*Bible, Leviticus 19:18*

The fundamental key to Judaism is Love.

—*Gustav Karpeles*

The noble deeds of our life are our passports to forever.

—*Paul Nathan*

Every man has three friends—his children, his money, and his good deeds. When the time comes for him to leave the world he calls upon his children, who reply, "Don't you know that no one can conquer death?" Then he calls upon his money, saying, "Day and night I have worked for you, save me now." The money replies, "Wealth cannot deliver you from death." He next calls on his good deeds and they reply, "Go in peace. By the time you arrive in the next world, we will be there before you to offer you help."

—*Talmud*

The world is based on three things: Torah, worship, and loving-kindness.

—*Simeon the Just, Mishneh Torah*

Deeds of kindness are equal in weight to all the commandments.

—*Talmud*

One may choose to observe or not to observe [Jewish Law], but one may not decide what Jewish Law demands to be observed.

—*Maurice Lamm*

Giving to charity and deeds of loving-kindness are equal to all the commandments in the Torah, but loving-kindness is the greater of the two.

Charity is given to the living, but deeds of loving-kindness are given to the living and the dead; charity is given only to the poor, deeds of loving-kindness are given to the poor and the rich.

In addition, acts of charity are done with one's money, deeds of loving-kindness with money and many other ways.

—*Talmud*

Kindness is more holy than piety.

—*Yiddish folk saying*

You shall love the Lord, your God, with all your heart, with all your soul and with all your resources. Let these matters which I teach you today be upon your heart. Teach them thoroughly to your children and speak of them when you sit in your home, while you walk on the way, when you go to bed at night and when you arise. Bind them as a sign upon your arm and let them be as frontlets between your eyes. And write them upon the doorposts of your house and upon your gates.

—*Bible, Deuteronomy 6:5–9*

God cares more for what you do than for what your ancestors did.

—*Midrash Rabbah*

When we observe Satan working with focus to have us do something wrong, we should understand that this is only Satan doing his duty as he understands it.

What we should learn from this is for all of us to do our duty, that we too should fight with persistence if we will persevere in our struggles with Satan.

—*Ba'al Shem Tov*

In the Ten Commandments we are addressed in the singular, because at Mt. Sinai [where the Commandments were given] all of Israel was of one heart.

—*Judah ha-Nasi*

Bars don't corrupt good men and temples don't transform bad ones.

—*Yiddish folk saying*

Worship motivated by fear is worship, but it does not rise to the highest. . . .
. . . [The highest] is reserved for worship motivated by love.

—*Zohar*

To cheat a Gentile is even worse than to cheat a Jew, for in addition to being in violation to moral law, this act brings the religion of Israel into contempt, and degrades the name of Israel's God.

—*Talmud*

The essence of religion is the human quest for salvation.

—*Mordecai M. Kaplan*

There are countless places of refuge, there is only one place of salvation; but the possibilities of salvation, again, are as numerous as all the places of refuge.

—*Franz Kafka*

As man acts, God reacts.

—*Ba'al Shem Tov*

The Torah warns us not to turn God's commandments into idols.

—*Menahem Mendel of Kotsk*

It is my desire to do God's will, not that God do my will.

—*Rabbi Isaac Meyer of Ger, the Gerer Rebbe*

Do not ask God for what you want, ask God what He wants for you.

—*"The Chofetz Chaim"*

Serve God in every effort, in every action, and in every place.
                                —*Nachman of Bratslav*

Naturally, God will forgive me. That's his business.
                                —*Heinrich Heine*

If only we deserved as much as God could give us.
                                —*Yiddish folk saying*

Be cautious of a pious fool, and a wise sinner.
                                —*Solomon ibn Gabirol*

The sinner does evil, the wicked man is evil.
                                —*Martin Buber*

Be as strong as the leopard, light as the eagle, swift as the deer, and brave as the lion, to do the will of your Father who is in heaven.
                                —*Rabbi Judah ben Tema, Pirke Avot*

. . . A person's real work in this world is the work of the Blessed Holy One.
                                —*Rabbi El'azar, Zohar*

We do not ask that our past sins be forgiven in the sense that their effects may be cancelled . . . All we can do and ask for is better insight, purer faith, fuller strength.
                                —*Claude G. Montefiore*

No smoke, no fire.
                                —*Zohar*

Your words are truth.
                                —*Bible, II Samuel 7:28*

I bring heaven and earth to witness that the Divine Spirit rests upon a non-Jew as well as upon a Jew, upon a woman as well as a man, upon a maidservant as well as a manservant. All depends on the deeds of the particular individual.
                                —*Yalkut Shimoni*

Always be . . . on sentry duty for the chance to do good deeds.
—*Johanan ben Nappha*

When your enemy falls it is not a time to rejoice.
—*Bible, Proverbs 24:17*

. . . even a non-Jew who occupies himself with the study of Torah
is equal to a high priest.
—*Rabbi Meir, Talmud*

If you feel the Evil Urge starting to overwhelm you, go to
someplace no one knows you, dress in black, and do the awful act, but
do not disgrace the Name in the open.
—*Ilai, Talmud*

He has told you, O man, what is good, And what the Lord requires
of you: Only to do justice, And to love goodness, And to walk
humbly with your God.
—*Bible, Micah 6:8*

Although pure reason was given to angels, human beings must
observe Torah and commandments.
—*Joseph Yaabetz*

A Nazarite is considered a sinner. . . . This is so because he afflicted
himself by abstaining from wine. . . .
If a person who abstained only from wine is called a sinner, how
much more so is the person who ascetically refrains from all
enjoyment?
—*Talmud*

Never offer Satan an opening.
—*Jose ben Halafta, Talmud*

It is not as some have said that being a mensch, a good man, is the
same as being a Jew. First you become a mensch and from there you
can aspire to becoming a Jew.
—*Ephraim Rottenberg*

The feeding of those who are hungry is a form of contemplation.
                                        —*Simone Weil*

There are times that call for voiding the law in order to work for the Lord.
                                        —*Rabbi Nathan on Psalm 119:126*

All sins are attempts to fill voids.
                                        —*Simone Weil*

Behold all souls are Mine; as the soul of the father, so also the soul of the son is Mine.
                                        —*Bible, Ezekiel 18:4*

. . . Fear to sin in private, where only God will see you, as much as you fear to sin in public, where all the world will see you.
                                        —*Rabbi Johanan ben Zakkai, Talmud*

God desires the heart.
                                        —*Talmud*

To withstand temptation is a deed of great merit.
                                        —*Isaac Nappha, Midrash*

God knew that humankind would be inclined to sin. God therefore created Repentance even before He created man.
                                        —*Otzar Midrashim*

There is no hereditary evil in Israel.
                                        —*Pesikta Kahana*

Truth will properly blame those who without reason dismiss all involvement with everyday life, and tell others that they have no respect for either pleasure or their reputation.

These people are only making pretentious statements, and they really do not have disregard for these issues.

These people travel in torn clothes and with stern faces, live the life of poverty and difficulty to bring attention to themselves, to try and make others believe they are of good conduct, restraint, and self-control.

With all this in mind, be drunk in a sober manner.

—*Philo*

No person sins for someone else.

—*Talmud*

Who is a person of piety and still a fool?

Imagine a man who sees a woman drowning, but says, "It would not seem right for me, a religious man, to touch a woman, and therefore I cannot pull her out."

—*Talmud*

For Judaism the center of gravity is here and now.

Though we are immortal, yet eternity is only a succession of todays. The whole problem of life faces us today.

—*Israel Zangwill*

Who is the pious fool?

Imagine a man who sees a child fighting to stay afloat in the water, and the man says, "When I have taken off my tefillin [phylacteries, a ritual of prayer] I will go and save the child," and while the man does this, the child is lost.

—*Jerusalem Talmud*

The soul consists of three parts: the power of life, the power of endurance, and the power of higher feeling.

—*Zohar*

Watch over your own soul and your neighbor's body rather than your body and your neighbor's soul.

—*Menahem Mendel of Kotsk*

Israel is redeemed because of the pious women of the generation.

—*Yalkut Shimoni*

Often we are less willing to do something about a negative urge than we are about the disturbance of a fly. For example, if a fly lands on us, at the least we will brush it away.

Often we are less willing to do something positive than the effort we would exercise for the smallest coin. For example, if along our way, we see a coin we will not hesitate to bend, and make an effort to retrieve it.

—Rabbi Isaac Meyer of Ger, the Gerer Rebbe

Repentance should be realized through joy.

—Nachman of Bratslav

Humankind's ladder to God is a ladder of deeds.

—Sholem Asch

Repentance: a fierce fight with the heart.

—Orhot Tzaddikim

A righteous person is a prince because he is obeyed by his senses, his mental and physical self.

—Judah Halevi

We are sinful not simply because we have eaten from the Tree of Knowledge, but also because we haven't eaten yet from the Tree of Life.

—Franz Kafka

A person came to the Ba'al Shem Tov. "Master, why does the Bible so often tell us about the bad acts of good people? Wouldn't it be more effective for convincing people to be good if the Bible taught that good people are always good?"

And the Ba'al Shem Tov answered, "If the Bible didn't show us the weaknesses, the vulnerabilities, the sins of our heroes, we might have deep questions about their true virtue."

—Ba'al Shem Tov

The religion of Israel freed mankind from that worship of Luck and Fate which is at the basis of all savagery.

—Joseph Jacobs

"Rabbi Bunam, Rabbi Bunam," requested a follower, "I need an explanation. In the Talmud, Erubin 13a, it is written that when a person flees from great honor, honor will follow him.

"I have been running from recognition, but accolades are not following me."

"The reason this is happening," reasoned Rabbi Bunam, "is because your expectation persists in looking behind you."

—*Simcha Bunam*

Anyone who does not follow a king's order because he is involved with a commandment of God, no matter how small, is free of any blame. . . .

And obviously, if a king orders you to do something that is against God's commands, the king is not to be followed.

—*Maimonides*

Justify not yourself in the sight of God.

—*Wisdom of Ben Sira*

The servant of God does not withdraw himself from worldly contact, because he might become a weight to the world and the world to him. . . .

He loves this world and a long life, because they give him a chance to deserve the world to come.

—*Judah Halevi*

[Those] who try to figure when the Redemption will happen will have no share in it.

—*Jose, Talmud: Tosefta Derek Eretz*

[The Garden of] Eden has no limit.

—*Talmud*

Just as it is forbidden to permit that which is prohibited, so it is forbidden to prohibit that which is permitted.

—*Jerusalem Talmud*

Rabbi Samuel bar Nahman said: "Repentance is like the vast sea laid out before humankind allowing us to purify ourselves at any time;

but prayer is like a bath and sometimes it is difficult to get into the bath."

—*Pesikta Buber*

Man's good deeds are single acts in the long drama of redemption.
—*Abraham Joshua Heschel*

Rabbi Simeon ben Lakish said: "Those who repent out of fear of the consequences cause their sins to be seen as unwitting errors.

"But those whose repentance comes from the far more ethical motive—love of God—cause even their sins to be treated as righteous deeds."

—*Talmud*

Judaism has not allowed the doctrine of original sin to be grafted on to it.

—*Abraham Geiger*

For there is not a righteous man upon earth, that doeth good, and sinneth not.

—*Bible, Ecclesiastes 7:20*

Seven attributes help bring a person closer to God, and these are: wisdom, righteousness, judgment, grace, mercy, truth, and peace.
—*Rabbi Nathan, Pirke Avot*

God forgives those who invent what they need.
—*Lillian Hellman*

Don't try to drive impropriety from your mind by force.
Instead, ignore evil thoughts, and focus on God.
—*Shenor Zalman*

Rabbi Eleazar said: "In life, when a person has insulted another in public and after a time wants to be friends again, the abused will say: 'You insulted me in public, and now you want to be friends again when we are by ourselves? Leave and bring together the others in front of whom you insulted me. Then I will be at one with you.'"

God, however, is not like this. A person may stand alone and shout and be sacrilegious in the center of the market and the Holy One says: "Do penance between only the two of us, and I will accept you."

—*Pesikta Buber*

. . . Not religion as duty, but duty as religion.

—*Felix Adler*

CHAPTER 6

God and Nature

The earth, O Lord, is full of Thy mercy.

—*Bible, Psalms 119:64*

Holy, holy, holy, is the Lord of hosts; the whole earth is filled with His glory.

—*Bible, Isaiah 6:3*

In former days men interpreted earthquakes and tidal waves as afflictions sent by God for the sins they had committed. The knowledge since acquired of the working of natural law has negated any connection between human sin and the tremors of the earth. But unfortunately this tendency to deny any relationship between human misery and human sin has been carried over to the domain of men's dealings with one another where the relationship is inextricable.

—*Mordecai M. Kaplan*

The Lord was not in the wind . . . not in the earthquake . . . not in the fire . . . but in a still, small voice.

—*Bible, I Kings 19:11*

There is not a single blade of grass that has not its own star in heaven that strikes it and says, "GROW!"

—*Genesis Rabbah*

Everything above and below is one unity.

—*Ba'al Shem Tov*

Why was Adam created on the sixth day, after all the other creatures?

So that in case a person would become arrogant, he would be reminded that even the gnats preceded him in the order of creation.

—*Talmud*

What is contrary to nature is contrary to God.

—*Leopold Kompert*

God does not play dice with the universe.

—*Albert Einstein*

As thou knowest not what is the way of the wind, nor how the bones do grow in the womb of her that is with child; even so thou knowest not the work of God Who doeth all things.

—*Bible, Ecclesiastes 11:5*

Revelation is the silent, imperceptible manifestation of God in history.

It is the still, small voice: it is the inevitableness, the regularity of nature.

—*Herbert M. J. Loewe*

Eternity is the very core of God.

—*Baruch Spinoza*

God is the space of the world.

—*Zohar*

He hides Himself in His manifestations, and shows Himself in His concealments.

—*Ba'al Shem Tov*

And God said . . .

"I will see in the rainbow an everlasting covenant between God and every living creature of all flesh that is upon the earth."

—*Bible, Genesis 9:16*

He is God in heaven above, and on earth beneath.

> —*Bible, Joshua 2:11*

God made all things, great and small, and anyone who disdains anyone disdains the face of the Lord.

> —*Apocrypha, II Enoch*

The details make life holy.

> —*Noah benShea*

Yours, Lord, is the greatness, the strength, the splendor, the triumph, and the glory, even everything on heaven and earth.

> —*Bible, I Chronicles 29:11*

PART TWO

Be a Master of
Your Will and a Servant
to Your Conscience

IT IS A PREMISE IN JUDAISM THAT A PERSON MUST NOT COME TO prayer inflated with self-pride. Such pride fills us and occludes our experience of the Divine. If we would be more, we must be prepared to be less. Nevertheless, although humility is a necessary aspect of prayer, self-abnegation should be cautioned against; we are reminded in the Talmud: "If I am not for myself, what am I?"

Finding our way means not just knowing the right path but also choosing it. In the evolution of an individual, character counts as much as intellect; and as Jews, character is our compass.

At the end of his life Moses is directed by God to the top of a mountain. There the land of Israel is revealed to him; but Moses is informed that he will never arrive there—for even Moses can have a place too far for this life. Like Moses, what life affords each of us is a view from the heights of our achievements. And it is by virtue of this perspective that we might see where we, in our wanderings, have both found and lost our way.

CHAPTER 7

Self, Self-Respect, Humility, Identity

The center of the world is exactly where you stand.

—*Talmud*

Progress never marches in a parade.

—*Walter Winchell*

One feels inclined to say that the intention that man should be "happy" is not included in the plan of "Creation." . . . We are so made that we can derive intense enjoyment only from a contrast and very little from a state of things.

—*Sigmund Freud*

Do what you can while you can; while you have the chance, the capability, and the strength.

—*Simeon ben Eleazar, Talmud*

The world is a mirror: what looks in looks out. It gives back only what you lend it.

—*Ludwig Boerne*

Be a master of your will, and a servant to your conscience.

—*Hasidic folk tradition*

The First Man was not created from the dust of this world, but out of the dust from the Upper Holy Temple.

—*Zohar*

Allow the truth and right by which you appear the loser to be desirable to you over the falseness and wrong by which you would appear to have gained.

—*Maimonides*

When something does not insist on being noticed, when we aren't grabbed by the collar or struck on the skull by a presence or an event, we take for granted the very things that most deserve our gratitude.

—*Cynthia Ozick*

Man can be defined as the animal that can say 'I.'

—*Erich Fromm*

People who lack the power to be in charge of or control their emotions [are subject to] what I call enslavement. . . .

. . . [Such people are] enslaved by fortune . . . forced to trail in the wake of the worst, even though they can see what is better right in front of them.

—*Baruch Spinoza*

When in doubt, do without.

—*Viscount Herbert Samuel*

Rabbi Eleazar taught:
"A person should bend like a reed, and not be hard like a cedar."

—*Talmud*

A young tree bends, an old tree breaks.

—*Yiddish folk saying*

At times it is strangely sedative to know the extent of your own powerlessness.

—*Erica Jong*

Those who can't dance say the musicians can't keep time.
—*Yiddish folk saying*

A man's variances are always explicable enough to himself.
—*André Maurois*

All [life] is pattern . . . but we can't always see the pattern when we're part of it.
—*Belva Plain*

Can the Ethiopian change his skin, or the leopard his spots?
—*Bible, Jeremiah 13:23*

. . . All people should love themselves and seek what is good for them.
—*Baruch Spinoza*

Equality of opportunity is an equal opportunity to prove unequal talents.
—*Viscount Herbert Samuel*

If you lose your self-respect you also lose the respect of others.
—*Yiddish folk saying*

In my life's chain of events nothing was accidental. Everything happened according to an inner need.
—*Hannah Senesh*

Once you have distanced yourself from anger, the experience of humility will enter your heart.
—*Nachmanides*

There is no ornament as attractive as humility.
—*Nachmanides*

Compassion directed to oneself is humility.
—*Simone Weil*

Don't be so humble. You're not that great.

—*Golda Meir*

Anyone well aware of their humility is no longer humble.

—*Jacob Klatzkin*

Getting out of bed in the morning is an act of false confidence.

—*Jules Feiffer*

If I am not for myself, who is for me?
And being only for my own self, what am I?
And if not now, when?

—*Hillel the Elder, Pirke Avot*

Little troubles are really a positive thing—for someone else.

—*Shalom Aleichem*

There is not a man that has not his hour, and there is not a thing that has not its place.

—*Ben Azzai, Pirke Avot*

The right to be left alone is the most comprehensive of rights and the right most valued in civilized man.

—*Louis D. Brandeis*

Relax. Little things affect little minds.

—*Benjamin Disraeli*

We are generally the better persuaded by the reasons we discover ourselves than by those given to us by others.

—*Marcel Proust*

The eye, the ear, and the nose are independent of man's will.

—*Wayyira, Tanhuma*

Man is not the creature of circumstances. Circumstances are the creatures of men.

—*Benjamin Disraeli*

What happens to a man is less significant than what happens within him.

—*Louis L. Mann*

Exaggerated sensitiveness is an expression of the feeling of inferiority.

—*Alfred Adler*

You cannot be everything if you want to be anything.

—*Solomon Schechter*

Try not to become a man of success but rather try to become a man of value.

—*Albert Einstein*

The danger in the past was that men became slaves. The danger of the future is that men may become robots.

—*Erich Fromm*

Who is a mighty man?
He who curbs his Evil Impulse.

—*Ben Zoma, Pirke Avot*

Learn the great art of being small.

—*Joseph Hayyim Brenner*

Think of all the beauty still left around you and be happy.

—*Anne Frank*

When God created Adam, the angels by mistake thought he was a god. . . . But when God put him to sleep, they knew he was a mortal.

—*Genesis, Midrash Rabbah*

We have inherited new difficulties because we have inherited more privileges.

—*Abram Leon Sachar*

It's always something.

—*Gilda Radner*

A person will be called to account on Judgment Day for every permissible thing that he might have enjoyed but did not.

—*Jerusalem Talmud*

To be a hero, one must give an order to oneself.

—*Simone Weil*

As a man thinks of himself, so will he be.

—*Moses Gentili*

It is a fault to wish to be understood before we have made ourselves clear to ourselves.

—*Simone Weil*

Keep calm, and be quiet.

—*Bible, Isaiah 7:4*

Let me listen to me and not to them.

—*Gertrude Stein*

I never refuse. I contradict. I sometimes forget.

—*Benjamin Disraeli*

He who promises runs in debt.

—*Talmud*

We often need most the unnecessary.

—*Berthold Auerbach*

We live on the leash of our senses.

—*Diane Ackerman*

Once I make up my mind, I'm full of indecision.

—*Oscar Levant*

In this world a person who is a dog can become a lion, and a person who is a lion can become a dog.

—*Ruth, Midrash Rabbah*

Pessimism is not a philosophy, it is a temperament.
—*Max Nordau*

Each person should say: "The world was created for my sake."
—*Sanhedrin, Mishnah*

Ben Zoma said:
"Who is wise? Those who can learn from everyone.
Who is strong? Those who can control their passions.
Who is honored? Those who honor others."
—*Pirke Avot*

The true value of a human being is determined primarily by the measure and the sense in which he has attained liberation from the self.
—*Albert Einstein*

The Universe does not exist for man's sake, but all things in the Universe exist for their own sake.
—*Maimonides*

The faint memory of forbidden fruit is the earliest event in the memory of each of us, and in the memory of mankind.
—*Henri Bergson*

Have confidence in yourself and others will have confidence in you.
—*Hasidic folk saying*

Each human being is often referred to as a small world. The way this is understood is this:
If a person sees himself as "small" in his own vision, then he is in fact a "world."
But if a person sees himself as a "world" in his own vision, then he is in fact "small."
—*Rabbi Noah Lekhivitzer*

The person who cannot find a moment when he is a disappointment to himself has a diminished conscience.
—*Jacob Klatzkin*

We cannot achieve self-respect if we are afraid of self-knowledge.
                                                    —*Morris Raphael Cohen*

Joy waits for no man.

                                                    —*Talmud*

Every person's life is given to him in trust for safekeeping, and to hold that trust for yourself is a closer duty than to hold that trust for your neighbor.

                                                    —*Ahad Ha-Am*

If there is any miracle in the world, any mystery, it is individuality.
                                                    —*Leo Baeck*

The idea that egotism is the basis of general welfare is the principle on which competitive society has been built.

                                                    —*Erich Fromm*

Lead me to a rock that is too high for me.
                                                    —*Bible, Psalms 61:3*

In a fight between you and the world, back the world.
                                                    —*Franz Kafka*

You will not obtain what you love if you do not bear a great deal that you hate, and you will not be released from what you hate if you do not bear a great deal from what you love.

                                                    —*Moses ibn Ezra*

A person can shoulder more than ten oxen can pull.
                                                    —*Yiddish folk saying*

A man is led in the direction he wants to follow.
                                                    —*Huna, Talmud*

The fault is in us.

                                                    —*Hannah Arendt*

Be whole-hearted.

—*Bible, Genesis 17:1*

Ten enemies will do less harm to us than we are quite capable of doing to ourselves.

—*Yiddish folk saying*

Men commit errors not because they think they know what they do not know, but because they think others do not know.

—*Shalom Aleichem*

A student was waiting in the rain to seek Jacob's advice. The boy ran alongside Jacob and matched his stride.

"Jacob, what are the limits of a man?"

"Ask the man!" said Jacob, without losing his pace.

"And what if the man acknowledges no limits?"

"Then you've discovered his."

"But," the student persisted, "what then is the route to wisdom?"

"Humility!" came the reply.

"How long is the route?"

And Jacob answered, "I don't know."

—*Noah benShea*

Life is too short to be little.

—*André Maurois*

Who would ever think that so much can go on in the soul of a young girl?

—*Anne Frank*

Rabbi Simeon said: "There are three crowns: the crown of learning, the crown of priesthood, and the crown of royalty. But greater than any of these is the crown of a good name."

—*Pirke Avot*

A horse does not need an excuse for being a horse and not being a man, but the horse must be a horse and not a man.

—*Baruch Spinoza*

The Soul of Man was created on the first day; the Angels on the second. If people keep the Spirit of God dominant within them, they are told: "You are greater than the angels."

—*Bereshit Rabbah*

The purpose of man's life is not happiness, but worthiness.

—*Felix Adler*

The human soul has a need for security and risk. The fear of violence or of hunger or of any other extreme evil is a sickness of the soul. The boredom produced by a complete absence of risk is also a sickness of the soul.

—*Simone Weil*

All must respect those who respect themselves.

—*Benjamin Disraeli*

It is easier to live through someone else than to become complete yourself.

—*Betty Friedan*

In spite of everything I still believe that people are good at heart.

—*Anne Frank*

Nobody has a worse servant than he who is his own master.

—*Moritz Gottlieb Saphir*

Every person has three names: one that his father and mother give him, one that others call him, and one that he gains by his own actions.

—*Ecclesiastes Rabbah*

We do not succeed in changing things according to our desire, but gradually our desire changes. The situation that we hoped to change because it was unacceptable becomes unimportant. We have not managed to surmount the obstacle, as we were totally determined to do, but life has taken us around it, led us beyond it.

—*Marcel Proust*

CHAPTER 8

Finding One's Way, Conducting One's Self, Will, and Self-Confidence

Inner superiority to worldly fortune is the essence of genuine nobility.

—*Morris Raphael Cohen*

The Tzupenester Rebbe discovered his followers playing a game of checkers and told them: It is possible to achieve much learning by observing the rules of this game.

You must give up one in order to take two.

It is impossible to make two moves at one time.

You are allowed to move up but not down.

Once you have reached the top, you may move where you want.

—*The Tzupenester Rebbe*

Destiny and freedom are solemnly promised each to the other. [But] only the man who makes freedom real to himself achieves his destiny.

—*Martin Buber*

Be Here Now.

—*Ram Dass (Richard Alpert)*

When someone behaves like a beast, he says: "After all, one is only human." But when he is treated like a beast, he says: "After all, one is human."

—*Karl Kraus*

Some miss many pleasures through caring too much for comfort.
—*Viscount Herbert Samuel*

A person should associate with good people and regularly be in the company of those who are wise so he may learn from what they do.

Similarly, a person should give distance to those who carry themselves in the shadow, so he does not mimic them. . . .

Therefore, if you are in an area where the habits are evil, and the people there walk the path of evil, you should move to another place where the habits are good and the people carry themselves as those who are righteous.

—*Maimonides*

What we anticipate seldom occurs; what we least expected generally happens.

—*Benjamin Disraeli*

First you should put together your house, then your town, then the world.

—*Israel Salanter Lipkin*

The best we can do to achieve holiness is to make a beginning and persevere in our efforts.

—*Moses Luzzatto*

If you can't bite, don't show your teeth.

—*Yiddish folk saying*

Ambition is its own bondage.

—*Solomon ibn Gabirol*

A great deal of what we want we would not like if we got it.
—*Berthold Auerbach*

Those who reflect on their own conduct add to themselves.
—*Midrash Rabbah*

It is the will that is the father of the deed.

—*Benjamin Disraeli*

Those who try to be everywhere end up nowhere.
—*Yiddish folk saying*

Those who do not grow, grow smaller.
—*Hillel the Elder, Pirke Avot*

If a man does not know what is impossible, he will do it.
—*Michael Todd*

Short-range defeats are often long-range victories.
—*Alexander H. Pekelis*

Always do one thing less than you think you can do.
—*Bernard M. Baruch*

Sometimes small things lead to great joys.
—*Samuel Joseph Agnon*

All our final decisions are made in states of mind that do not last.
—*Marcel Proust*

If you are not able to get what you desire, desire what you are able to get.
—*Solomon ibn Gabirol*

Don't be like a bird who sees the seeds but not the snare.
—*Judah ibn Tibbon*

If you don't know where you are going, then any road will take you there.
—*Talmud*

People look caringly only at the blossom and the fruit, and disregard the long period of transition when one is ripening into the other.
—*Berthold Auerbach*

Postpone not till tomorrow what you can do today.
—*Yiddish folk saying*

One should despise much, forgive often, and never forget.

—Sarah Bernhardt

Our concern is not how to worship in catacombs but how to remain human in skyscrapers.

—Abraham Joshua Heschel

An ideal is a port toward which we resolve to steer.

—Felix Adler

I have often thought that morality consists singularly in the courage of making a choice.

—Léon Blum

You may be disappointed if you fail, but you are doomed if you don't try.

—Beverly Sills

Man is not imprisoned by habit. Great changes in him can be wrought by crisis—once that crisis can be recognized and understood.

—Norman Cousins

All beginnings are difficult.

—Mekilta to Jethro

Let another person praise you, and not your own mouth.

—Bible, Proverbs 27:2

Akabya ben Mahalalel said: "Remember three things and you will avoid the consequences of evil: know from where you came, to where you are going, and before Whom you will have to explain what you have done and become."

—Pirke Avot

The righteous person falls seven times and gets up again.

—Bible, Proverbs 24:16

Do not run too far, for you must return the same distance.

—Midrash Rabbah

The perfection of Torah leads us to perfection . . . it aims at a person following a path of moderation, following the laws of Nature, eating, drinking, enjoying moral sexual intercourse, all with moderation, and residing among people honestly and righteously, but not living in distant wildernesses or on mountain peaks, or dressing ourselves in uncomfortable clothes, or in any way afflicting the body.

—*Maimonides*

Modesty is submissiveness and wisdom combined.

—*Solomon ibn Gabirol*

Grasp what is good, even if it is meager; put your hand on it, hold on to it, and do not let it go.

—*Berechiah ben Natronai ha-Nakdan*

There is moderation even in excess.

—*Benjamin Disraeli*

. . . Controversy is hateful, and peace is wonderful. Set your heart to pursue peace, for if peace is lacking then there is nothing.

—*Rashi*

The middle road is in reality the royal road.

—*Philo*

You are not allowed to deceive anyone, Jew or non-Jew.

—*Talmud*

If we fight against the waves that pass over us in life, we are overpowered.

If we move with the waves in life as they roll over us, the wave passes on.

—*Pesikta Zutarti*

We are what we will to be.

—*Max Weiner*

The world is a rocky sea of unfathomable depth and size, and time is a vulnerable bridge crossing this sea. . . .

We human beings spend our lives traveling this bridge from the day we are born.

—*Jedaiah of Béziers*

If you desire life, expect pain.

—*Azariah, Midrash Tehillim*

Hillel said: Among those who stand, do not sit, and among those who sit, do not stand. Among those who laugh, do not weep; and among those who weep, do not laugh.

—*Tosefta Berakot*

When one changes one's place, one changes one's fortune.

—*Yiddish folk saying*

There is no roadway without ambushes, and there is no roadway without crossroads.

—*Sifrei*

Do not walk the path taken by those who are unethical, And do not take the path of those who are meanspirited . . . Turn from these roads and move on.

—*Bible, Proverbs 4:14–15*

We have to try and cure our faults by attention and not by will.

—*Simone Weil*

The worm in the radish doesn't think there is anything sweeter.

—*Shalom Aleichem*

I believe in the tragic element of history. I believe there is the tragedy of a man who works very hard and never gets what he wants. And then I believe there is even the more bitter tragedy of a man who finally gets what he wants and finds that he doesn't want it.

—*Henry Kissinger*

When you must, you can.

—*Yiddish folk saying*

CHAPTER 9

Growing Older,

Experience, Time, Fate

Time and chance happen to all of us.

—*Bible, Ecclesiastes 9:11*

The best minister is the human heart;
the best teacher is time;
the best book is the world;
the best friend is God.

—*Yiddish folk saying*

Experience is a good school, but the fees are high.

—*Heinrich Heine*

Experience is what we call our mistakes.

—*Yiddish folk saying*

The present is the spinning wheel, the past the thread with which
we spin, the future the wool for men to weave their years.

—*Benjamin Mandelstamm*

Life, despite their frantic yoohooings, had passed them by.

—*Bernard Malamud*

After a certain number of years, our faces become our biographies.
—*Cynthia Ozick*

In middle age, you go to bed hoping you'll feel better in the morning.
In old age, you go to bed hoping you'll have a morning.
—*Groucho Marx*

Experience: a comb life gives you after you lose your hair.
—*Judith Stern*

What recalls another to us most vividly is precisely that which we had forgotten because it was unimportant: it has remained as it was, unchanged by our thought.
—*Marcel Proust*

Remember God in the days of your youth . . . Before the silver cord snaps in two, And the golden bowl is broken . . . And the dust returns to the earth as it was, And the breath of life returns unto God, Who gave it.
—*Ecclesiastes 12:1, 6–7*

I am a sojourner on the earth.
—*Bible, Psalms 119:19*

We want what we do not have, and what we have we do not prize.
—*Yiddish folk saying*

Growth is a greater mystery than death. All of us can understand failure, we all contain failure and death within us, but not even the successful man can begin to describe the impalpable elations and apprehensions of growth.
—*Norman Mailer*

Middle age is when a man is warned to slow down by a doctor instead of a policeman.
—*Sidney Brody*

Conditioned to operating as a machine for making and spending money, with all other relationships dependent upon its efficiency, the moment the machine is out of order and beyond repair, one begins to feel like a ghost without a sense of reality.

—*Abraham Joshua Heschel*

The time that we have for our use every day is elastic; the passions that we feel expand it, the passions we inspire contract it, and habit fills up what remains.

—*Marcel Proust*

Wisdom doesn't automatically come with old age. Nothing does— except wrinkles. It's true, some wines improve with age. But only if the grapes were good in the first place.

—*Abigail Van Buren*

I must govern the clock, not be governed by it.

—*Golda Meir*

Rabbi Joshua ben Levi once said: "Have respect and honor for the old and saintly whose physical powers are broken just as you would for the young and healthy; for the broken Stone Tablets just as the whole ones were given a place in the Holy Ark of the Covenant."

—*Talmud*

People think all I have to do is to stand up and tell a few jokes. Well, that's not as easy as it looks. Every year it gets to be more of an effort to stand up.

—*George Burns*

Youth is a blunder;
Manhood a struggle;
Old Age a regret.

—*Benjamin Disraeli*

Your old men shall dream dreams, your young men shall see visions.

—*Bible, Joel 2:28*

Time will teach more than all our thoughts.
　　　　　　　　　　　—*Benjamin Disraeli*

The disappointment of manhood succeeds the delusion of youth.
　　　　　　　　　　　—*Benjamin Disraeli*

Being an old maid is like death by drowning, a really delightful sensation after you cease to struggle.
　　　　　　　　　　　—*Edna Ferber*

Old age is the most unexpected of all things that happen to a man.
　　　　　　　　　　　—*Leon Trotsky*

There is an ever-rotating wheel in this world.
　　　　　　　　　　　—*Midrash Rabbah*

Like all great travellers, I have seen more than I remember, and remember more than I have seen.
　　　　　　　　　　　—*Benjamin Disraeli*

It would be correct to say that the world was not made in time, but that time was created by the world, because it is the movement of the heavens that is the index for the nature of time.
　　　　　　　　　　　—*Philo*

You can't push a wave onto the shore any faster than the ocean brings it in.
　　　　　　　　　　　—*Susan Strasberg*

We make our fortunes and we call them fate.
　　　　　　　　　　　—*Benjamin Disraeli*

If you want the present to be different from the past, study the past.
　　　　　　　　　　　—*Baruch Spinoza*

If we do not know our own history, we are doomed to live it as though it were our private fate.
　　　　　　　　　　　—*Hannah Arendt*

Those who want to know everything become old while they are young.

—*Yiddish folk saying*

Time is a circus always packing up and moving away.

—*Ben Hecht*

Middle age is when your classmates are so grey and wrinkled and bald they don't recognize you.

—*Bennett Cerf*

There are two myths regarding the Phoenix in Jewish literature. In the first, only the Phoenix of all the living creatures did not eat fruit from the Tree of Knowledge in the Garden of Eden, and therefore never dies. The second myth recalls that when the Phoenix was in the Ark with Noah, the Phoenix observed how hard Noah had to work caring for the needs of all the animals. Not wanting to be a burden, the Phoenix went off by itself and hid unseen. Time passed, and when Noah discovered the Phoenix half-starved, Noah so appreciated the bird's goodwill he blessed the Phoenix with eternal life. Since then, the Phoenix lives a thousand years, passes through a flame, and reappears newborn.

—*Talmud*

We do not leave this world with even half of what we want answered.

—*Midrash Rabbah*

For the ignorant, old age is winter. For the wise, old age is a time of harvest.

—*Hasidic folk saying*

You shall stand before those who are old, and show respect for those who are old.

—*Bible, Leviticus 19:32*

Nobody grows old by merely living a number of years. People grow old only by deserting their ideals.

—*Samuel Ullman*

A man lives with himself for seventy years, and doesn't know who he is.

—*Israel Salanter Lipkin*

Life is not a matter of extent but of content.

—*Stephen Samuel Wise*

Sound within silence, struggle within serenity, war within peace—these are confusions that dissolve as the mind matures.

—*Richard H. Guggenheimer*

It was said by Rabbi Yose ben Kisma:
"Life is a sorrow for the one thing which leaves and does not return."
"What is that?" he was asked.
"One's childhood."

—*Talmud*

To me, old age is fifteen years older than I am.

—*Bernard M. Baruch*

A beautiful lady is an accident of nature. A beautiful old lady is a work of art.

—*Louis Nizer*

. . . No loss like the loss of time.

—*Samuel Uceda, Midrash Samuel*

I didn't belong as a kid, and that always bothered me. If only I'd known that one day my differentness would be an asset, then my early life would have been much easier.

—*Bette Midler*

Each day, as I look, I wonder where my eyes were yesterday.

—*Bernard Berenson*

Living in the past is a dull and lonely business; looking back strains the neck muscles, causes you to bump into people not going your way.

—*Edna Ferber*

Jehuda ben Tama used to say: "At the age of five a person is ready to study the Bible, at ten to study the Mishna, at thirteen to observe the Commandments, at fifteen to study the Talmud, at eighteen to get married, at twenty to start earning a living, at thirty to come into one's full strength, at forty to show discernment, at fifty to give counsel, at sixty to start feeling old, at seventy to turn white, at eighty for worry and trouble, at ninety for senility; and at one hundred . . . for death."

—*Pirke Avot*

To be old is a glorious thing when one has not unlearned what it means to begin.

—*Martin Buber*

PART THREE

We Are Born

for Community

IN JUDAISM THE INDIVIDUAL, AS A REFLECTION OF THE DIVINE, IS RAISED to divine heights. And yet as Jews we are, at the root of our history, each members of one of the Twelve Tribes of Israel. Consequently, we glorify the self but are bound by the sanctity of others.

We are taught in the Talmud to treat others with the same respect with which we would hope to be treated. Clearly, self-respect is essential in order for this principle to operate at its highest levels. And as we have been formed by the Hand of God, we are a people to whom lending others a hand is a sacred obligation.

Vulnerability and insecurity nurture anger, jealousy, fear, and conceit. By witnessing the ways by which we arrive at these emotions, we can observe the patterns that bind all of us. Although we may not have the answer to whether we are our brother's keeper, the question itself no more shields us than it did Cain from the responsibility of his actions toward others.

CHAPTER 10

Self and Others,
Humankind, Social Class,
Community

Behold, how good and pleasant it is for brothers to dwell together in unity!

—*Bible, Psalms 133:1*

In the beginning, God created only one person in order to teach us the lesson that if you destroy a single person it is as if you have destroyed the whole world. And, the Scripture reminds us, if you save the life of a single person, it is as if you have saved the whole world.

—*Mishneh Torah*

A giant is more than a man surrounded by dwarfs.

—*Yiddish folk saying*

Despise no man and consider nothing impossible. For there is no man who does not have his hour, and there is nothing that does not have its place.

—*Ben Azzai, Pirke Avot*

If you insist you're right long enough, you'll be wrong.

—*Yiddish folk saying*

We are born for community.

—*Josephus*

Observe the waters: when they flow together, they sweep along stones, trees, earth, and many other things; but if the waters are divided into many streams, the earth swallows them, and they disappear. So shall you also be if you allow yourself to be divided.

—*Apocrypha*

Man . . . can develop into an individual only in society.

—*Karl Marx*

Am I my brother's keeper?

—*Bible, Genesis 4:9*

Do not attribute a fault within yourself to the person next to you.

—*Talmud*

To show that no person can sin only for himself alone, Rabbi Simeon ben Yohai explained:

"A number of people were seated in a boat, and one of them took out a drill and began drilling a hole beneath where he sat. The fellow travelers shouted: 'What are you doing there?'

"The person with the drill shouted back, 'What does it matter to you? Aren't I drilling a hole under my seat?'

"The others answered: 'It is absolutely our business. If the water fills the boat, we will all drown.' "

—*Midrash Rabbah*

Who is honored? He who honors mankind.

—*Ben Zoma, Pirke Avot*

If a prince were to wear a Bohemian glass stone on his finger, it would be taken for a diamond; should a beggar wear a genuine diamond ring, everyone would be equally convinced it was only glass.

—*Heinrich Heine*

One who desires the attention of others has not yet found himself.

—*Shlomo Wolbe*

There are people who are followed all through their lives by a beggar to whom they have given nothing.

—*Karl Kraus*

Pleasing everyone is an impossible aim, and escaping all criticism is an unattainable goal.

—*Moses ibn Ezra*

Each social class has its own pathology.

—*Marcel Proust*

Not the power to remember, but its very opposite, the power to forget, is a necessary condition for our existence.

—*Sholem Asch*

Those who persuade others to perform a good deed, it is as if they themselves have performed it.

—*Talmud*

One glorious chain of love, of giving and receiving, unites all creatures.

—*Samson Raphael Hirsch*

There are so many sorts of people in the world: asses . . . dogs . . . pigs . . . worms.

—*Shalom Aleichem*

In the coming world, I will not be asked, "Why weren't you Moses?" Rather, I will be asked, "Why weren't you Zusya?"

—*Rabbi Zusya*

What hurts the most is what you can't tell others.

—*Yiddish folk saying*

Rabbi Aibo said: "When the Angels objected to the creation of man, God replied: 'And of what use are all of the good things I have created unless people are there to enjoy them?' "

—*Midrash Rabbah*

An old man sat outside the walls of a great city.

When travelers approached they would ask the old man: "What kind of people live in this city?"

And the old man would answer: "What kind of people lived in the place where you came from?"

If the travelers answered: "Only bad people lived in the place where we came from."

Then the old man would reply: "Continue on, you will only find bad people here."

But if the travelers answered: "Only good people lived in the place where we have come from."

Then the old man would say: "Enter, for here, too, you will only find good people."

—Adapted from the Yiddish folk tradition

What should be done, if one of two travelers in the desert has a little water and the other has none?

If one of the two drinks all the water, he will survive.

If they divide the water, they both will die.

Ben Paturi said they should share the water and die because it is written: "And your brother shall live with you."

But Rabbi Akiba answered: "Your brother shall live with *you,* and this means that your life takes precedence over his life."

—Sifrei

Take a companion.

—Joshua ben Perahia, Mishneh Torah

Those who think they can live without others are wrong. But those who think that others cannot survive without them are even more in error.

—Hasidic folk saying

Do not put a stumbling block in front of the blind.

—Bible, Leviticus 19:14

No one has the vision to observe his own faults.

—Judah Al-Harizi

To do evil to another human being is worse than to do evil toward God. The person you hurt may leave and go to a place you do not know or are incapable of reaching. Therefore you will not have the opportunity to ask to be forgiven for what you had done. God, however, so completely surrounds us with His presence that it is always possible to find Him if you are truly seeking.

—*The Amshinover Rebbe*

The first human being who hurled an insult instead of a stone was the founder of civilization.

—*Sigmund Freud*

I cannot give you the formula for success, but I can give you the formula for failure—which is: Try to please everybody.

—*Herbert Bayard Swope*

If the community is in trouble, a person must not say, "I will go home, and eat and drink, and my soul will be at peace."

A person must share in the concerns of the community as Moses did.

Those who share in the community's troubles are worthy to see its consolation.

—*Talmud, Ta'anit*

CHAPTER 11

Kindness, Friendship, Mercy, Forgiveness, Sympathy, Hospitality, Patience, Pleasure, Happiness

Seek the good in everyone, and reveal it, bring it forth.

—*Nachman of Bratslav*

From a slight distance we all remain closer friends.

—*Yiddish folk saying*

Say not, "I will do to him as he has done to me."

—*Bible, Proverbs 24:29*

Whenever I met someone for whom my heart felt no affection, I forced myself to speak kindly to this person, so my heart would feel affection.

—*Joel ben Abraham Shemaria*

Before honor goes humility.

—*Bible, Proverbs 15:33*

Those who chase happiness are often fleeing from contentment.

—*Yiddish folk saying*

Consider as significant the small slights you do to others, and minimal the large wrongs done to you.

—*Talmud*

Don't visit your neighbor in the hour of his disgrace.
—*Mishneh Torah*

Guests and rain are the same. If they stay long they are a nuisance.
—*Yiddish folk saying*

Cast not pearls before swine, for they can do nothing with them.
—*Solomon ibn Gabirol*

What business does a drunk peasant have in God's world? But if God gets along with him, can I deny him?
—*Moshe Leib of Sasov*

To pull a friend from the mud, don't hesitate to get dirty.
—*Ba'al Shem Tov*

To have a friend, be one.
—*Viscount Herbert Samuel*

Kindness is remembered, meanness is felt.
—*Yiddish folk saying*

When King David had finished writing the Book of Psalms, he was filled with a great pride, and said: "Lord of the Universe, do You have another creature who sings more praises of You than me?"

Then God sent a frog to David. The frog, croaking, said: "Do not be so filled with pride. I sing the praises of my Creator more than you do.

"And in addition, I perform a great deed when my time to die comes. At that point, I go down to the sea and allow myself to be swallowed by one of the sea's creatures.

"In this way, even my death is an act of kindness."
—*Yalkut Shimoni*

Sentimentality is the emotional promiscuity of those who have no sentiment.
—*Norman Mailer*

Too much modesty is half conceit.

—*Yiddish folk saying*

Happiness is not something you experience, it is something you remember.

—*Oscar Levant*

Too few is as many as too many.

—*Gertrude Stein*

Come now and let us reason together.

—*Bible, Isaiah 1:18*

A soft answer turneth away wrath.

—*Bible, Proverbs 15:1*

If a Gentile blesses thee, respond, "Amen."

—*Talmud*

Whoever blesses you, respond, "You, also."

—*Talmud*

Forgiveness is the key to action and freedom.

—*Hannah Arendt*

An optimist is the kind of person who believes a housefly is looking for a way to get out.

—*George Jean Nathan*

The love of our neighbor in all its fullness simply means being able to say to him, "What are you going through?"

—*Simone Weil*

Love demands infinitely less than friendship.

—*George Jean Nathan*

Accustom yourself to speak gently to all people at all times.

—*Nachmanides*

It is of high value to compromise.

—*Joshua ben Karha*

Boredom is an emptiness filled with insistence.

—*Leo Stein*

Friendship is a very taxing and arduous form of leisure activity.

—*Mortimer Adler*

King Solomon received an incredible gift from the Lord, an amazing silk carpet that flew through the air. The king and his courtiers would have breakfast in Damascus and supper in Media, carried back and forth on the glorious carpet.

Once the king passed over an anthill. And, as Solomon understood the language of all living creatures, he overheard the queen ant order all the subjects under her reign to hide from Solomon.

"Why have you demanded this?" Solomon shouted down to the queen ant.

"Because I was afraid my citizens might look up at you, and then they would see pride in the place of humility, diligence, and praise for their Maker."

"I have a question for you," said the king.

"Bring me up to you, then," replied the queen ant.

Holding the small ant in his hand, Solomon asked: "Is there anyone in the world greater than myself?"

"But of course," answered the ant. "I am greater than you, as God has sent you to carry me."

—*Midrash Rabbah*

A Persian king, Arteban, once happened to visit the Emperor Marcus Aurelius Antonius when he was in Syria.

On meeting, the emperor introduced his friend the Patriarch Rabbi Judah I to the Persian king.

The king later sent to Rabbi Judah I a priceless gemstone as a gift, and the rabbi in turn sent to the king a mezuzah [a small, rectangular object, containing sacred passages, that Jews attach to the door frames of their homes].

When the king later met the rabbi he said: "I have sent you a very expensive gift, but you have sent me something of relatively little expense."

Rabbi replied: "[Inside the mezuzah] the portion of the Torah inscribed upon it is of more worth than all valuable objects, because I must keep your gift safe, but my gift will keep you safe, as it is written: 'When you lie down, it shall watch over you' [Proverbs 6:22]."

—Midrash Rabbah

The punishment doled out to those who say bad things is also delivered to those who have the chance to say something good and do not.

—Zohar

You shall not harm any widow or orphan. If you ever wrong them and they cry out loud to Me, I will be sure to hear their cry, and My anger will be hot.

—Bible, Exodus 22:21–22

In choosing a friend, go up a step.

—Talmud

They say to fruit trees:
"Why do you not make any noise?"
The trees reply:
"Our fruit is sufficient publicity for us."

—Midrash Rabbah

All of life's misfortunes can be hidden beneath a smile.

—Yiddish folk saying

The entire value of a kind deed depends on the love that inspires it.

—Talmud

Those who steal another person's confidence are chief among thieves.

—Mekilta

It is a responsibility to nurture kindness.

—Aaron Halevi

An understanding of false humility can be learned from this tale:

A man was knowledgeable, talented, and considerate, but bore the scar of hubris, self-pride.

This same person was told that if he mastered humility he would develop into a perfect person.

Now the man, taking the advice, began to study humility day and night until all the learning concerning humility had been committed to memory.

But, almost immediately, while walking down a street, a stranger failed to show the student of humility the anticipated elevated respect.

"Are you an idiot?" he shouted to the stranger. "Don't you realize that I have now mastered humility and am a person of flawless virtue?"

—*Ba'al Shem Tov*

If you are looking for a friend who has no faults, you will have no friends.

—*Hasidic folk saying*

The most attractive act a person can engage in is to forgive.

—*Eleazar ben Judah*

. . . If we are seeking to be genuinely sympathetic to others, then we must not think one emotional blanket will cover all when God by design and act shows sympathy for each of us as individuals.

—*Moses Mendelssohn*

Judah ha-Nasi was in the middle of a lecture when he noticed that the smell of garlic filled the room.

"One of you has eaten garlic and must leave," said ha-Nasi.

First Rabbi Hiyya rose, and then all the other scholars rose and followed him from the room.

The following morning, Rabbi Simeon, the son of Judah ha-Nasi, went to Rabbi Hiyya and asked, "Were you the one who had been eating garlic?"

"Of course not," said Rabbi Hiyya, looking to heaven, "but by our leaving we kept the individual responsible from being humiliated."

—*Talmud*

Understand that the Lord wants your heart, and the intention of your heart is the measure of what you do. It is for this reason that our sages declare, the righteous among the non-Jews have a place in the world after. . . .

Have no confusion that every person who raises his soul by the elevation of his morality and wisdom out of faith in God absolutely is a member of the community of people in the world after.

—*Maimonides*

Putting sugar in your mouth won't help if you are bitter in your heart.

—*Yiddish folk saying*

Those who are compassionate when they should be stern end up being stern when they should be compassionate.

—*Midrash Rabbah*

Heaven offers us solace; from our neighbors we look for help.

—*Ludwig Boerne*

Those who have compassion for others may be considered true descendants of Abraham.

—*Talmud*

Only feeling comprehends feeling.

—*Heinrich Heine*

Anguish awaits those whom nobody likes, but be very cautious of those whom everybody likes.

—*Hasidic folk saying*

Great is hospitality, even greater than early attendance at the House of Study, or to receive the Holy Spirit.

—*Talmud*

It does not say anywhere in the Torah to invite your guest to pray; but it [the Torah] does require us to offer food, drink, and a bed.

—*"The Chofetz Chaim"*

The habit of loving-kindness is necessary to saintliness.

The Hebrew word that connotes saintliness comes from the same base word that implies kindness.

Conducting oneself with loving-kindness toward others is one of the three foundations wherein the world, according to our sages, is premised.

—*Moses Luzzatto*

My friend is someone who tells me my faults in private.
—*Solomon ibn Gabirol*

The test of good manners is being able to bear patiently with bad ones.
—*Solomon ibn Gabirol*

What is the ultimate virtue?
Patience with the vices of others.
—*Solomon ibn Gabirol*

A true friend is someone who is there for you when he'd rather be anywhere else.
—*Len Wein*

A friend is someone who allows you distance but is never far away.
—*Noah benShea*

Make no friendships with a man given to anger.
—*Bible, Proverbs 22:24*

The highest wisdom is kindness.
—*Talmud*

CHAPTER 12

Jealousy, Envy, Flattery, Gossip, Sentimentality, Arrogance, Indifference, Conceit, Anger, Hate

I never went to the fair without taking into consideration the feelings of my neighbors.

If I was successful and peddled everything I took, and came home with my pockets stuffed with money, and my heart singing, I would tell my neighbors that I had lost all my money and was a failed man.

The outcome of this was that I was happy and my neighbors were happy.

—*Shalom Aleichem*

The worst part of being a success is to try to find someone who is happy for you.

—*Bette Midler*

He is less upset by his poverty than by your wealth.

—*Yiddish folk saying*

Envy is hatred without a remedy.

—*Bahya ben Asher*

Destructiveness is the outcome of unlived lives.

—*Erich Fromm*

He that is slow to anger is better than the mighty; and he that ruleth his spirit is greater than he who captures a city.

—*Bible, Proverbs 16:32*

Anger is born mad and dies with regret.

—*Abraham Hasdai*

Anger locks a person in his own house.

—*Noah benShea*

Most of the terrible things that happen to people are caused by lust and anger.

—*Joseph ibn Shem Tov*

A hurtful act is the transference to others of the degradation that we bear in ourselves.

—*Simone Weil*

All men of anger are men of pride.

—*Midrash Rabbah*

Anger is blindness.

—*Apocrypha*

If you see your neighbor's ox or sheep wander away, do not pretend you have not seen, return it to your neighbor.

If your neighbor does not live close to you or you do not know him, you should still bring the animal home and keep it until your neighbor comes to claim it and then you should give it back to him.

You should do the same if it's a donkey, and the same if it's clothing, and the same no matter what it is that your neighbor loses and you find, you must not say it doesn't matter.

—*Bible, Deuteronomy 22:1–3*

What three people know is no secret.

—*Yiddish folk saying*

We are more likely to find faults in others than virtue in ourselves.
                                              —*Yiddish folk saying*

A number of the Ba'al Shem Tov's followers, Hasidim, sought him out and said: "Those who oppose us, the wise men of Brody, needle us without end, saying that we do not follow the ancient Law and are disrespectful to the traditions of our ancestors. We can't bear up under this aggravation any longer. We must say something to them."

"Those who oppose us with these accusations," said the Ba'al Shem Tov, "believe they are doing this from religious motives. They think that what they are doing are positive deeds and they find joy in this. Who are we to diminish their joy?"
                                              —*Ba'al Shem Tov*

Because of gossip, if you want to know what is happening in your own home, ask your neighbors.
                                              —*Yiddish folk saying*

Gossip is nature's telephone.
                                              —*Shalom Aleichem*

Flattery is diseased friendship.
                                                        —*Philo*

Time wounds all heels.
                                              —*Bennett Cerf*

He who shames his fellow is shamed.
                                              —*Mesikta Kallah*

What Paul says about Peter tells us more about Paul than about Peter.
                                              —*Baruch Spinoza*

Envy looks with a thousand eyes but none of them can see clearly.
                                              —*Isachar Hurwitz*

. . . When we describe what the other person is really like, I suppose we often picture what we want. We look through the prism of our need.
                                              —*Ellen Goodman*

To some extent you may praise a person in his presence, but to praise him fully in his presence is forbidden.

—*Talmud*

If you speak evil of Esau [a non-Jew], you will in the long run speak evil of your fellow Israelite [a Jew].

—*Tanhuma Buber*

. . . All is vanity!

—*Bible, Ecclesiastes 1:2*

A man may flatter his wife for the sake of marital peace.

A man may flatter a creditor for the sake of obtaining another chance.

A man may flatter a teacher for the sake of obtaining more attention.

—*Otzar Midrashim*

A man who owned a store sought out the Premislaner Rebbe with a disturbing concern. The shopkeeper heard that someone else was going to start another business near his, and he was concerned with the implications for his livelihood.

"Have you observed," asked the rebbe, "that a horse, when he bows his head to drink water at a pond, pounds his hooves in the pond?"

"I have," said the man.

"And do you know why?" asked the rebbe.

The man raised his shoulders, implying ignorance.

"Well, let me explain it to you," said the rebbe. "As a horse bends his neck to drink, next to him in the pool is his reflection, another horse. Afraid now that there will not be enough water for both of them, the horse bangs his hooves, hoping to scare the other horse away.

"What do we learn from this? We learn that the horse is imagining a competitor, fears his own reflection, and ignores the fact that regardless there is plenty of water for many horses.

"Your foe also is your own fear. God's plenitude runs as a great river with enough for each of us."

—*Aaron Leib Premislaner, the Premislaner Rebbe*

Don't seek the opinion of a person who is suspicious of you or tell your plans to those who envy you.

—*Wisdom of Ben Sira*

Do not go about as a gossip among your neighbors.

—*Bible, Leviticus 19:16*

Someone who shames another in public is like someone who has caused bloodshed.

—*Talmud*

The devil is an optimist if he thinks he can make people meaner.

—*Karl Kraus*

If a person in anger breaks something, the broken item represents a sacrifice on Satan's altar.

—*Zohar*

If one of us is capable of saving another person and does not save him, we have broken the commandment "Neither shall you stand idly by the blood of your neighbor" [Leviticus 19:16].

—*Maimonides*

. . . Forgive those who insult you.

—*Rabbi Nathan, Pirke Avot*

A mirror fools none but the ugly.

—*Yiddish folk saying*

Humility in the hope of approval is the worst arrogance.

—*Nachman of Bratslav*

Show me someone who never gossips, and I'll show you someone who isn't interested in people.

—*Barbara Walters*

If you want people to think you are wise, agree with them.

—*Yiddish folk saying*

CHAPTER 13

Enemies, Prejudice, Equality

The man who never made an enemy never made anything.

—*Paul Muni*

Respect one another.

—*Eleazar ben Azariah, Talmud*

An enemy is not hidden in adversity.

—*Wisdom of Ben Sira*

Even one enemy is one too many.

—*Asher ben Yehiel*

Who is a hero? He who turns an enemy into a friend.

—*Avot de Rabbi Nathan*

When a man points a finger at someone else, he should remember that four of his fingers are pointing at himself.

—*Louis Nizer*

All colors look alike in the dark.

—*Yiddish folk saying*

Rabbi Levi, in the name of Rabbi Simeon ben Lakish, said: "The gazelle is the animal most loved by God. When the gazelle gives birth to a fawn, God sends a herb to heal her. When she is thirsty, she digs her horns into the ground and moans. God hears her prayer and helps her to find water in the deep pits. When she goes forward to drink, she is at first afraid of the other beasts, but God gives her courage. She stamps her feet and uses her horns, and the beasts then run from her.

"Why does God love her? Because the gazelle harms no one, and never disturbs the peace."

—*Midrash Rabbah*

The eye of a needle is not too narrow for two lovers, but the entire world is not wide enough for two enemies.

—*Solomon ibn Gabirol*

The person we hate fills our mind far more than the person we love.

—*Jacob Klatzkin*

I am very careful in the choice of enemies.

—*Ahad Ha-Am*

Every man's enemy is under his own ribs . . .

—*Bahya ben Joseph ibn Pakuda*

Inflate beyond its size the small wrong you did to someone else, and [consider] as nothing the huge wrong done to you.

—*Talmud*

A friend costs nothing. An enemy you must pay for.

—*Yiddish folk saying*

Even a paranoid can have enemies.

—*Henry Kissinger*

We might define an eccentric as a man who is a law unto himself, and a crank as one who, having determined what the law is, insists on laying it down to others.

—*Louis Kronenberger*

A policy that the Gastininer Rebbe made for himself was as follows: Whenever he was offended or took offense at something someone said to him, he would never say anything on the same day to that person about how he felt.

Instead, he would let his emotions sleep on the matter, and on the next day approach the offender, saying, "I was not happy with you on the day before."

—*The Gastininer Rebbe*

Those who welcome their fellow human beings are like those who welcome Shekinah [God's presence].

—*Talmud*

If you remove from your midst those things which enslave others,
The denigration of others, the saying of evil things about others,
And share what you have with those who have not,
And respond to the needs of those who call out to you,
Then shall your light be a beacon in the darkness,
And your darkness will be washed in the full day's light,
And the LORD will walk beside you as a guide,
And shall richly fill and nourish your life;
And God will renew your strength,
And you will be like a garden wealthy with water,
A spring of water,
Whose waters fail not.

—*Bible, Isaiah 58:9–11*

If two people ask for your help, and one of them is your enemy, help that person first.

—*Talmud*

Rabbi Johanan ben Torta said: "Why was the First Temple destroyed? Because the Israelites were guilty of idolatry, lewdness, and murder.

"But in the days of the Second Temple they were sincere about Torah and gave tithes; so why was the Second Temple also destroyed?

"The answer is that the people . . . hated one another.

"This teaches us that hatred of one's brothers and sisters is a terrible sin in God's eyes, and as wrong as idolatry, lewdness, and murder."

—*Tosefta Menahot*

Release the displeasure you bear toward those who have made mistakes of character in their life.

If these people had been of your character, perhaps they would not have made the mistake.

And if you had been of their character, perhaps you would have made the mistake.

The errors in a lifetime do not always come about from free choice. Often there are many other factors that lean in on us.

—*The Kariver Rebbe*

Those who have no money to lend friends make no enemies.

—*Yiddish folk saying*

No barber cuts his own hair.

—*Yiddish folk saying*

It was a wise man who said that there is no greater inequality than the equal treatment of unequals.

—*Felix Frankfurter*

In a city where there are both Jews and Gentiles, those who collect money should collect from both the Jews and Gentiles, and feed the poor of both, visit the sick of both, bury both, comfort the mourners regardless if they are Jews or Gentiles, and restore the lost goods of both.

—*Jerusalem Talmud*

People are not as good as their friends represent them, and they are not as bad as their enemies depict them.

—*Judah Leib Lazerov*

And a stranger you shall not wrong; neither shall you oppress him; for you were strangers in the land of Egypt.

—*Bible, Exodus 22:20*

PART FOUR

And a Little Child
Shall Lead Them

WITH THE DESTRUCTION OF THE SECOND TEMPLE BY THE ROMANS IN the first century and the expulsion of the Jews from their land, the role of family, already strong in a tribal community, gained new significance. Though the world exercised little regard—if not outright hostility—for its minorities, the social unit of the Jewish family defended itself by reminding its members that they had responsibility for one another, were worthy of love, and had the capacity to love. This core community, the family nucleus, still remains central to understanding the Jewish courage to carry on and flourish.

The same Ten Commandments wherein God demands reverence require one to *Honor Thy Father and Mother.* For Jews, these linked tenets help to hold the world together. Additionally, the significance of honoring parents is that parents are then challenged to conduct themselves in a manner deserving of their children's esteem. The nature of this interaction is a nurturing and embracing circle of respect.

The concept of *dor l'dor,* "generation to generation" in Hebrew, means the passing down of religious belief and participation in a collective consciousness. The Jewish people have been immigrants and wanderers for countless generations, often carrying with them little more than the hope that things would somehow be better for their children. Across the centuries (and in the face of evil), Jewish parents tied themselves to their sons and daughters with cords fashioned from hope and belief. Parents persevered so that their progeny might climb Jacob's ladder from the mire of the parents' struggle. So often, in fact, have Jewish parents sacrificed for their children that it has become memorialized in our humor. Thus tears *and* laughter testify to the truth between generations.

CHAPTER 14

Family, Parents, Siblings, Grandparents, Orphans, Home

To give honor to your parents is even more important than honoring God.

—Simeon ben Yohai, Jerusalem Talmud

After a certain age, the more one becomes oneself, the more obvious one's family traits appear.

—Marcel Proust

I grew up to have my father's looks—my father's speech patterns—my father's posture—my father's walk—my father's opinions—and my mother's contempt for my father.

—Jules Feiffer

The love of parents is for their children; the love of the children is for their children.

—Proverb, quoted by Huna, Talmud

A father bird began a journey through the winds above a broad sea with three of his children who could not yet fly.

The nature of the elements was such that the father was forced to turn back and attempt the journey again, taking the children one at a time in his claws.

Flying with the first child, the winds turned ferocious and the father looked down to the baby bird in his grasp and said: "Dear child, do you see how I am putting my life on the line for you? When you have become an adult and I am old, will you look after me, doing no less then I have done for you?"

"Father," answered the baby bird, "just bring me safely to the other side of this sea, and when you are old I will provide whatever you want."

On hearing this, the father let the baby drop from his grasp and drown in the sea, saying, "That's what happens to a liar like you."

The father returned for the second child, and once again began his flight, and once again asked the same question, and once again received the same answer, and once again dropped the child, and once again said, "That's what happens to a liar like you."

At last, the father began his journey with the third child, encountered the same winds, and asked the same question, but received this answer: "My father who I love, it is obvious that you are working hard and putting your life on the line on my behalf, and I would be mistaken not to try and find a way to compensate you when you are old for what you are doing, but I cannot tie myself to promise to this commitment. What I can promise is that when I am an adult and have my own children, I will do for them as you have done for me."

On hearing this the father said: "You speak with wisdom, my child, and I will save your life, and I will take you safely to the other side."

—*Adapted from Glueckel of Hameln*

Honi ha-Meaggel once saw on his travels an old man planting a carob tree. He asked him when he thought the tree would bear fruit. "After seventy years," was the reply.

"Do you expect to live seventy years and eat the fruit of your labor?"

"I did not find the world desolate when I entered it," answered the old man, "and as my fathers planted for me before I was born, so do I plant for those who will come after me."

—*Talmud*

The rich don't have children: they have heirs.

—*Yiddish folk saying*

God could not be everywhere, so He created mothers.

—*Leopold Kompert*

Rabbi Joseph, when he heard his mother's approaching footsteps, used to say, "I stand for the approach of the *Shekinah*" [God's presence].

—*Talmud*

At work, you think of the children you have left at home. At home, you think of the work you've left unfinished. Such a struggle is unleashed within yourself. Your heart is rent.

—*Golda Meir*

The reason grandparents and grandchildren get along so well is that they have a common enemy.

—*Sam Levinson*

How goodly are your tents, O Jacob, your dwellings, O Israel.

—*Bible, Numbers 24:5*

Sanctifying the Jewish home as a temple of God . . . is the purpose of the mezuzah, the sacred writing on the entry.

—*Samson Raphael Hirsch*

It happens that a poor man became so distressed, both because of how small his home was and how crowded it was, that he went to see his *rebbe*.

"Rebbe, I have so many children and relatives living with me, my wife and I cannot breathe in our own home."

The rabbi listened and then asked the man, "Do you have a goat?"

"A goat?" asked the man incredulously. "Why do you ask me this question? Of course I have a goat."

"Good," said the rabbi. "My advice to you is to move the goat into your house and visit me again next week."

The man did as he was told even though the situation at home went from bad to intolerable. A week later he was at the rabbi's door.

"How is it now?" asked the rabbi.

"Impossible," said the man.

"Let me ask you a question. Do you by any chance have any chickens?" asked the rabbi, scratching his beard.

"Yes," said the man, throwing up his hands, "I have chickens."

"Good," said the rabbi, smiling. "My advice to you is to also move the chickens into your house, and come back to see me in a week."

The man could barely wait the week to return. He stood there, banging on the rabbi's door.

"So, now, how is it?" asked the rabbi.

"Impossible, simply impossible," said the man. "I cannot go on like this."

The rabbi smiled. "My advice to you is to go home and to take the chickens and the goat out of your house and come back to see me next week."

"Yes, Rebbe," said the man, anxious now to leave and do as he was told.

Next week the man stood at the rabbi's door with a broad grin and a well-rested manner.

"So how was it this past week?" asked the rabbi.

"A blessing on you, Rabbi. You are a saint. Only you could have solved this. My life is so much better. I don't know how to thank you."

—*Adapted from a Hasidic folktale*

Honor thy father and thy mother, even as thou honorest God; for all three have been partners in thy creation.

—*Zohar*

Rabbi Simeon ben Yohai said: "Great is the honoring of father and mother, for God makes more of it than of honoring Himself. About God, it is written: 'Honor the Lord with your substance' [Proverbs 3:9]; if you have substance, you must do this, and if you have no substance, you are not obligated to do this. But when it comes to honoring your father and mother, whether you have substance or not, 'Honor thy father and thy mother,' even if it means you have to beg your living from door to door."

—*Talmud*

Two women came to King Solomon and stood in front of him, and one woman spoke up: "My lord, this woman and I live in the same house, and I gave birth to a child while she was there. Then, three days later this woman also gave birth. We were the only people in the house.

"That night, the newborn child of this woman died. Then she took my child and put it on her chest and put her dead child at my bosom.

"In this way, when I woke just before dawn to nurse my child, I discovered it dead. But with the morning light I could see that this was not the child I had delivered."

On hearing this, the second woman burst into speech: "This is not true. The living child is mine, and the child that is dead is yours."

And the first woman said, "No, the living child is mine and the dead child is yours."

In this way, the two women argued before the king.

Then King Solomon said, "One of you says, 'This is my child, the living one, and your child is dead.' While the other insists, 'No; but your son is dead, and my child is the living one.' So, now bring me a sword."

A sword was brought in and put down in front of the king. The king then said, "Cut the child that is alive in two and give half to one and half to the other."

But the mother whose child lived spoke out to the king because her heart was stirred for her child: "Oh, my great lord, give this woman the child that lives, but do nothing to harm the child."

The other woman shouted, "It shall belong to neither of us. Cut the child in half. Divide it."

Then King Solomon answered by saying, "Give the first woman the living child, and by no means kill it, for she is the child's mother."

Now when all of Israel heard of this case and the king's judgment, they stood in great respect of the king; for they saw that the wisdom of God was in him to administer justice.

—*Bible, I Kings 3:16–28*

Teach your family to make the simple needs of life their habit.
—*Talmud*

It is incumbent on a man to consume food and drink that cost less than he can afford, to wear clothes that he can afford, and to show honor to his wife and children beyond what he can afford.

This is done because a man's family relies on him, and he relies on God who spoke, causing the world to come into existence.

—Talmud

An advantage you gain over someone in your family is a disadvantage.

—Apocrypha II

Once there were two farmers who were brothers.

One of the brothers was married and lived with his wife and children on one side of a high hill.

The other brother was not married and lived by himself on the other side of the same hill.

As it happened, in this year, there was a harvest of good fortune for both the brothers.

While he tried to sleep, the brother who was married thought to himself:

My life is blessed. I have had not only a wonderful crop this year but also my wife and children who have helped me to reap my crop. My brother, on the other hand, has no one to help him. I will load a wagon with grain from my field and carry it to my brother.

Also during this night, the brother who was not married lay in bed unable to sleep and thought to himself:

My life is blessed. My crops have been bountiful and my needs are few. My brother, on the other hand, has a wife and family, and I am concerned if they will have enough. I will load a wagon with grain from my field and carry it to my brother.

So, with the moon climbing into the night, the brothers loaded their wagons, and each beginning from their side, began their ascent of the hill.

At the top, with the moon directly overhead, the brothers met. Each immediately understood the intention of the other and they fell into each other's arms and cried.

—Legend, adapted from the tradition

Moral action is the meeting-place between the human and the divine.

—Leon Roth

When you raise an orphan in your home, it is the opinion of the Scriptures that it is the same as if the child had been born to you.

—*Talmud*

If the mind of a person's mother or father becomes diminished or injured, the child should do whatever he can to respond to the demands of the affected parent until God exercises His mercy.

Nevertheless, if the parent's situation grows even more difficult and the child can no longer bear the burden, the child may leave and assign others to give his parents the concern and rightful proper care.

—*Maimonides*

A bastard [on account of his birth] can have a place in the World-to-Come.

—*Midrash Rabbah*

When a person conducts himself by honoring his mother and father, God is heard to say, "It is as though I were living with them and they honored Me."

—*Talmud*

The man who raises a child is the one to be called its father, not he who is only the birth father.

—*Midrash Rabbah*

Hear, my son, the teaching of your father.

—*Rashi*

No matter how many children parents have, each child is the only one they have.

—*Yiddish folk saying*

Those who don't themselves do good cannot count on their father's efforts and merits.

—*Midrash Rabbah*

You don't know how much you don't know until your children grow up and tell you how much you don't know.

—*S. J. Perelman*

☙

CHAPTER 15

Birth, Parenting

The greatest esteem I can give my children is love for our people, loyalty to self.

—*Theodor Herzl*

A person on a ship waits without patience for the day when the boat will reach its port. As the ship approaches the shore, a sudden storm drives the ship back out to sea, upsetting the passenger.

It is in this way that parents are filled with concern until they have seen their children become adults.

Then once the children have become adults, parents hope they no longer have to worry; the shore, they believe, is in sight.

But then, without warning, the eldest son returns home with financial needs, and the father's plans are put off because of the son's requirements.

After this, the daughter returns with requests of her parents, and the quiet of the parents' home is disturbed. Once again, the ship is blown back from the shore.

Only a very limited number of people live without worries or the continuous effort of trying to make port.

—*Adapted parable of Solomon ha-Kohen Rabinowich of Radamsko*

Don't threaten a child: Either punish him or forgive him.

—*Talmud*

Eggs think they are smarter than hens.

—*Yiddish folk saying*

Parents once taught their children to talk; today children teach their parents to be quiet.

—*Yiddish folk saying*

When you teach your son, you teach your son's son.

—*Talmud*

Listen, my son, to what your father tells you and do not forget what you have learned from your mother.

Learn to speak gently to all people at all times . . . as it is written: "Remove anger from your heart. . . ."

Absent of anger, you will find the quality of humility growing in your heart, and this is better than many things you may think are good. . . .

Lower your voice, and bow your head. Turn your eyes to the ground at your feet and your heart toward heaven. . . .

Every person you meet should appear to you as greater than yourself. It doesn't matter if this person is wise or wealthy, it is your duty to show respect.

If the person is poorer than you, or you are wiser than they, think in your heart that you are more guilty, and they are more innocent. See to it that if they sin, it is from error, but if you sin, it is with purpose.

Every week read this letter and follow what is said. . . .

Then you will be considered as worthy by all that is good and held to have value by those who are righteous.

—*Judah ben Samuel ha-Hasid*

A father who quickly loses his temper teaches his sons to be fools.

—*Nachman of Bratslav*

The best security for old age—respect your children.

—*Sholem Asch*

The life of the mother takes precedence over the life of the unborn child.

—*Talmud*

Train up a child in the way he should go; and when he is old he
will not depart from it.

—*Bible, Proverbs 22:6*

Once there was a man who in his will said that his son should
inherit nothing until he became a fool.

Two sages went to discuss this with Rabbi Joshua ben Karha. As
they approached his home, they were surprised to see him crawling
around on his hands and knees with a piece of straw in his mouth,
playing with his little son.

The two waited in hiding until the rabbi's game with his son
ceased, and then they came over to the rabbi and asked him his
opinion of the will.

Rabbi ben Karha laughed and explained the will: "The father
clearly meant for his son to marry and have children, for you have
seen that once a man has children he is willing to act like a fool to play
with them."

—*Midrash Rabbah*

Obeying from love is better than obeying from fear.

—*Rashi*

A person should not promise to give a child something and then not
give it, because in that way the child learns to lie.

—*Talmud*

A person is bound to treat his parents honorably less for having
given birth to him than for the moral manner in which he was
brought up. The reason for this is because, in creating a child, self-
pleasure was the parents' motive.

—*Adapted from Israel ben Joseph Al-Nakawa*

Make your children your students when they are young, and they
will not make you their students when you grow old.

—*Hasidic folk saying*

In the nature of things, a father works with his son in the hope that
the son will become a wise and religious Jew.

The son, in his own lifetime, goes through the same process with
his own son.

But the question is, when is there a time when the father attempts to become a wise and religious Jew in his own right, rather than making this singularly the work of his son.

—*Yerachmiel of Parsischa, the "Yud"*

Those who do not teach their child an occupation are as those who would teach their child to rob.

—*Talmud*

When God decided to create Adam, the father of all of us, He took the dust from which humankind would be made, not from Israel, the land of the Jew; not from Jerusalem, the Holy City; not from Zion, the site of the Holy Temple; but He took a little earth from every corner of the globe, from East and West, from North and South.

Why?

The rabbis answered: "So that in the future no nation shall say, from the earth of my place was Adam created; so that no one people could say, we are more important, better than our neighbors, because Adam was born from this place."

—*Talmud*

Rab Huna said: "There once was a Sage who opened a shop for perfumes for his son on a street occupied by prostitutes.

"Between the products sold, the location of the store, and the boy's youth, he was naturally led to the bed.

"The boy's father, on catching the boy with a prostitute, became incredibly angry, shouting: 'I'll kill you!'

"But another Sage intervened, asking the father: 'How can you blame the boy? You yourself caused the boy to lose his way. Of all the occupations, you brought him close to women with the perfumes, and of all the women to bring him near, you placed him on a street of prostitutes!'"

—*Midrash Rabbah*

Nothing brings me more joy on earth than to see [my children] doing well, and I can experience no pain or worry greater than [my children's] misconduct.

—*Judah ben Asher*

One father can support ten children, but ten children cannot support one father.

—*Yiddish folk saying*

A ewe follows a ewe: the acts of a daughter can be seen in the mother.

—*Talmud*

Push your child away with the left hand and draw him closer with the right hand.

—*Talmud*

If you hit a child, hit him only with a shoelace.

—*Talmud*

My son, in the house of learning don't speak idly but listen to the words of the wise. Don't discount whatever you hear, and despise no person. For many pearls are found in a poor man's tunic.

My son, be sure to visit the sick, for sympathy lessens pain . . .

My son, comfort those in mourning, and speak to their hearts. . . .

My son, give honor to the poor person, and offer him your soul. . . .

My son, do not hurt the poor person with hard words, for the Lord will plead their cause . . .

Do not make yourself so important or feared in your home, because this is the cause of much evil.

My son, rid your heart of anger, "for anger lives in the chest of fools, and a strange god rests on the fool's head."

My son, love the wise, and become one with them. Search to know your Maker, "for the soul to be without knowledge is not good." Salute all people and speak the truth . . .

My son, do not walk alone, do not judge alone, do not testify alone, do not be a judge and witness at the same time. No one may judge alone but the One . . .

My son, "Do not rejoice when your enemy falls, and do not let your heart be happy when your enemy stumbles, or the Lord will see it and it will make Him angry, and He will turn His anger from your enemy on to you." But "if your enemy is hungry give him bread to eat."

My son, hurry to do your duty and do not diminish its importance to yourself. Do not think or say that your duty is unimportant, for you do not know how each moral act is rewarded. Let all your deeds be done in the Name of Heaven.

My son, do not be overrighteous.

—The Testament, Eleazar the Great

. . . Do not forget me, God, until I have shouted of Your strength to the next generation.

—Bible, Psalms 71:18

Who is ignorant? He who does not educate his children.

—Jonathan ben Joseph, Talmud

CHAPTER 16

Children, Childhood

Almost everything that is great has been done by youth.
—*Benjamin Disraeli*

It came to be that when the people of Israel stood prepared at Mount Sinai to accept the Torah, God spoke to them, saying:

"Bring Me promises to assure that you will hold to My Torah, and at that time I will allow you to have it."

The people said, "Those who came before us are our promise."

"Those who came before you," said God, "have had failings. . . ."

The people said, "King of the Universe, our prophets will be our promise to you."

"Your prophets," said God, "have had failings. . . ."

And then the people said to the Lord, "Our children will be our promise. . . ."

When God heard this, He said, "Surely, these are promises that assure me and I will give you the Torah for the sake of your children."
—*Midrash Rabbah*

Children without childhood are a dreadful sight.
—*Mendele (Moscher Sforim)*

Adolescence is a kind of emotional seasickness. Both are funny, but only in retrospect.

—*Arthur Koestler*

After murdering his mother and father, the defendant asked the court for mercy because he was an orphan.

—Yiddish folk saying

Youth is the trustee of posterity.

—Benjamin Disraeli

. . . If a child has great learning we must honor the child as if he were an elder.

—Zohar

An embryo is like a scroll rolled together with a candle burning at one of the ends. Looking forward, the embryo can see from itself to the end of its world.

As its view will never be greater, the embryo is taught the entire Torah.

But when the child is born and emerges into the atmosphere of this world, an angel arrives. The angel touches the child's mouth as it gulps its first breath of air, and the child suddenly forgets everything it has learned of the Law.

—Adapted Hebrew legend

The king trembled, he was so deeply moved. He went up to the chamber above the gate and cried and cried, moaning the following as he moved:

"O my son Absalom, my son, my son Absalom!
Could it only be, I would die for you,
O Absalom, my son, my son!"

—Bible, II Samuel 19:1

And a little child shall lead them.

—Bible, Isaiah 11:6

Small children interfere with your sleep, big children your life.

—Yiddish proverb

PART FIVE

More People Die from

Overeating than from

Undernourishment

BECAUSE OUR BODIES ARE A GIFT FROM GOD, ANYTHING THAT WOULD harm our health is considered an insult to the Divine. And while Jews do not glorify the body as in the Greco-Roman tradition, we do esteem those who would heal the body.

Issues of food and cleanliness are woven into the mitzvoth, the commandments of the Torah. Restraint and respect with regard to our body, food, and eating allow us to live with our appetites and enjoy the bounty that the Lord has provided.

The term for penance in Hebrew is *tshuva*. The word literally means to turn and look back at oneself. This ancient concept established an intellectual, moral, and theological disposition toward critical self-examination and reflection. A great deal of 20th-century psychology is sympathetic to—and perhaps has borrowed much from—the Jewish mind-set of *tshuva* and the perspectives it affords.

CHAPTER 17

Body, Diet, Doctors, Physical Health, Food, Drink, Cleanliness, Drugs, Alcohol

The body is the soul's house. Shouldn't we therefore take care of our house so that it doesn't fall into ruin?

—*Philo*

Illness is the doctor to whom we all listen. To kindness, to knowledge, we only make promises; pain we obey.

—*Marcel Proust*

Hillel's disciples were walking with him once and when he was about to leave their company, they asked: "Where are you going?"

He answered: "I'm going to fulfill a religious duty."

"What duty?"

"To bathe in the bathhouse."

"Is this a duty?"

"Yes," answered Hillel. "The statues of the king are set in theaters and circuses. And he who is assigned to look after the statues cleans and polishes them. He is sustained by the king for this purpose. . . . I, who have been created in the image and likeness of God, how much more must I keep my body clean and untainted."

—*Midrash Rabbah*

There is no wealth like health, no enjoyment like happiness.

—*Solomon ibn Gabirol*

The proverb says: The door that is closed to a good deed is open to a physician.

—*Midrash Rabbah*

It is a fact that the movement from disease to ease gives us more pleasure than continual ease.

—*Maimonides*

The dietary laws teach us to control our hungers . . . and not to think . . . eating and drinking are the end of our being.

—*Maimonides*

Blessed are You, the Lord our God, who brings forth the bread from the earth.

—*Blessing over bread*

. . . There is nothing better for man under the sun than to eat, drink, and be happy.

—*Bible, Ecclesiastes 8:15*

Blessed are You, the Lord our God, who brings forth the fruit of the vine.

—*Blessing over wine*

Let us eat and drink; for tomorrow we shall die.

—*Bible, Isaiah 22:13*

When wine goes in, secrets come out.

—*Yiddish folk saying*

We are told five things concerning garlic: It fulfills one's hunger; it makes the body warm; it turns one's face bright; it multiplies a man's potency; and it destroys parasites in the bowels. There are those who say that garlic also enhances love and gets rid of jealousy.

—*Talmud*

More people die from overeating than from undernourishment.

—*Nachman of Bratslav*

In life, one person has no appetite for his food, while the other has no food for his appetite.
— *Yiddish folk saying*

When a poor man eats a chicken, one of them is sick.
— *Yiddish folk saying*

A doctor can heal everything but poverty.
— *Yiddish folk saying*

Because God loves our soul it is impossible for Him to think lowly of our bodies, which are necessary for the continuation of us as individuals and as a genus.
— *Jacob Anatoli*

God sends the remedy with the disease.
— *Yiddish folk saying*

In the World-to-Come a person will be asked to account for that, which being excellent to eat, he looked at and did not eat.
— *Talmud*

Where there's wine, there's immortality.
— *Midrash Rabbah*

Don't ask the doctor. Ask the patient.
— *Yiddish folk saying*

A merry heart doeth good like a medicine.
— *Bible, Proverbs 17:22*

If you're in pain, go to a physician.
— *Talmud*

When you need a doctor, you raise him to a god;
When he's saved your life, you think he's a king;
When you're better, he's a person just like you are;
And when you get his bill, he's a devil.
— *Jedaiah of Béziers*

Wine cheers God and man.

—*Bible, Judges 9:13*

Health is not simply the absence of sickness.

—*Hannah Green*

It purifies our spirit when we keep our body clean.

—*Pseudo-Phocylides*

It is forbidden to live in a town that does not have a physician.

—*Jerusalem Talmud*

If a doctor fails to treat a patient when he can, he is considered a murderer, regardless if there is another doctor who can deal with this patient, as it is possible that the initial physician has particular talents which would help the healing in this case.

—*Joseph Caro, Shulhan Aruk*

There are no such things as incurables; there are only things for which man has not found a cure.

—*Bernard M. Baruch*

Rabbi Ishmael bar Joseph visited Rabbi Simeon ben Jose ben Lekonya. The visitor was handed a glass of wine, which he swallowed in a single swig. Rabbi Simeon smiled slightly and said, "Apparently you do not agree with the ruling that he who drinks wine in a single swallow is a drunkard."

Rabbi Ishmael answered, "The opinion does not apply to your wine, which is sweet; to your cup, which is small; and to a man like myself, who is stout."

—*Talmud*

No person in the world is free from pain.

—*Yalkut Shimoni*

Do not take drugs.

—*Talmud*

You should not take drugs, because they create their own need and your heart will yearn for them.

You will also be giving away money.

Even if you are taking the drugs as medicine, do not take them if you can find another medicine that can be of aid.

—*Samuel ben Meir, the Rashbam*

Personal cleanliness is the foundation of spiritual purity; it is the path by which one attains the Kingdom of Heaven.

—*Talmud*

There is more appetite than there is meat on the planet.

—*Theodor Herzl*

No person of learning should live in a town where you cannot get vegetables.

—*Huna, Talmud*

Eat a third, drink a third, and leave the remaining third of your stomach empty.

Then if anger takes you over, there will be room in your stomach for gas.

—*Talmud*

The health of the soul can only be achieved after the health of the body has been achieved.

—*Maimonides*

Eat to live, do not live to eat.

—*Abraham ibn Ezra*

A person should never eat except when he is hungry, nor drink except when he is thirsty. . . .

A person should not eat until he has walked before a meal a distance sufficient for the body to begin feeling warm, or has done some work, or other exercise.

The abiding principle should be to exercise the body and make it tired every morning, until the body grows warm, then to rest until the body has recovered, and then to eat.

—Maimonides

Work prior to eating, rest after eating.

—Maimonides

Sleep faster, we need the pillows.

—Yiddish folk saying

When a person develops a habit of eating and drinking with good appetite, he is distressed if he happens to miss his next meal.

—Moses Luzzatto

We often mistake a desire of the body for a yearning of the soul.

—Harry Austryn Wolfson

When we eat and enjoy the incredible taste of food, we should remember that it is God who has given food the qualities we enjoy. In this understanding, we will serve God by eating.

—Ba'al Shem Tov

The Holy One, blessed be He . . . made in people as He made in His world:

He made forests in the world and He made forests in people, i.e., a person's hair . . .

He made wind in the world and He made wind in people, i.e., a person's breath . . .

Salt water in the world and salt water in people, i.e., a person's tears . . .

Flowing water in the world and flowing water in people, i.e., a person's blood . . .

In this way you see that no matter what the Holy One, blessed be He, created in His World, He created in people.

—Avot de Rabbi Nathan

Give the doctor honor for what he does, for the Lord created him.
. . . The Lord made medicines from the earth and a person with common sense would not diminish them. . . .

. . . There is no end to the creations of the Lord, who covers the whole world with health.

—*Wisdom of Ben Sira*

It was the habit of Moshe Leib Sassover, the Sassover Rebbe, to stay by the bed and nurse any of the boys in his community who were very sick no matter how grievous their illness.

The Sassover Rebbe would say, "Any of us who are not willing to suck the pus from the boil of a child with the plague have not yet climbed even halfway up the ladder of love for our fellow human beings."

—*Rabbi Moshe Leib Sassover, the Sassover Rebbe*

To boost the essential strength [of people who are ill] you should use musical instruments and tell those who are sick happy tales that will cause their heart to fill with joy and descriptions of events that cause people to forget their circumstance and cause laughter for them and those around them.

The people who are hired to work with those who are ill must have the ability to bring a smile to a patient's disposition.

—*Maimonides*

Moses was given 613 commandments: 365 of these were negative [You shall not . . .], the same as the number of days in the year, and 248 were positive [You will . . .], the same as the number of joints in the human body.

—*Talmud*

Someone came to spend time with a sick man and asked the patient what was wrong with him.

After the illness was explained, the visitor pawed at the air with his hand, and said, "Oh, that's the same disease that killed my father."

On hearing this, the patient became visibly disheartened and the visitor said, "Don't worry, I'm going to pray to God to make you better."

And the sick man said, "Listen, when you pray, also ask God if I may be saved from any more visits from idiots like you."

—*Adapted from the Yiddish folk tradition*

For any dish, hunger is an excellent seasoning.

—*Moses Gentili*

Wine leads the list of all medicines.

—*Talmud*

Washing your hands and feet in warm water each night is superior to any of the medicines in the world.

—*Talmud*

Revere your own body as the container, messenger, and instrument of the spirit.

—*Samson Raphael Hirsch*

CHAPTER 18

Psychology, Mental Health

When the head is a fool, the body is in trouble.
> —*Yiddish folk saying*

People usually hate what they don't understand.
> —*Moses ibn Ezra*

Avarice, ambition, lust . . . are kinds of madness.
> —*Baruch Spinoza*

You don't get ulcers from what you eat. You get them from what's eating you.
> —*Vicki Baum*

What you can't avoid—welcome.
> —*Yiddish folk saying*

It is difficult to right oneself from the sin of melancholy.
Knowing one has sinned draws one deeper into the depths of the sin.
> —*The Bershider Rebbe*

Sanity is a cozy lie.
> —*Susan Sontag*

. . . Much will be gained if we succeed in transforming your hysterical misery into common unhappiness.

—*Sigmund Freud*

If a physician cannot give a patient medicine for the body, he should somehow find and give medicine for the patient's soul.

—*Zohar*

I have seen the best minds of my generation destroyed by madness, starving hysterical mad.

—*Allen Ginsberg*

After you have been bitten by a snake you are afraid of a piece of rope.

—*Yiddish folk saying*

Work and love—these are the basics. Without them there is neurosis.

—*Theodor Reik*

Analysis makes for unity, but not necessarily for goodness.

—*Sigmund Freud*

Anybody who is twenty-five or thirty years old has physical scars from all sorts of things. . . . It's the same with the mind.

—*Moses R. Kaufman*

A sigh breaks half the body.

—*Talmud*

We are the carriers of health and disease—either the divine health of courage and nobility or the demonic diseases of hate and anxiety.

—*Joshua Loth Liebman*

Neurosis does not deny the existence of reality, it merely tries to ignore it: psychosis denies it and tries to substitute something else for it.

A reaction that combines features of both of these is the one we call normal or "healthy"; it denies reality as little as neurosis, but then, like a psychosis, is concerned with effecting a change in it.

—Sigmund Freud

To worry is a sin. The only worry that is permitted is: if one worries because one worries.

—Noah Lekhivitzer

Two men came to a rabbi with the hope that he would settle a long-running argument between the two of them.

The rabbi listened, and listened, and listened, and then finally gave his opinion.

He turned to the first man and said, "You're right."

Then he turned to the second man and said, "You're right."

Just then, the rabbi's wife, who had stood as witness during the conversation, spoke up: "How is it possible for both these men to be right?"

"Shh," said the rabbi, turning to his wife, "you're right too."

—Yiddish folk tradition

The great majority of people have a strong need for authority that they can admire, to which they can submit, and which . . . sometimes even ill-treats them.

. . . It is the longing for the father that lives in each of us from his childhood days.

—Sigmund Freud

Don't allow yourself to always be sad or make yourself sad on purpose.

A happy heart keeps a person alive, and joy will add days to our lives. . . .

Envy and anger diminish a person's life, and concern creates early old age.

—Wisdom of Ben Sira

The world cannot be changed by chiding or laughing.

—Yiddish folk saying

The eye says what the heart means.

—*Judah Leib Lazerov*

The Bible is the great medicine cabinet of humanity.

—*Heinrich Heine*

PART SIX

Love Is Based on

Equality and Freedom

IN KABBALA (A TERM GENERALLY USED FOR THE ESOTERIC TEACHINGS of Judaism and Jewish mysticism) there is a school of thought that says we are both male and female prior to our birth. The teaching holds that at birth we are split from our sexual complement and spend our days trying to re-create that union. This effort of *tikkun,* coming together with ourselves, involves an external search for the mate who makes us whole. *Tikkun* also implies that, regardless of finding the perfect husband or wife, we are like an amputee who can "feel" his missing phantom limb; and each of us should make an effort to "get in touch with" our missing male or female aspects in a search for balance and self-wholeness. In Judaism both the male and female are glorified; but the greater glory is in knowing we are one of One.

The famed sage Maimonides said that of all the conduct restraints placed on humankind none is more difficult than those involving sexuality. Nevertheless, beauty and desire are also God's gifts, and without them life would be diminished. In dealing with this dilemma, teachings from divine literature to rabbinic commentary are laced with a common thread: respect. Equality between the sexes is clearly a present-day social issue, but respect between the sexes in Judaism is a prescribed tradition.

CHAPTER 19

Male, Female

And God created man in His image, in the image of God He created him; male and female He created them.

—*Bible, Genesis 1:27*

The bond between male and female is the secret of true faith.

—*Zohar*

In a place where there are no men, strive to be a man.

—*Hillel the Elder, Pirke Avot*

For every woman who makes a fool out of a man, there is another woman who makes a man out of a fool.

—*Samuel Hoffman*

Better to talk to a woman and think of God, than to talk to God and think of a woman.

—*Yiddish folk saying*

What passes for woman's intuition is often nothing more than man's transparency.

—*George Jean Nathan*

Alexander the Great came to a city inhabited only by women. Alexander desired to make war on the women, but they sent a message to him:

"If you destroy us, the world will say, 'He conquered women.' If we destroy you, the world will say, 'What kind of king was this? Women destroyed him!'"

Then Alexander said, "Bring me bread."

The women brought him a loaf of gold on a table of gold.

"Can I eat gold?" asked the great conquerer.

The women answered, "Have you come so far from your own kingdom because bread is what you wanted?"

Alexander left the city, leaving behind a note on the walls of the gate:

"I, Alexander, was a madman, having come to Africa only to be taught by women."

—Tanhuma Buber

The great question that has never been answered, and which I have not yet been able to answer despite my thirty years of research into the female soul, is: What does a woman want?

—Sigmund Freud

Female passion is to masculine as an epic is to an epigram.

—Karl Kraus

Everything unfolds from the woman.

—Midrash Rabbah

In our civilization, men are afraid that they will not be men enough and women are afraid that they might be considered only women.

—Theodor Reik

Show me a woman who doesn't feel guilty and I'll show you a man.

—Erica Jong

The ideal man has the strength of a male and the compassion of a female.

—Zohar

She openeth her mouth with wisdom; and in her tongue is the law of kindness.

—*Bible, Proverbs 31:26*

A woman's voice is an excitement.

—*Talmud*

God has endowed women with a special sense of wisdom that man lacks.

—*Talmud*

A woman's weapons are always with her.

—*Talmud*

Talk to women as much as you can. This is the best school.

—*Benjamin Disraeli*

The emperor said to Rabbi Gamaliel: "Your God is a thief because He made Adam fall asleep and then stole one of his ribs."

Just then, the rabbi's daughter cut into the conversation and cried to the emperor to call for some guards.

"Why? What has happened?" asked the emperor.

"Well, a thief entered our home last night and took away a silver pitcher, but left a gold one in its place."

"Well," said the emperor, "if only a thief like this would come to me every night."

And the daughter of Gamaliel answered: "How can you say that and speak poorly of our God? Did God not steal a rib from Adam only to enrich him with a wife?"

—*Talmud*

A true conception of the relation of the sexes will not admit of conquerer and conquered; it knows of but one great thing: to give of one's self boundlessly, in order to find one's self richer, deeper, better.

—*Emma Goldman*

A group of Hasidim were meeting with their rebbe, and as it is not unusual in any group to find one who doubts amid those who believe, the one who doubted thought he would make a joke at the rebbe's expense.

"Rebbe," said the man, "since you know so much, can even you tell us what Eve did whenever Adam came home late in the evening?"

"She counted his ribs," replied the rebbe.

—Hasidic folk tale

It happened that one day King Solomon, who understood the language of animals, listened in on the conversation between a male bird and a female.

"All you have to do is ask if you want me to destroy the great King Solomon's throne," said the male bird.

Angered at hearing this, the king had the bird taken to the throne room and told it to explain.

"You have the audacity to speak of destroying my throne?" asked Solomon.

"O great King Solomon, have you lost your wisdom? Have you forgotten that to win a woman's interest men always enlarge their strength and brag of their incredible talents?"

—Adapted from Hebrew legend

CHAPTER 20

Love, Marriage,

Infidelity,

Divorce

. . . Whither thou goest, I will go; and where thou lodgest, I will
lodge; thy people shall be my people, and thy God, my God.
—Bible, Ruth 1:16–17

A man is only as good as what he loves.
—Saul Bellow

When love is concerned, it is easier to renounce a feeling than to
give up a habit.
—Marcel Proust

Love is the best relationship, wisdom the best ancestor.
—Joseph Zabara

God is forever creating new worlds. How is this done? By bringing
about new marriages.
—Zohar

A true woman loves a strong man because she knows his
weaknesses.
—André Maurois

Those who can't love, flatter.
—Yiddish folk saying

Love is based on equality and freedom.

—*Erich Fromm*

When he was a young man, the famed Rabbi Akiba was a lowly shepherd for a wealthy man named Kalb Savu'a in Jerusalem.

This nobleman had a daughter who was a shy beauty. The girl noticed in Akiba a very special quality and asked him:

"If I promise to marry you, will you leave and promise to learn Torah?"

And Akiba replied, "With my whole heart, I answer 'Yes.' "

The boy and girl married in secret, and he left to begin his studies.

When the girl's father discovered what had taken place, he forced his daughter to leave the house, and said that for as long as he lived he would allow her nothing from his estate.

For twelve years, Akiba was gone from his wife. On his return, he traveled with twelve thousand followers. As he came close to where his wife lived, Akiba overheard an old man talking to her.

"Why do you persist on living like a widow?"

"If my husband would listen to me, I would send him away for another twelve years to further his learning," said Akiba's wife.

When he heard this, Akiba turned and left. He went to the center of learning for another twelve years.

Returning home this time, Akiba traveled with twenty-four thousand followers.

Now hearing of her husband's return, Akiba's wife prepared to greet him. Her friends said to her, "Let us lend you something decent to wear so you look a little nicer." But she said, "No."

As Akiba approached her, she bent to the ground and kissed his feet. The followers moved to take her from the path, and then Rabbi Akiba said, "Let her be. All that we have belongs to her."

In this voice, Akiba made his disciples aware that none of what he had achieved, and they through him, would have been possible without this woman.

When Akiba's father-in-law was told that a famous sage had arrived, he thought he would go and seek out the sage, hoping to be freed from his vow against his daughter, which he now regretted having sworn.

Pleading his case before Akiba, whom he did not recognize, the father-in-law said to the sage, "If I knew my son-in-law might be a great teacher, I would not have made the vow. If I knew my son-in-law might have known even one chapter of one law, I would not have made that vow."

Then Akiba revealed himself, saying, "I am the youth who once guarded your sheep and who left at your daughter's insistence that I go and study because she believed in me."

When the father-in-law understood what had happened, he begged for Akiba's forgiveness, knelt to honor him, and gave him half of all that was his.

—*Talmud*

A woman should see as her responsibility that there is peace between her and her husband, and that she offer love and kindness to him.

—*Jonah ben Abraham Gerondi*

Go understand a girl: she can't wait for the wedding, yet weeps on the way to the canopy.

—*Shalom Aleichem*

The heart knows its own bitterness; and with its joy no stranger can interfere.

—*Bible, Proverbs 14:10*

If you dance at every wedding, you'll weep at every funeral.

—*Yiddish folk saying*

When a man who has been previously married marries a woman who has been previously married, four people go to bed.

—*Talmud*

I have yet to hear a man ask for advice on how to combine marriage and a career.

—*Gloria Steinem*

A woman prefers poverty with love over luxury without it.

—*Joshua ben Hanania, Mishneh Torah*

Love is like butter: it's good with bread.

—*Yiddish folk saying*

A man too good for the world is no good for his wife.

—*Yiddish folk saying*

A wife is the joy of a man's heart.

—*Talmud*

A woman of valor, who can find? For her price is far above rubies. The heart of her husband does safely trust in her, and she has no lack of gain. She does him good and not evil all the days of her life.

. . . Her children rise up and call her blessed; her husband also, and he praises her.

—*Bible, Proverbs 31:10–12, 28 (sung by a husband to his wife on
every Sabbath)*

The tongue is the pen of the heart.

—*Yiddish folk saying*

A man likes his wife to be just clever enough to comprehend his cleverness, and just stupid enough to admire it.

—*Israel Zangwill*

I have said, The world is built by love.

—*Bible, Psalms 89:3*

When a soul comes down from Heaven, it is both male and female. The male aspects enter a male child and the female aspects enter a female child. If they are deserving, God will cause them to find each other and to join in marriage. This is a true union.

—*Zohar*

Finding a wife is finding a great good.

—*Bible, Proverbs 18:22*

He who is full of joy is full of love.

—*Ba'al Shem Tov*

. . . Love is as strong as death.

—*Bible, Song of Songs 8:6*

I ask you, my friend, who began all this business of marriages and wives?

—*Shalom Aleichem*

. . . I am sick with love.

—*Bible, Song of Songs 5:8*

The calmest husbands make the stormiest wives.

—*Isaac D'Israeli*

Why does a woman work ten years to change a man's habits and then complain that he's not the man she married?

—*Barbra Streisand*

Men often marry their mothers.

—*Edna Ferber*

Chains do not hold a marriage together. It is threads, hundreds of tiny threads, which sew people together through the years.

—*Simone Signoret*

People relate love with feelings of sentiment alone. But love includes a great deal more. The act of love should bring every level of the human being into play . . . intuitions . . . emotions . . . logic and mind.

—*Zvi Judah Kook*

This is a story told by Rab Id: a woman and her husband lived together for ten years but had no children. The couple asked Rabbi Simeon ben Yohai to give them a divorce.

The rabbi, however, could see that the two were still very much in love and was saddened to think of their divorcing.

He said to the couple, "Because your lives were joined, one to the other, at a feast, be separated also after a feast."

The two invited many many friends and the party was like that of a wedding. When the guests had all gone home, the husband said, "You may take with you to your father's house whatever you most desire in our house."

That night, when the husband had fallen asleep, his wife told the servants to gently carry him to her father's house.

In the morning, the husband awoke and shouted, "Where am I?"

The woman answered, "You are in my father's home."

"But," asked the man, "what am I doing here?"

"My dear, you are the thing that I most desire from our house, and by your promise, I have a right to keep you."

The couple went back to see the rabbi, who blessed them and asked God to remember them, and the following year Rabbi Simeon offered the prayers at the circumcision of their son.

—*Midrash Rabbah*

When a person is newly married, he is not to go out with the army, nor be counted on for any duty; he is to be free at home for at least one year, to enjoy himself with his mate whom he has married.

—*Bible, Deuteronomy 24:5*

A man should not marry a woman with the thought in mind that he may divorce her.

—*Talmud*

Love does not remember dignity.

—*Simeon ben Eleazar, Talmud*

There once was a leopard whose life was filled with joy and plenty. He always found plenty for his wife and family.

Nearby lived the leopard's neighbor and friend, the fox.

The fox, although a neighbor and friend, felt nervous that his safety was dependent on the leopard always finding enough prey for his family. So the fox thought of a plan to end what he saw as a dangerous friendship.

Before the bad things arrive, the wise say it is wise to think about what you would do. "So I will move the leopard," thought the fox. . . .

The next day, the fox went to the leopard and told him of a wondrous place . . . a place of beautiful flowers and fawns. . . .

The leopard went with the fox to see this place and was incredibly happy to have discovered this "secret."

"Ah," said the fox to himself, pleased to see his plan working, "often joy concludes with weeping."

The leopard, however, was totally pleased and wanted to move to this new area. Nevertheless, said the leopard, "I first must ask my wife what she thinks. She is my partner, my mate from my youth."

The fox was concerned to hear this, because he knew the cleverness of the wife and her wisdom. So the fox said to the leopard, "Don't trust your wife. A woman's advice is both silly and foolish. Her heart is like a stone. . . . Ask her opinion and do just the opposite."

The leopard came home and told his wife that he was convinced they should move.

But his wife said, "Be cautious of the fox. . . . Have you not heard the story about how the fox tied up the lion and killed him?"

"How could the fox," asked the leopard, "even dare to do such a thing, even come close enough to the lion to do such a thing?"

The leopard's wife began her story: The lion cared for the fox, but the fox did not trust the lion, and planned to kill the lion. So the fox came to the lion complaining of a terrible pain banging in his head. "I have been told," said the fox to the lion, "that when this pain happens the patient should be completely tied in ropes." The lion agreed to do this and wrapped the fox in cords.

Shortly later, the fox said, "Ahh, my anguish has left." And the lion untied the fox.

After some time, the lion came down with a terrible headache. He came to the fox, like a bird to the trap, and asked, "Please, brother, tie me up so I can be made better as you were."

The fox took new rope and tied the lion tightly. Then the fox found huge stones and crushed the lion's skull.

"So, my dear leopard husband," said his wife, ending the story, "do not trust the fox. He is too sly. If he tells you how wonderful this other place is, why does he not move there?"

—*Joseph Zabara*

In time, a man leaves his father and mother and joins to his wife so they become as one flesh.

—*Bible, Genesis 2:24*

A tradition in old Judea was for a cedar tree to be planted when a male child was born and an acacia tree when a female child was born. When they became adults and married, the canopy for their marriage was to be constructed from branches of these two trees.

—Talmud

Everything in life can be substituted but the wife you chose when you were young.

—Talmud

When a man divorces his first wife, the altar where they married begins to cry.

—Talmud

He who loves his wife as himself, and honors her more than himself—to him the Scriptures promise: "There shall be peace in your tent."

—Talmud

An old man can climb a sand dune with greater ease than a quiet man can live with a wife who nags.

—Wisdom of Ben Sira

It is necessary for a Jew to honor his wife even more than he chooses to honor himself.

If he hits his wife, he should be treated more harshly than he might for hitting someone else. The reason for this is because a man is held responsible for honoring his wife but may not be responsible for honoring the other person.

—Meir ben Baruch Rothenburg

He who wins a wise woman by his own worth has won the chief victory in life.

—Zohar

It used to be a matter of practice for Rabbi Meir to offer talks to the community on Friday after sundown. And one woman, who enjoyed what the rabbi had to say, used to come often.

After one of the rabbi's talks went a little late, the woman came home to find her husband extremely angry.

"And tonight? Where were you?" demanded the husband.

"It was Friday. I went to hear the rabbi speak," answered the woman demurely.

"Well," said the husband, enjoying his anger, "if the rabbi's speeches are so important to you, I will teach you a lesson. I make a vow that you will never be allowed back into our home until you go to the rabbi and spit in his face. In this act, he will find his payment for being so entertaining to you."

The wife was stunned by this announcement, and being forbidden to enter her own home, went to live with a friend nearby.

Stories of what had transpired between husband and wife passed to the rabbi, and he asked that the wife be brought to his office.

When the woman arrived, Rabbi Meir began to complain about a terrible ache he was experiencing in his eyes. Did the wife, the rabbi asked, know anything about a cure for this pain.

The woman, confused, answered quietly, "No."

"I have heard that if you spit in my eyes seven times," said the rabbi, "that I will become better."

Unsure, but urged on by the rabbi, the woman did as she was told.

"And now," said the rabbi, wiping his face, "return to your husband and tell him that you spit in the rabbi's face seven times. Six times more than he requested."

After the woman left, the followers of the rabbi came to him and said they were stunned to see how he had allowed himself to be debased.

"You are wrong," said Rabbi Meir to his students, "nothing is below one if the result is to help the cause of peace and well-being between a wife and her husband."

— *Adapted legend, Midrash Rabbah*

Love when there is not criticism is not love.

— *Jose ben Hanina*

The Berditschever Rebbe found himself thought of as an enemy by another man. And one day as the rebbe was walking through the streets, his opponent's wife ran up to the rebbe and dumped a bucket of water over him.

The rebbe said nothing, but ran to the House of Worship. There he prayed, "Dear God, do not harm this woman. It is obvious that her husband told her to do this and she should be praised for conducting herself as a willing wife."

—The Berditschever Rebbe

An emotion ceases to be a passion as soon as we form a clear and distinct idea of it.

—Baruch Spinoza

No one should put himself between two people sleeping on the same pillow.

—Yiddish folk saying

A man once said: "When our love was vibrant, we could sleep in a bed no wider than the edge of a sword; but now that our love has diminished, a bed sixty feet across seems too narrow for us."

—Talmud

As a rule, people love one another from a distance.

—Shalom Aleichem

If your wife is short, bend down so you can hear her whisper.

—Talmud

Love me a little, but love me long.

—Yiddish folk saying

The loneliest person is someone who loves only himself.

—Yiddish folk saying

There are three views of life that . . . are considered beautiful in the eyes of the Lord and of man: harmony between brothers, closeness among neighbors, and a man and his wife who are as one.

—Wisdom of Ben Sira

CHAPTER 21

Beauty, Desire,

Sexual Relations

The act of sexual union is sacred and pure . . . The Lord created all things in accordance with His wisdom, and whatever He created cannot possibly be filled with shame or ugly . . . When a man is in union with his wife in a spirit of holiness and purity, the Divine Presence is with them.

—Nachmanides

Nothing is restricted in the Torah that is as arduous to adhere to as forbidden unions and illegal relations between the sexes.

—Maimonides

Stolen waters are sweet, and bread eaten in secret is pleasant.

—Bible, Proverbs 9:17

The sexual organs are the most sensitive organs of the human being. . . . They are not diplomats. They tell the truth.

—Isaac Bashevis Singer

There is no greater adultery for a woman than for her to think of another man while she is having intercourse with her husband.

—Tanhuma Buber

A man is not allowed to make his wife have sexual relations with him.

—Talmud

In expressing love we belong among the underdeveloped countries.
—Saul Bellow

A man . . . should make himself holy when he is to have sexual relations.

—Maimonides

A husband is not allowed to coerce his wife to meet his sexual demands, because the Spirit of the Divine is never with the mate who has sexual relations without real desire or love.

—Nachmanides

A husband is forbidden to hold back from his wife her matrimonial rights for sexual relations.
If the husband does this to taunt his wife he has gone against a negative precept of the Torah.

—Maimonides

A man [who travels] . . . when he returns home has a duty to offer his wife [sexual] pleasure . . . for two reasons. The first is because for him to find pleasure is a religious pleasure. . . . The second is that should his wife become pregnant, the Heavenly partner gives to the still–unborn a sacred soul.

—Zohar

In the theatre, a hero is one who believes that all women are ladies, a villain one who believes that all ladies are women.
—George Jean Nathan

[Due to a high incidence of street assaults, the members of the Israeli cabinet asked Golda Meir, Minister of Labor, to enact a curfew for women. Ms. Meir responded:]
"It is men who are attacking women. If there needs to be a curfew for anyone, lock up the men, not the women."

—Golda Meir

It is better to behold beauty and live with wisdom than vice versa.
                                        —*Yiddish folk saying*

For a little love you pay all your life.
                                        —*Yiddish folk saying*

Beauty is often half the dowry.
                                        —*Yiddish folk saying*

I am the vessel; You, God, art the Master; fashion me in beauty so you may receive praise for your workmanship.
                                        —*Midrash Rabbah*

A woman who cannot be ugly is not beautiful.
                                        —*Karl Kraus*

Charm is more than beauty.
                                        —*Yiddish folk saying*

Oh, what lies there are in kisses!
                                        —*Heinrich Heine*

Lust isn't all there is to sex. Sex isn't all there is to love. But love is almost all there is to life.
                                        —*Eddie Cantor*

Long ago in London, I heard the story of the old gentleman who, when buying a book for his daughter, timidly asked, "No sex in it, I hope?"
The saleswoman replied, "No, sir, it's a love story."
                                        —*André Maurois*

Desire is the essence of man.
                                        —*Baruch Spinoza*

Power is the great aphrodisiac.
                                        —*Henry Kissinger*

Passions are fashions.
                                        —*Clifton Fadiman*

[The prophet Nathan offered this parable to King David.]

"There were two men who lived in one city, the one rich, and the other poor. The rich man owned many, many flocks and herds. But the poor man had nothing but a single ewe lamb, which he had purchased. The poor man raised the ewe and it grew up with him and the man's children. The ewe would eat from the man's plate and drink from his cup, and it lay on his chest, and it was like a daughter to him.

"Now a visitor came to see the rich man, but he refused to take a lamb from his own herds to make food for the visitor. Instead the rich man took the poor man's lamb and made a meal of it for the visitor."

[After hearing this story] David became outraged with anger and said to the Prophet Nathan: "As the LORD lives, the man that does this should be put to death; he will be forced to replace the lamb times seven, because he did this, and because he showed not pity."

Now, the Prophet Nathan cried out to David: "You are the man! And this is what the LORD God of Israel says to you: 'I anointed you king over Israel and I took you out of the hand of Saul . . . I also gave you the house of Israel and of Judah, and if this were not enough, I have added to you ever beyond this.

" 'Why then have you despised the LORD by doing this which is evil in my sight? You have slain Uriah the Hittite with the sword, and you have taken his wife [Bathsheba] to be your wife.'"

—Bible, II Samuel 12:1–10

. . . Sexual intercourse between a man and his wife is both unsoiled and sacred . . . God made everything . . . and didn't make anything unattractive or disgraceful. . . .

. . . The male is the unknown of wisdom and the female is the unknown of understanding. And the unblemished act of sex contains the unknown of knowledge. . . .

. . . The proper joining of a man with a woman can be a way to heightened spirituality.

—Nachmanides

In this manner was how people would sing songs to the bride before her wedding in Palestine:

"No powder and no paint, and no waving of the hair, and still a graceful gazelle."

—Talmud

Give no one praise for their beauty; think less of no one for their appearance.

—*Wisdom of Ben Sira*

Grace is deceitful and beauty is vain.

—*Bible, Proverbs 31:30*

PART SEVEN

Patriotism . . . Begins with

Human Allegiance

THROUGHOUT HISTORY, WHILE OTHERS MAY HAVE SEEN THE JEWS AS A people who chose to set themselves apart, a very real impulse in the Jewish social personality has been to do just the opposite. Though the God of Israel is often referred to as the King, approximately three thousand years ago the children of Israel came to the prophet Samuel and asked for an earthly king, "So," they entreated, "we may be governed like all other nations."

Samuel first warned the people, "He [the king] will take your sons," but upon the people's insistence and God's counsel, Samuel anointed Saul, from the tribe of Benjamin.

This intrusion of political structure into a theologically centered community added form to tribal life and then wreaked havoc. By the time Roman soldiers marched triumphantly through a crushed and smoldering Jerusalem almost a thousand years later, in the first century of the Common Era, two alarming realities were a part of the Jewish experience: Political supporters across the spectrum had grafted theories of government, often cabals of self-interest, onto a jurisdiction premised on the monarchy of divine faith; and the Jewish people were cut adrift, sent into the great dispersion known as *galut* ("exile" in Hebrew).

Over the next two thousand years and across the world Jews lived only as minorities in other cultures, devoid of any "sovereign" power of their own until the creation of the modern state of Israel in 1948. This reality, and the fact that even today more Jews live outside than inside Israel, forced the Jewish people to deal with nations and politics—because nations as well as religious and political figures had every intention of "dealing" with the Jews.

CHAPTER 22

Politics, Diplomacy, Nations, Nationalism, Patriotism, Leadership, News, Publicity, Propaganda, Elections, Conservatives, Liberals

Seek the welfare of the land into which I have seen you carried in exile, and pray to the LORD on this land's behalf; for in its welfare shall you find your welfare.

—Bible, Jeremiah 29:7

Give me your tired, your poor,
Your huddled masses yearning to breathe free,
The wretched refuse of your teeming shore.
Send these, the homeless, tempest-tossed to me,
I lift my lamp beside the golden door.

*—Emma Lazarus,
inscription on the Statue of Liberty*

Religion must move forward to help the state . . . to make plain that the responsibilities to man are also responsibilities to God . . . that charity is God's most sacred will; and a true insight into God will not allow antisocial attitudes.

—Moses Mendelssohn

We must not appoint a leader over the community before consulting the people.

—Talmud

A sage is more of value to a country than is its king.
                                                —*Maimonides*

Patriotism . . . begins with human allegiance.
                                                —*Norman Cousins*

Be sure you have the backing of your equals before you stir your
superiors.
                                                —*Yiddish folk saying*

What we call public opinion is generally public sentiment.
                                                —*Benjamin Disraeli*

An elder statesman is somebody old enough to know his own mind
and keep quiet about it.
                                                —*Bernard M. Baruch*

Diplomacy is to do and say the nastiest things in the nicest way.
                                                —*Isaac Goldberg*

No man can think clearly when his fists are clenched.
                                                —*George Jean Nathan*

Well-chosen phrases are a great help in the smuggling of offensive
ideas.
                                                —*Vladimir Jabotinsky*

The secret of the demagogue is to make himself as stupid as his
audience so that they can believe they are as clever as he.
                                                —*Karl Kraus*

If we all pulled in one direction the world would fall over.
                                                —*Yiddish folk saying*

. . . The Messianic hope . . . [is] a hope which the nation cannot
forget without ceasing to be a nation. A time will come when there
will be neither enemies nor frontiers, when war shall be no more, and
men will be secure in the dignity of speech.
                                                —*Chaim Weizmann*

I believe it to be a rule that tyrants of genius are succeeded by scoundrels.

—*Albert Einstein*

Politics is the diversion of trivial men who, when they succeed at it, become more important in the eyes of more trivial men.

—*George Jean Nathan*

How is the world ruled and how do wars start? Diplomats tell lies to journalists and then believe what they read.

—*Karl Kraus*

Real politics are the possession and distribution of power.

—*Benjamin Disraeli*

Men and nations behave wisely once they have exhausted all the other alternatives.

—*Abba Eban*

People will give up their rights before their customs.

—*Moritz Gudemann*

The duty of a wise man is to be exacting in his faith to the religious laws of his country, and not to abuse those of others.

—*Josephus*

Propaganda is the art of persuading others what you don't believe yourself.

—*Abba Eban*

The state must perish if man becomes tied to it in such a way that the welfare of the state, its power and its glory, become the criteria of good and evil.

—*Erich Fromm*

[Do not allow the political state to] reward or punish any belief or hold out promise or gain for the adopting of a religious belief.

—*Moses Mendelssohn*

When a person is capable of smiling while being abused, he is acceptable to become a leader.

—*Nachman of Bratslav*

Do not put your trust in princes.

—*Bible, Psalms 146:3*

Be sure that you pray for the well-being of the government, for it is respect for authority that saves people from swallowing up one another alive.

—*Pirke Avot*

Laws will not cause people to change their beliefs.

—*Moses Mendelssohn*

All revolutions are the work of a minority.

—*Max Nordau*

An empty stomach is not a good political adviser.

—*Albert Einstein*

Vote for the man who promises least. He'll be the least disappointing.

—*Bernard M. Baruch*

I must follow the people. Am I not their leader?

—*Benjamin Disraeli*

[Rabbi] Shemaiah's saying was: Love labor, shun office, and do not cultivate intimacy with authorities.

—*Pirke Avot*

Without moral and intellectual independence, there is no anchor for national independence.

—*David Ben-Gurion*

There is an interesting resemblance in the speeches of dictators, no matter what country they may hail from or what language they may speak.

—*Edna Ferber*

We should remember that Liberty, Equality, Fraternity do not belong to the world of facts but to the world of ideals.

—*Israel Zangwill*

The law is incapable of preventing us from believing as true what our reason wants us to believe.

—*Levi ben Gerson*

The Emperor Antoninus said to Rabbi Judah I: "The patricians make my life unbearable. What shall I do?"

Rabbi Judah I led the emperor into the garden and pulled out a plant. The next day the rabbi again led the emperor into the garden and again pulled up another plant.

Antoninus then understood. He should get rid of those who troubled him one at a time instead of trying to get rid of them all at one time.

—*Adapted from the Talmud*

Because humans had denied God's presence in life, even in nature, and instead found the premise of life in owning objects and the purpose in pleasure . . . a people [were] brought into the ranks of the nations who, through their history and life, would declare God the single creator of all existence, [and] realization of His will the only purpose in life.

—*Samson Raphael Hirsch*

If the man of learning participates in public affairs and serves as a judge or arbitrator, he establishes the land. But if he sits at home and says to himself, "What have the affairs of society to do with me? Why should I concern myself with the lawsuits of the people? Why should I trouble myself with their voices of protest? Let my soul dwell in peace!"—if he does this, he overthrows the world.

When Rabbi Ammi's hour to die was at hand, his nephew saw him weeping bitterly. He said: "Uncle and Teacher, why do you weep? Is there any Torah that you have not learned and taught? Is there any form of kindness that you have not practiced? And above all else, you have never accepted a public office and you have kept yourself apart from sitting in judgment."

The rabbi replied: "It is for this very reason that I weep. I was granted the ability to weigh justice between those who argue in Israel and I have not conducted myself according to my capability."

—*Tanhuma*

A nation is a work of art and a work of time.

—*Benjamin Disraeli*

This is the manner of the king who will reign over you: he will take your sons and use them for himself for his chariots and for his horsemen; and they will run ahead of his chariots; and he will make them serve him as captains of thousands and as captains of hundreds, and some of them he will make do his plowing and reap his harvests and make his weapons of war and the equipment for his chariots.

He will take your daughters to make perfumes, cook food, and bake bread. He will take over the best of your fields and your vineyards and your olive orchards, and give these to those who serve him in his court.

He will take a tenth of your fields of grain and of your vineyards and give them to his eunuchs and to those who do his dirty work.

He will take . . . the best of your cattle and asses, and use them to do his work. He will take a tenth of your flocks; and you yourselves will become his slaves.

Then you will cry out on that day because of the king who you will have taken on yourselves; but the LORD will not answer you on that day.

—*Bible, I Samuel 8:11–18*

The office seeks him who would run from it.

—*Tanhuma*

Happy is the generation where the great listen to the small, for it follows that in such a generation the small will listen to the great.

—*Talmud*

Perfection of means and confusion of goals seem to characterize our age.

—*Albert Einstein*

One who accepts any office in order to profit by it is no better than an adulterer.

—*Pesikta Rabbati*

Just as a man of muscle may be attracted to pugilism, so a man without character is drawn into politics. It is a calling that turns flaws into assets.

—*Ben Hecht*

If people's minds were as easy to control as their tongues, every king could rest easy on his throne.

—*Baruch Spinoza*

To give strength to a weak government, we must diminish its power.

—*Ludwig Boerne*

A person in political office who wants a law observed that they helped to create, should first observe it.

—*Midrash Rabbah*

Praised is he who fills the people of a community with a love for it.
—*Simeon ben Lakish, Midrash Rabbah*

It is obvious that there is a very real distinction between the nation state and the nation's religion. . . .
The state has physical force at its disposal and uses it if necessary. The strength of religion is love and caring.

—*Moses Mendelssohn*

The most important office [we can hold] is that of private citizen.
—*Louis D. Brandeis*

The nations of the world are so preoccupied with their anxieties and ambitions that they do not realize that the very foundation of civilized life is being undermined.

—*Mordecai M. Kaplan*

No man can be a conservative unless he has something to lose.
—*James Paul Warburg*

A conservative government is an organized hypocrisy.
—*Benjamin Disraeli*

Liberals feel unworthy of their possessions. Conservatives feel they deserve everything they've stolen.
—*Mort Sahl*

A man who is not a Liberal at sixteen has no heart; a man who is not a Conservative at sixty has no head.
—*Benjamin Disraeli*

History is not merely the record of a string of occurrences. It is the attempt to seize occurrences in their pattern.
—*Leon Roth*

When the shepherd blunders and has lost his way, his flock blunders after him.
—*Pirke de Rabbi Eliezer*

To save a people, leaders must be lost.
—*Israel Zangwill*

The rabbis commended all acts done for the public good, and among such acts they included the lighting of dark alleys and the keeping of roads in good repair.
—*Midrash Rabbah*

All nationalism is bad which turns out to be an ultimate value in and by itself; [nationalism can] be good while serving a higher value and aim than itself.
—*Ernst Simon*

Nationalism is an infantile disease. It is the measles of mankind.
—*Albert Einstein*

There's never been a good government.

—*Emma Goldman*

No government can be long secure without formidable opposition.

—*Benjamin Disraeli*

Ninety percent of the politicians give the other ten percent a bad reputation.

—*Henry Kissinger*

CHAPTER 23

Freedom, Democracy, Peace, War, Revolution

If one soldier knew what the other one was thinking there would be no war.

> —*Yiddish folk saying*

The final purpose of government is not to rule, or bind by fear, not to demand obedience, but on the contrary, to liberate every person from fear so they may live their lives with the highest security.
. . . The true purpose of government is liberty.

> —*Baruch Spinoza*

You are free and that is why you are lost.

> —*Franz Kafka*

Freedom is not the absence of slavery; it is the memory.

> —*Noah benShea*

Whereas each man claims freedom as a matter of right, the freedom he accords to other men is a matter of toleration.

> —*Walter Lippmann*

In this world it is very dangerous to be weak.

> —*Isaac Leibush Peretz*

All power is a trust.

—*Benjamin Disraeli*

The distinguishing factors between liberty and liberties are as great as those between God and gods.

—*Ludwig Boerne*

Love peace and pursue peace.

—*Hillel the Elder, Pirke Avot*

Democracy is moral before it is political.

—*Louis Wirth*

A rabbi happened to meet the prophet Elijah in a crowded marketplace environment.

"Master," asked the rabbi, "who among all who are present is most likely of eternal life?"

Elijah, answering, pointed toward two men of unpretentious manner. The rabbi was struck that these common-looking souls could be so special.

"What," he asked, upon confronting these two, "make you worth special merit?"

"We are not," the men answered, "unless you want to take into consideration that whenever people are having trouble we try to comfort them, and when people quarrel we make them friends again."

—*Talmud*

It is impossible for you to find peace anywhere but in your own self.

—*Simcha Bunam*

All lies are forbidden unless they are spoken for the sake of making peace.

—*Baraita*

If peace is not present, everything is lessened no matter what else we have.

—*Moshe Leib Sassover*

God is present whenever a peace treaty is signed.

—*Nachman of Bratslav*

The wolf also shall dwell with the lamb, and the leopard shall lie down with the kid.

—*Bible, Isaiah 2:4*

They tried their best to find a place where I was isolated. But all the resources of a superpower cannot isolate a man who hears the voice of freedom, a voice I heard from the very chamber of my soul.

—*Anatoly B. Scharansky*

The ultimate end of all revolutionary social change is to establish the sanctity of human life, the dignity of man, the right of every human being to liberty and well-being.

—*Emma Goldman*

You shall not follow the many to do evil.

—*Bible, Exodus 23:2*

Every revolution evaporates and leaves behind only the slime of a new bureaucracy.

—*Franz Kafka*

Every policeman is aware that although governments change, the police remain.

—*Leon Trotsky*

Every dogma has its day.

—*Israel Zangwill*

The most radical revolutionary will become a conservative on the day after the revolution.

—*Hannah Arendt*

We should treat our enemies like a treasure. We should bury them with care and affection.

—*Yiddish folk saying*

The greatest menace to freedom is an inert people.
—*Louis D. Brandeis*

Always come to the aid of those who are being oppressed.
—*Nachman of Bratslav*

Democracy is always a beckoning goal, not a safe harbor. For freedom is an unremitting endeavor, never a final achievement.
—*Felix Frankfurter*

In critical times men can save their lives only by risking them.
—*Léon Blum*

War is, at first, the hope that one will be better off; next, the expectation that the other fellow will be worse off; then, the satisfaction that he isn't any better off; and, finally, the surprise at everyone's being worse off.
—*Karl Kraus*

In a quarrel, each side is right.
—*Yiddish folk saying*

As long as there are sovereign nations possessing great power, war is inevitable.
—*Albert Einstein*

War is no more inevitable than the plague is inevitable.
War is no more a part of human nature than the burning of witches is a human act.
—*Meyer London*

It simply is not true that war never settles anything.
—*Felix Frankfurter*

War never ends war.
—*Stephen Samuel Wise*

God can never be saved by the devil.
—*Heinrich Heine*

Victory is the Lord's.

—*Bible, Proverbs 21:31*

When force is necessary, it must be applied boldly, decisively, and completely. But one must know the limitations of force; one must know when to blend force with a maneuver, the blow with an agreement.

—*Leon Trotsky*

The lust for power is not rooted in strength, but in weakness.

—*Erich Fromm*

Man had achieved freedom from—without yet having achieved freedom to—to be himself, to be productive, to be fully awake.

—*Erich Fromm*

Proclaim liberty throughout the land and to all the people therein.

—*Bible, Leviticus 25:10*

Henceforth the adequacy of any military establishment will be tested by its ability to preserve the peace.

—*Henry Kissinger*

War is the unfolding of miscalculations.

—*Barbara Tuchman*

Competing pressures tempt one to believe that an issue deferred is a problem avoided; more often it is a crisis invented.

—*Henry Kissinger*

The sword conquered for a while, but the spirit conquers forever!

—*Sholem Asch*

The story of man is the history, first, of the acceptance and imposition of restraints necessary to permit communal life; and second, of the emancipation of the individual within that system of necessary restraints.

—*Abe Fortas*

We cannot live by power, and a culture that seeks to live by it becomes brutal and sterile. But we can die without it.

—*Max Lerner*

Great is peace! Peace is the name of God.

—*Midrash Rabbah*

Iron, the weapon of destruction, cannot be used to build an altar to the God of life and peace.

—*Mekilta*

When you go out to do battle against your enemies . . . the officers shall say to the people, "Those who have built a new home, but have not dedicated it, may leave and return home, in case you die in the battle, and another dedicates it. Those who have planted a vineyard, but have not yet had a chance to enjoy it, may leave and go home, in case you die in battle, and another gets the use of it. Those who are engaged, but have not yet married, may leave and return home, in case you die in battle, and another marry the person you love."

In addition, the officers shall say to the people, "Any of you who are afraid and faint of heart must leave and return home. . . ."

—*Bible, Deuteronomy 20:5–8*

The evolution of mankind, though marked by frequent and disheartening reactions, moves irresistibly in the direction of universal security and freedom.

—*Mordecai M. Kaplan*

When you want to capture a city and for this purpose lay siege to it, you are not allowed to encircle the community on all four sides but only on three sides so that those who want the chance to escape can leave and keep their lives. . . .

We have learned from our tradition that this policy was given to Moses.

—*Maimonides*

The Jewish belief in democracy is based simply on the faith that God created man in His image, that all men are His equal children,

and that each possesses within him a spark of the divine which may not be violated.
—*Simon H. Rifkind*

When is a man free? Not when he is driftwood on the stream of life . . . free of all cares or worries or ambitions.
. . . To be free in action, in struggle, in undiverted and purposeful achievement, to move forward toward a worthy objective across a fierce terrain of resistance, to be vital and aglow in the exercise of a great enterprise—that is to be free. . . . A man is free only when he has an errand on earth.
—*Abba Hillel Silver*

Independence is never given to a people, it has to be earned; and having been earned, it has to be defended.
—*Chaim Weizmann*

When we observe one person ruling over a people, dictating to the entire state, we are watching a large group of human beings conducting themselves with fear. But whom do they fear? In reality the slaves are immeasurably superior to their master in terms of power. But each slave sees himself as one against all his fellow slaves. If they desire to rebel, they are afraid of one another.
. . . It is not the ruler who is the source of fear, but the army of slaves who follow his orders. Or, if you will, they fear themselves. Their weakness is an imagination, a misconception, a slave's error.
. . . All great revolutions are really the correcting of this misconception, a trifling error in the minds of the enslaved.
—*Jacob Klatzkin*

Moses was the author of the great principle that the governments and religions of nations must be built upon the same basis of truth as is individual character.
—*Isaac Mayer Wise*

A large political state whose citizens do not lift arms against the government because they shrink in fear are rather a people living without war than a people well enjoying a peace.
—*Baruch Spinoza*

Under conditions of tyranny it is far easier to act than to think.
—*Hannah Arendt*

We have learned in a hard school that, while you can have power without freedom, you cannot have freedom without power.
—*Lionel Morris Gelber*

A slave is free if he is at peace with his lot.
A free man is a slave if he wants more.
—*Yiddish folk saying*

The greatest dangers to liberty lurk in the insidious encroachment of men of zeal, well meaning but without understanding.
—*Louis D. Brandeis*

There may be a time when we are powerless to prevent injustice, but there must never be a time when we fail to protest.
—*Elie Wiesel*

Your primary purpose in life on the planet earth is to be at peace with all people, Jew and Gentile.
Do not be contentious with anyone.
Make your home a place of quiet and happiness, absent of hard language, and filled with love, friendship, modesty, and a continual air of the gentle and reverent.
This attitude should not be limited to the home.
In your interaction with the larger world, don't let either money or ambition distract you to disturbance.
Bend to others if necessary and bear envy for no one.
The central theme is peace, peace with the whole world.
Let all people receive your sincere respect, offer them your faith and absolute integrity.
—*Joel ben Abraham Shemaria*

CHAPTER 24

Israel, Zionism, Jews, Converts, Anti-Semitism, Holocaust

You have chosen us from among all the nations. Why, O Lord? What do you have against us?

—*Yiddish folk saying*

I have set you for a light unto the nations.

—*Bible, Isaiah 42:6*

My father often spoke in military terms: the Jews were the vanguard of mankind, the reconnaissance troops, and therefore prone to taking the highest casualties. But we would succeed one day in establishing the Kingdom of God on earth. Of that he had no doubt.

—*Chaim Potok*

The people's heart is the foundation on which the land will be built.

—*Ahad Ha-Am*

If you will it, it is not a dream.
        —*Theodor Herzl (on creating the modern state of Israel)*

Building a State means for us a return to the soil. We found hundred of Arab villages. We didn't take them away. . . . We established hundreds of new Jewish villages on new soil. . . . We didn't merely buy the land, we re-created the land. . . . In the swamps of Hedera hundreds of Jews died of malaria, and they refused to leave that place until it was made healthy. . . . With our toil, our sweat, and with our love and devotion, we are remaking the soil to enable us to settle there, not at the expense of anybody else.

—David Ben-Gurion

This is what our philosophy and propaganda aims at. To return to the Land, and within the Land to the soil; to cure that nervous over-strungness of exile and dispersion; to liquidate the racial inferiority complex and breed a healthy, normal earthbound race of peasants.

—Arthur Koestler

Our emancipation will not be complete until we are free of the fear of being Jews.

—Mordecai M. Kaplan

They shall sit every man under his vine and under his fig tree, and none shall make them afraid.

—Bible, Micah 4:4

If my theory of relativity is proven successful, Germany will claim me as a German and France will declare that I am a citizen of the world. If my theory should prove to be untrue, then France will say that I am a German, and Germany will say that I am a Jew.

—Albert Einstein

The great wrong that Shakespeare did the Jewish people was . . . that by emphasizing at every evil point Shylock's race and religion, he made him as a type of his people . . . Shakespeare painted many other villains . . . yet never did he associate their religious creed with them. . . . The villainies they executed were individual, the villainy of Shylock was made to be Jewish.

—Edward N. Calisch

To the Christian the Jew is the incomprehensibly obdurate man, who declines to see what has happened; and to the Jew the Christian is the incomprehensibly daring man, who affirms in an unredeemed world that its redemption has been accomplished.

—Martin Buber

Hatred for Judaism is at bottom hatred for Christianity.
—*Sigmund Freud*

It was as though in those last minutes he [Eichmann] was summing up the lessons that this long course in human wickedness had taught us—the lesson of the fearsome, word-and-thought-defying banality of evil.
—*Hannah Arendt*

If a person says to his representative, "Go and kill that person," and if the representative does so, he, the person who does this, is guilty.
—*Talmud*

There's no difference between one's killing and making decisions that will send others to kill. It's exactly the same thing, or even worse.
—*Golda Meir*

The question asked by many of us after the nightmare of the Holocaust was:
"At Auschwitz, where was God?"
And the answer that was given:
"Where was man?"
—*Dialogue of Holocaust survivors*

The pursuit of knowledge for its own sake, an almost fanatical love of justice and the desire for personal independence—these are the features of the Jewish tradition which make me thank my stars that I belong to it.
—*Albert Einstein*

A Jew is never on time. . . . He gets married, has children, grows old, and dies before his time.
—*Mendele (Moscher Sforim)*

When there is a possibility of danger, do not depend upon a miracle.
—*Talmud*

The State of Israel will prove itself not by material wealth, not by military might or technical achievement, but by its moral character and human values.

—*David Ben-Gurion*

All Israelites are mutually accountable to one another.

—*Talmud*

Put three Zionists in a room, and they'll form four political parties.

—*Levi Eshkol*

We are perhaps the children of rag peddlers, but we are the grandchildren of prophets.

—*Chaim Weizmann*

It is not that I belong to the past, but that the past belongs to me.

—*Mary Antin*

We should leave the ghetto but we should leave as Jews, [taking with us] our own spiritual treasures.

—*Isaac Leibush Peretz*

We Jews have a secret weapon in our struggle with the Arabs: we have no place to go.

—*Golda Meir*

Zionism is not simply national or chauvinistic caprice, but the last desperate stand of the Jews against annihilation.

—*Arthur Ruppin*

Those who persecute Israel are unwearying.

—*Talmud*

He who defends Israel is uplifted by God.

—*Pesikta Buber*

The school of Shammai put forth its own interpretations and acceptance of behavior regarding the laws of the Torah. The school of

Hillel held opinions that were often opposite to Shammai. Still, the two houses were friendly to each other and had respect for each other's opinions. The families intermarried, they ate with each other, and never sought to confuse or mislead the other as it is written: "Love ye both truth and peace" [Zechariah 8:19].

—Tosefta

Anti-Semitism cannot be stopped by the good behavior of the individual Jew.

—Kurt Zadek Lewin

In every generation, it is for each of us to think as if we, ourselves, went forth from Egypt.

—Talmud

Let my people go!

—Bible, Exodus 5:1

Palestine has the size of a county and the problems of a continent.

—Arthur Koestler

The stranger who gives himself to God's will is dearer to God even than Israel was at Sinai, for the stranger comes without the influencing terror of thunder and lightning, and voluntarily making himself at One with the Highest, gives himself to the "yoke of the kingdom of Heaven."

—Tanhuma

To be a Jew is to be a friend of mankind, to be a proclaimer of liberty and peace.

—Ludwig Lewisohn

It came to the attention of the emperor that his kinsman, Aquila, had become a proselyte of Judaism. The emperor then sent guards to summon him. When the guards arrived they began speaking with Aquila, and all of them became proselytes.

Once more the emperor sent messengers to bring Aquila forth, but they were warned not to speak with him. Aquila said, "Among

Romans an officer of a lower rank holds the lamp before his superior, but with the God of Israel, it is written that He went before Israel to light the way." Now all these messengers also became followers of Judaism.

For a third time the emperor sent messengers commanding them not to even listen to Aquila's words. Aquila simply placed his hand over a mezuzah and smiled broadly.

"Why are you smiling?" asked the messengers.

And Aquila answered: "Among the Romans, the king sits within, and his subjects guard him from without. Of God it is said that His subjects sit within, and He guards them from without" [Psalms 121:8].

Once again all these men became proselytes. But after this, the emperor sent no more messengers to Aquila.

—Talmud

Zionism is the return of Jews to Judaism, before they return to the Jewish land.

—Theodor Herzl

One day, Papus ben Judah discovered Rabbi Akiba teaching the Torah openly in public, a practice which was outlawed by the Roman government.

Papus asked, "Aren't you afraid of the government?"

The rabbi replied, "Let me tell you a parable. Once while walking downstream next to a river, a fox saw some fish racing back and forth in the stream. 'Tell me what you are running from,' asked the fox.

" 'From the nets,' answered the fish.

" 'Well then,' asked the fox, 'why don't you come out of the water onto the dry land next to me, where we can live together?'

" 'We have heard of you,' shouted the fish, 'you are the most cunning of animals. In the water we are in our element no matter our chances of being caught. But if we come out of the water we will surely die!'

"In this way," Rabbi Akiba continued, "those of us who study Torah are like the fish . . . for if we suffer for studying Torah, how much more would we suffer if we neglect it?"

—Talmud

The attempt of Zionism to lead Israel, nation and land, into the "normalcy" of the other nations has no future. It is only God's will as king, God's revealed Torah, that can shelter Israel, the people and the land.

—*Isaac Breuer*

You must not begin to imitate the abominable practices of the immoral nations.

—*Bible, Deuteronomy 18:9*

. . . Along with redemption of the land there must also be redemption of the soul.

—*Judah Leib Gordon*

To those who desire to come and live under the same laws as us, he [Moses] gives a gracious welcome, saying that it is not only the family bonds alone that create relationship, but ties between people also come from agreement in the principles of conduct.

—*Josephus*

In Judaism social action is religiousness, and religiousness implies social action.

—*Leo Baeck*

This country made us a people; and our people made this country.

—*David Ben-Gurion*

The Holy One loves those who choose to be Jews . . .

A king had many sheep and goats that went out each morning to the pasture and returned home each evening to the stable.

One day a stag joined the flock and grazed alongside the sheep, and returned with them. On seeing this, the shepherd came to the king. "With the sheep there is a stag who has joined them, and grazes with them, and now has come home with them."

The king greatly loved the stag, and he told the shepherd, "Watch out for this stag and make sure no one hurts it in any way." The king also ordered that when the stag returned at nights with the sheep, that the stag, too, should be given food and water.

At last, the shepherd said to the king, "My Lord, you have many goats and sheep and kids, and you give us no directions about them. But regarding this stag you give us orders every day."

Then the king answered, "It is the custom of sheep to feed in the pasture, but stags dwell in the wilderness, and do not venture into our cultivated pastures. Consequently, it is only right that we should be grateful to this stag for having left the wilderness where many stags and gazelles find food, to come and live with us."

In this way also spoke the Holy One: "I owe great thanks to those who are strangers, because they have left their family and their father's house, and they have come to live among us. Because of this I declare in Law: 'You should love the stranger.' "

—*Midrash Rabbah*

We must not turn our country into an idol, but a stepping-stone toward God.

—*Simone Weil*

Closer to God is the proselyte who had come forward on his own than all the great crowds of Israelites who stood at the base of Mount Sinai.

If the Israelites had not witnessed the thunder and lightning, the shaking mountain and rams' horns, they would not have accepted the Torah.

But the proselyte, who didn't witness even one of these phenomena, nevertheless came and surrendered himself to the Holy One, blessed be He, and took the yoke of heaven upon himself.

Can anyone be dearer to God than this person?

—*Tanhuma Buber*

To preserve the past is half of immortality.

—*Isaac D'Israeli*

Yiddish far more than Hebrew or neo-Hebrew was the living Jewish tongue. It was the language of the Jewish masses; it vibrates with their history, follows the mould of their life and thought, and colors itself with their moods. It is to Yiddish we must look for the truest repository of specifically Jewish sociology.

—*Israel Zangwill*

. . . What is necessary in Israel is more belief for the "believers" and more freedom for the "free-thinkers," and, above all, love, a bit more love.

—*Zvi Judah Kook*

A man came to a Polish magnate and asked him: "What do you think of the Jews?" The answer was: "Swine, Christ-killers, usurers, not to be trusted."

"But what do you think of Isaac?"

"A man after my own heart. An honorable man. A kind man. He saved me from bankruptcy."

"And what do you think of Berl?"

"I have known Berl all my life. He's one of the best."

"And of Shmuel?"

"Shmuel is a saint, as everyone knows."

The same man went to a rich and pious Jew and asked him: "What do you think of the Jews?" The pious man answered: "A kingdom of priests and a holy nation, the elect of the Eternal, blessed be His name."

"And what do you think of Isaac?"

"That thief? That scoundrel? May his bones be broken. He looks at you and you are robbed!"

"And of Berl?"

"A fellow of the same kind, without truth or justice."

"And of Shmuel?"

"Do you think I am taken in by his piety? A pretentious idiot."

—*Ludwig Lewisohn*

The Occidental would rebuild *society;* the Oriental works to rebuild *man.*

—*Marcus Ehrenpreis*

The Jewish religion, although it has had its periods of mild proselytizing, has never had to be, like either Mohammedanism or Christianity, a missionary religion. For since it does not hold man and nature to be corrupt, it does not consider men damned automatically and thus in need of a specific nostrum of metaphysical salvation.

—*Ludwig Lewisohn*

The idea of Semitic superiority can no more be defended than the idea of Aryan superiority.

—*Bernard Lazare*

The Prophets address the Gentile and Jewish nations with the same tone of spirit.

. . . God does not seek to destroy the evil nations, but their evil.

—*Sholem Asch*

Assimilation is evaporation.

—*Israel Zangwill*

The future of Judaism, even more than that of other historical civilizations, depends upon its having the courage to commit itself to the cause of social idealism.

—*Mordecai M. Kaplan*

And how deep is our responsibility that the Law requires in the matter of converts?

We are told to honor our mother and father, and listen to our prophets. Here, a person may honor without love. But in the matter of "strangers" [converts] we are to love with all the energy our heart can bring to bear.

—*Maimonides*

Faith in Israel means faith in the spiritual strength of the world.

—*Nahman Syrkin*

Do not imagine that you, of all the Jews, will flee with your life because you are in the king's palace.

—*Bible, Esther 4:13*

Nothing gratifies the mob more than to get a simple name to account for a complex phenomenon, and the word "Jew" is always at hand to explain the never-absent maladies of the body politic.

—*Israel Zangwill*

Though all the nations under the king's power obey and follow him and give up the beliefs of their ancestors, though others have decided to follow the king's commands, still my sons and I will follow the covenant of our fathers. . . . We will not shift even in the slightest from our manner of worship.

—Mattathias, I Maccabees

. . . We were the very first that revolted against them, and we remain the last to fight against them. . . .

. . . The nature of our fortress, although it cannot be conquered, will not be the way of our deliverance. . . .

. . . Let our wives die before they are raped, and our children before they are forced to eat slavery; and after we have slain our families, let us give each other the benefit of the same release. . . .

. . . We have not been conquered.

—Josephus Flavius at Masada
(testimony before the community suicide)

At the place of assembly, surrounded by the electrified barbed wire, thousands of silent Jews gathered, their faces stricken.

Night was falling. Other prisoners continued to crowd in, from every block, able suddenly to conquer time and space and submit both to their will.

—Elie Wiesel

The last person to hate Jews will die only with the last Jew.

—Victor Adler

There is within us the infinite and universal Concept that rescues us from the common fate of the fleeting.

—Nahman Krochmal

There is not a street in all of Rome where someone is not killed by the sword, and this evil nation will continue to shed innocent Jewish blood. My last advice to you is: Care for one another, love peace and justice; perhaps there is yet some hope.

—Yeshebab the Scribe (last words before martyrdom)

What does the Voice of Auschwitz command? Jews . . . are commanded to survive as Jews. . . . They are forbidden to despair of man and his world, and to escape into either cynicism or otherworldliness.

—*Emile Ludwig Fackenheim*

We are a generation that lacks someone to pray for us.
—*Rashi (after witnessing the slaughter of the First Crusade)*

I believe in the sun even when it is not shining.
I believe in love even when not feeling it.
I believe in God even when He is silent.
—*Scratched on cellar walls by anonymous people hiding from Nazis*

I figure the Jew as the eldest-born of Time, touching the Creation and reaching forward into the future, the true base of the Universe; the Wandering Jew who has been everywhere, seen everything, done everything, led everything, thought everything, and suffered everything.

—*Israel Zangwill*

Is there anywhere a Jew could go and be an alien? No, since wherever a Jew goes, God is with him.

—*Midrash Rabbah*

I am a Jew because in all places where there are tears and suffering, the Jew weeps.

—*Edmond Fleg*

O sing unto the Lord a new song.

—*Bible, Psalms 98:1*

Zionism was the Sabbath of my life.

—*Theodor Herzl*

Five years ago, I submitted my application for exit to Israel. Now I'm further than ever from my dream. It would seem to be cause for regret. But it is absolutely otherwise. I am happy. I am happy that I lived honestly, in peace with my conscience. I never compromised my soul, even under threat of death.

> —*Anatoly B. Scharansky*
> *(closing words before being sentenced in a Moscow court)*

Jerusalem will be reconstructed only through peace.

> —*Nachman of Bratslav*

We did not invent the art of printing; we did not discover America . . . we did not inaugurate the French Revolution . . . we were not the first to utilize the power of steam or electricity . . . Our great claim to the gratitude of mankind is that we gave to the world the word of God, the Bible. We stormed heaven to snatch down this heavenly gift . . . we threw ourselves into the breach and covered it with our bodies against every attack; we allowed ourselves to be slain by hundreds and thousands rather than become unfaithful to it; and bore witness to its truth and watched over its purity in the face of a hostile world.

> —*Solomon Schechter*

To the millennial wanderer, no road, no matter how far, need be too long.

> —*Leo Pinsker*

Why are the children of Israel compared to the dove?
All other birds when they grow tired find rest upon a rock or the branch of a tree. But when the dove tires, she does not cease flying; instead she rests one wing and flies with the other.

> —*Midrash Rabbah*

PART EIGHT

Who Is Wealthy?
He Who Is Happy
with His Lot in Life

WITH ADAM AND EVE'S EXIT FROM THE GARDEN OF EDEN WORK WAS introduced to the human experience. And while observance of the Sabbath is ordained in the Ten Commandments, it is in labor that most of our days are spent.

If, as some thinkers have suggested, work is one of the two major issues in our life, the other being love, then how we interact with our work has a great deal to do with what we know about ourselves. The Jewish people today are no longer a tribal agrarian society; but although issues of success and failure have been redefined they still spur and torment us.

In Hebrew the word for charity has at its root the word *justice*. We are directed in the Bible that gleanings of our crops be left in the field and that corners of the harvest be ungathered so that those who had little would have something. In Judaism, caring for others is not a matter for self-congratulation but simply just the right thing to do. Charity is a requirement of a just world.

As Jews we are taught not to count on luck but to trust in God. Nevertheless, while fortune and opportunity may be heaven-sent, we're also taught not to count on miracles. Within a Jewish context, work is God-given, whether it is to labor at a task or to chip away at our blindness.

CHAPTER 25

Work, Money

In toil you shall eat . . . all the days of your life.
—*Bible, Genesis 3:17*

Nothing is better than for a man to rejoice in his work.
—*Bible, Ecclesiastes 3:22*

Merchants throughout the world have the same religion.
—*Theodor Herzl*

You can tell what God thinks of money by looking at some of the people he gives it to.
—*Yiddish folk saying*

The bigger the businessman, the smaller the Jew.
—*Isaac Leibush Peretz*

Money sometimes makes fools of important persons, but it also makes important persons of fools.
—*Walter Winchell*

Since people inevitably think of business while they are at the synagogue, is it asking too much that they should think of God while they are at business?
—*Nahman Kasovir*

Because of Roman occupation, Rabbi Simeon ben Yohai and his son fled to a cave where they hid. For many years they stayed in the cave and spent all their days in study and contemplation.

One day they ventured from the cave and watched the multitudes working the soil, preparing the fields. Rabbi Simeon turned to his pupils and said: "These people working in the fields neglect eternal life and busy themselves with momentary needs."

. . . Suddenly a Heavenly Voice was heard to say to the rabbi and students: "You came out to destroy My world; return to your cave."

—Talmud

If a person has work, he is blessed.

—Midrash Tehillim

The fundamental evil of the world arose from the fact that the good Lord had not created enough money.

—Heinrich Heine

You never work so hard as when you're not being paid for it.

—George Burns

The best form of prayer is work.

—Israel Zangwill

A curse? You should have a lot of money, but you should be the only one in your family with it.

—Ernst Lubitsch

No man can claim to be free unless he has a wage that permits him and his family to live in comfort.

—Sidney Hillman

Money is only important if you haven't got it.

—Michael Todd

Man does not live by bread alone.

—Bible, Deuteronomy 8:3

When you don't have butter for your bread, it is not yet poverty.
—*Yiddish folk saying*

It is not so good with money as it is bad without it.
—*Yiddish folk saying*

Love work.
—*Rabbi Shammai, Pirke Avot*

Neither woman nor man lives by work or love alone. . . . The human self defines itself and grows through love and work.
—*Betty Friedan*

Love your work, and work at love.
—*Noah benShea*

The day is short. The task is great. . . . You are not expected to finish the work but neither are you excused from it.
—*Rabbi Tarfon, Pirke Avot*

. . . We are like the servants in a large home. Every one of us is assigned to some task for which we are responsible both for staying at it and trying to do a good job.
—*Moses Luzzatto*

Do not be afraid of work that has no end [like learning Torah].
—*Avot de Rabbi Nathan*

He that loveth money will not be satisfied with money.
—*Bible, Ecclesiastes 5:9*

Money is a difficult master, but an exceptional servant.
—*Joshua Steinberg*

When you labor with your own hands happy shall you be.
—*Bible, Psalms 128:2*

One that slacks in his work is brother to him that is a destroyer.
—*Bible, Proverbs 18:9*

Those who submerge themselves in the desire for money are always in debt.

—*Nachman of Bratslav*

As a general rule, nobody has money who ought to have it.
—*Benjamin Disraeli*

Some people think they are worth a lot of money just because they have it.

—*Fannie Hurst*

Whether our work is art or science or the daily work of society, it is only the form in which we explore our experience which is different.
—*Jacob Bronowski*

A committee is a group that keeps minutes and loses hours.
—*Milton Berle*

Whoever withholds an employee's wages, it is as though he has taken the person's life from him.

—*Talmud*

In the same manner that an employer is forbidden to deny the poor employee his salary or hold back what is owed him in any way, the employee is also forbidden to deny the employer the true effort of his work by wasting his time, in pieces or the day in the whole.
—*Maimonides*

Money attracts money.

—*Yiddish folk saying*

Money doesn't talk, it swears.

—*Bob Dylan*

By abolishing private property one takes away the human love of aggression.

—*Sigmund Freud*

This new attitude towards effort and work as an aim in itself may be assumed to be the most important psychological change which has happened to man since the end of the Middle Ages . . . a striving to do something.

—Erich Fromm

More and more I am certain that the only difference between men and animals is that men can count and animals cannot and if they count what they mostly do count is money.

—Gertrude Stein

Money is a wonderful thing, but it is possible to pay too high a price for it.

—Alexander Bloch

When a habit starts to cost money, it is called a hobby.

—Yiddish folk saying

He who has a hundred wants two hundred.

—Midrash Rabbah

In his work the individual is at minimum well attached to a piece of reality, the human community.

—Sigmund Freud

It was a favored saying of the rabbis at Yavneh: I am a creation [of God], and my neighbor is also His creature; my work is in the city, and his in the field; I rise early to do my work, and he rises early to do his. As he cannot do well at my work, similarly, I cannot do well at his work.

Nevertheless, if you say, I do great things and he does unimportant things, I say: We have learned that [it doesn't matter if] a person does much or little, but only if he directs his heart to Heaven.

—Talmud

No work, no matter how humble, is a dishonor.

—Talmud

A person must not depend on the work of his ancestors. If a person does not do good in his lifetime, he cannot fall back on the work of those who came before him. No person will eat in the Time-to-Come of his parents' work, but only of his own.

—*Midrash Tehillim*

Rabbi Judah would go to the house of learning bearing a pitcher on his shoulders, and saying,

"Great is labor, for it honors the person who does it."

—*Talmud*

The right of the laborer always takes precedence over that of his employer.

—*Talmud*

Turnus Rufus asked Rabbi Akiba: "If you say that man's handiwork is better than God's, how do you answer why man cannot make the Heavens and the earth?"

"Do not ask me about things not in man's power to do, but about that which man can do," answered Rabbi Akiba.

"All right, then tell me why men are born uncircumcised?" asked the Roman.

"I knew you would ask me this and that is why I said man's work is better than God's. We are required to improve upon nature. For example, God gives us wheat, but we make it into loaves. Is man's work not an improvement on nature?"

—*Tanhuma*

If the study [of Torah] is not integrated with work, study will finally be avoided, and thus the absence of work becomes the cause of doing wrong.

—*Rabban Gamaliel, Pirke Avot*

When the study of Torah is accompanied by work in this world it is a safeguard against sin.

—*Pirke Avot*

Find work that is beneath you rather than becoming dependent on others.

—*Jerusalem Talmud*

There was a poor woman who sold apples near where the Rebbe Hayyim of Zanz lived.

The woman came to the rebbe complaining of her situation. "Rabbi, I have no money. Not even enough to buy something for the Sabbath."

The rebbe listened, and then asked, "And what about the apples?"

"People won't buy my apples, I am told they are bad."

Without saying anything, the rebbe went out into the street and began shouting, "I have good apples. Who would like some?"

Almost immediately, the rebbe was surrounded by people who bought all the apples.

The rebbe handed the woman the money as she stood unbelieving of what she had just seen. "How is this possible, Rebbe?"

"Is it so strange," said the Rabbi to the woman, "to see people buying when they are told something is good? Your apples were good. The only thing wrong was that people didn't know that."

—*Adapted from a story about Rabbi Hayyim ben Leibush of Zanz*

Great is labor! All the prophets engaged in it.

—*Midrash Hagadol*

Sometimes one pays the most for the things one gets for nothing.

—*Albert Einstein*

Labor honors.

—*Simeon ben Yohai, Talmud*

No person who is enthusiastic about his work has anything to fear from life.

—*Samuel Goldwyn*

Although Abba Joseph was a rabbi, he was a builder's laborer. And while he worked one day, he was confronted by a man who wanted to drag the rabbi into a long theological conversation.

The rabbi refused. "I am a day laborer," he said, "and I must not leave my work, so say what you want to quickly and leave."

—*Midrash Rabbah*

The sleep of a laboring man is sweet.

—*Bible, Ecclesiastes 5:11*

CHAPTER 26

Prosperity, Success, Fame, Debt, Poverty, Economic Failure

Who is wealthy?
He who is happy with his lot in life.

—*Ben Zoma, Pirke Avot*

Man is usually trying to make something for himself rather than something of himself.

—*Jascha Heifetz*

The door of success is marked "Push" and "Pull." Achieving success is knowing when to do what.

—*Yiddish folk saying*

The secret of success is constancy of purpose.

—*Benjamin Disraeli*

The one who persists in knocking [is the one] who will succeed in entering.

—*Moses ibn Ezra*

The toughest thing about being a success is that you've got to keep on being a success.

—*Irving Berlin*

Do not be fooled into believing that because a man is rich he is necessarily smart. There is ample proof to the contrary.

—*Julius Rosenwald*

What we get out of life is in direct proportion to what we put into it.

—*Herbert H. Lehman*

Quickly got, quickly lost.

—*Yiddish folk saying*

When you are experiencing prosperity be happy, and when things are going against you remember: God created both of these times.

—*Bible, Ecclesiastes 7:14*

Our failures . . . for the most part spring from our successes.

—*David Sarnoff*

In our rich consumer's civilization we spin cocoons around ourselves and get possessed by our possessions.

—*Max Lerner*

The true defense against wealth is not a fear of wealth—of its fragility and of the vicious consequences that it can bring—the true defense against wealth is an indifference to money.

—*Natalia Ginzburg*

Increased means and increased leisure are the two civilizers of man.

—*Benjamin Disraeli*

The rich also must love work, must find something to do worthy of their time rather than simply staying passive—because having nothing to do makes you do bad things.

—*Menahem ben Solomon ha-Meiri*

In dreams, even fools get rich.

—*Yiddish folk saying*

You can't make cheesecake from snow.
—*Yiddish folk saying*

Don't tire yourself to be rich.
—*Bible, Proverbs 23:4*

The difficult we do immediately. The impossible takes a little longer.
—*David Ben-Gurion*

If you carry your own lantern you will survive the dark.
—*Hasidic folk saying*

Those who do not depend on fortune forestall misfortune.
—*Talmud*

Moses did not desire to abolish the notion of private property.
Instead, Moses wanted everybody to own some property, so no person would be so poor so as to spend his life as a serf with the mindset of enslavement.
Freedom was the prevailing principle in Moses's thoughts.
—*Heinrich Heine*

Have witnesses when you lend but none when you give.
—*Yiddish folk saying*

A heavy purse carries a light heart.
—*Yiddish folk saying*

Winning may not be everything, but losing has little to recommend it.
—*Dianne Feinstein*

It's better to live rich than to die rich.
—*Ernst Lubitsch*

When I was a young boy I used to think that if you were very nice to very rich people they would give you fabulous presents, like a

Cadillac or a house on the French Riviera. But as I journeyed through life I discovered that rich people give you nothing—that's why they're rich. So now I insult them all I want.

—*Groucho Marx*

People say: when food is lacking in the pantry, quarrel knocks at the door.

—*Talmud*

Always say NO, first. I have become a millionaire by saying NO.

—*Solomon Loeb*

Misers worship idols.

—*Yiddish folk saying*

To sell something you have to someone who wants it—that is not business. But to sell something you don't have to someone who doesn't want it—that is business.

—*Joseph Seligman*

Rich men are often lean and poor men fat.

—*Yiddish folk saying*

Everyone knows where his shoe pinches.

—*Yiddish folk saying*

The desire for success lubricates secret prostitutions in the soul.

—*Norman Mailer*

Poverty is not a disgrace.

—*Seligman Ulman Ginzberger*

Two farmers each claimed to own a particular cow. While one of the farmers pulled at the cow's head, and the other yanked at the tail, the cow was milked by a lawyer.

—*Yiddish folk saying*

One who seeks more than he needs hampers himself from enjoying what he has.

—*Solomon ibn Gabirol*

A schlemiel is someone who falls on his back and bruises his nose.
　　　　　　　　　　　　　　　　—*Yiddish folk saying*

A speculator is a man who observes the future, and acts before it
occurs.
　　　　　　　　　　　　　　　　　—*Bernard M. Baruch*

The more poverty, the more hope.
　　　　　　　　　　　　　　　　—*Shalom Aleichem*

God will provide—but if only He would provide until he does.
　　　　　　　　　　　　　　　—*Yiddish folk saying*

. . . With righteousness shall he judge the poor,
And decide with equity for the meek of the land.
　　　　　　　　　　　　　　　—*Bible, Isaiah 11:4*

Most of the things worth doing in the world had been declared
impossible before they were done.
　　　　　　　　　　　　　　　　—*Louis D. Brandeis*

Competition brings out the best in products and the worst in people.
　　　　　　　　　　　　　　　　—*David Sarnoff*

The first question a person will have to answer on the Judgment
Day is: "Have you been honest in your business?"
　　　　　　　　　　　　　　　　　—*Talmud*

Being honest in business fulfills the whole Torah.
　　　　　　　　　　　　　　　　　—*Mekilta*

Wealth maketh many friends.
　　　　　　　　　　　　　　　—*Bible, Proverbs 19:4*

Glory in excess is a disgrace.
　　　　　　　　　　　　　　　—*Yiddish folk saying*

One sits uncomfortably on a too comfortable cushion.
　　　　　　　　　　　　　　　　—*Lillian Hellman*

A financier is a pawn-broker with imagination.
                                        —*Arthur Wing Pinero*

We only possess what we renounce; what we do not renounce escapes us.
                                        —*Simone Weil*

It takes twenty years to make an overnight success.
                                        —*Eddie Cantor*

Wealth means power: the power to subdue, to crush, to exploit, the power to enslave, to outrage, to degrade.
                                        —*Emma Goldman*

"Vanity," said Jacob, "is its own mirror, a way we are seduced by what we *want* to see."

"But I *want* to feel like somebody important," said the man.

Jacob smiled. "What is important is that you like the somebody you are."
                                        —*Noah benShea*

There are so many ways of earning a living, and most of them failures.
                                        —*Gertrude Stein*

Every cat likes fish but few of them will enter the water.
                                        —*Yiddish folk saying*

Diligence is the right hand of accomplishment.
                                        —*Solomon Rubin*

The dynamo of our economic system is self-interest which may range from mere petty greed to admirable types of self-expression.
                                        —*Felix Frankfurter*

. . . Economic independence lies at the very foundation of social and moral well-being.
                                        —*Felix Frankfurter*

No one is so poor as those who are ignorant of the Torah and its commandments, for this is all that can be considered as wealth.

—*Zohar*

It is within human nature to make an effort to gain money and add to it; and in our desire to seek more wealth and honor is the largest source of agony for human beings.

—*Maimonides*

Borrow, and you'll sorrow.

—*Yiddish folk saying*

See how all of God's creation borrow from one another: Day borrows from night, and night from day. . . . The moon borrows from the stars, and the stars from the moon. . . . Wisdom borrows from understanding, and understanding from wisdom. . . . The heavens borrow from the earth, and the earth from the heavens. . . . All the creations of God borrow from one another, but live in a state of peace without taking one another to court.

—*Midrash Rabbah*

Nothing is so negative that good cannot come from it.

—*Yiddish folk saying*

A man was running down the street looking only straight ahead.

The rabbi in the community saw the man and asked him: "Why are you in such a rush?"

"I'm trying to make a living," said the man, hesitant to even slow down to answer the question.

"Do you think," asked the rabbi, "that it is possible that the living you are trying to make is not ahead of you but behind you and all that is required of you is to stand still?"

—*Rabbi Levi Isaac ben Meir of Berdichev*

All shoemakers go barefoot.

—*Yiddish folk saying*

Nothing in the world exists that is worse than poverty—it is the most awful of anguishes.

—*Midrash Rabbah*

What is too heavy for you, don't lift.

—*Wisdom of Ben Sira*

Those who cannot find the strength to survive bad times will not discover good times.

—*Hasidic folk saying*

It's not what you know how to do but what you have the character to do that leads to wealth or poverty.

—*Rabbi Tanna Meir*

Lend someone money and you've made an enemy.

—*Yiddish folk saying*

Who are the people of God? The poor.

—*Midrash Rabbah*

If I sold candles, the sun would never set.

—*Yiddish folk saying*

There must be more to life than having everything.

—*Maurice Sendak*

If you have too much, something is missing.

—*Yiddish folk saying*

Just as God infuses the wicked with the strength to bear their punishment, so does God give the good the strength to bear their rich rewards.

—*Talmud*

I've never been poor, only broke. Being poor is a frame of mind. Being broke is only a temporary situation.

—*Michael Todd*

CHAPTER 27

Charity

The greatest charity is to enable the poor to earn a living.
—*Yiddish folk saying*

Early one morning, a rich man who seldom gave to charity happened to approach the rebbe's house. On seeing the rebbe at his window, the man invited himself up and joined the rebbe at the window overlooking the street.

"When you look out the window, what do you see?" asked the rebbe.

"People," answered the miser, with disregard.

"And now?" asked the rebbe, pulling the man over until he stood in front of a tall mirror.

"And now," said the man, thinking the question ridiculous, "I see myself."

"Ah," said the rebbe, "think about this. In both the window and in the mirror there is glass, *but* the glass in the mirror is backed with silver. What do we learn from this? From this we learn, that as soon as silver was added to the equation, you no longer saw others and saw only yourself."

—*Adapted Hasidic folktale*

When you feed strangers you occasionally feed angels.
—*Yiddish folk saying*

Before prayer, give to charity.

—*Nachman of Bratslav*

Is this the fast I want, a day for men to starve their bodies? Is it bending the head like a bullrush and lying in sackcloth and ashes? Do you call that a fast, a day when the Lord is disposed to you?

No, this is the fast I desire:

To unlock the bindings of wickedness and untie the cords of the yoke. To let the oppressed go free; to break off every yoke.

It is to share your bread with the hungry and to take the suffering poor into your home; when you see the naked to give them clothes, and not to ignore your own family . . .

—*Bible, Isaiah 58:5–7*

Even a poor man who lives off charity should perform acts of charity.

—*Talmud*

Charity is also a habit.

—*Yiddish folk saying*

Deeds of loving-kindness are greater than charity.

—*Talmud*

The reward of charity depends entirely upon the extent of the kindness in it.

—*Talmud*

Those who lend without interest are more worthy than those who give charity; and those who invest money in the business of a poor person are the most worthy of all.

—*Talmud*

Those who do not pay their debts but give to charity commit robbery.

—*Yiddish folk saying*

It happens that once there was a very poor man who struggled with the way to approach God concerning his poverty.

Then one day, it dawned on him.

"Dear God," began the man, "if you give me twenty thousand dollars I will make an arrangement with you. I will give ten thousand dollars of what you give me to charity and keep only the rest."

When the money didn't suddenly appear, the man prayed again.

"Dear God, it is obvious that you question my integrity. And so I offer this suggestion. Give me ten thousand dollars and give the other ten thousand to charity Yourself."

—Anonymous, from the Yiddish

Tithes are a fence for wealth.

—Rabbi Akiba, Mishneh Torah

Those who feed the hungry also feed God.

—Agadat Shir ha-Shirim

Do not neglect the children of the poor.

—Eleazar ben Pedat, Talmud

A rabbi reminded his wife: "When a beggar comes to the door, give him bread in order that one day the same will be offered to our children."

The wife shouted, "You are cursing our children."

"No," said the rabbi, "there is a wheel that revolves in the world. On this wheel the poor become rich and the rich become poor."

—Talmud

During a great famine, King Monoboaz of Adiabene distributed all his treasures to the poor. His relatives complained, "Your ancestors stored these riches, but you waste them."

The king replied, "My ancestors stored these treasures for life on the lower level where force controls—riches which give no fruit; riches of money, riches of consequence in this world only. I, on the other hand, am storing riches for the World Above: a sacred place where force does not control—riches which deliver fruit; riches of the soul; riches of value; riches in the World-to-Come."

—Talmud

There was a terrible famine sweeping the country and a certain tzaddik [righteous man] realized it was in his capacity to help by going to those who could give and asking for something for those who were starving.

Knocking at the door of a man well-known for his disregard of others, the tzaddik made his presentation of the need and received instead of a contribution a smack in the face.

Wiping the blood from his lower lip, the tzaddik said to the wealthy man, "The punishment was obviously for me, but *now* what will you give to the poor?"

—*Hasidic folktale*

Collectors of charity receive a reward equivalent to the reward of all those who donate.

—*Zohar*

Each of us is required to give to charity.

Even the poor who are on charity should give a piece of what they receive. . . .

We should do what ever we can including finding the courage to bear our misery to avoid depending on the charity of others. . . .

Ransoming captives is of more importance than feeding or clothing those who have less.

There is no deed of charity that is a higher deed than to ransom captives.

—*Joseph Caro, Shulhan Aruk*

The commandment to be charitable is in its weight as much as all the rest of the commandments in total. . . . Those who give to charity in secret are greater than Moses.

—*Talmud*

If you live in a community for thirty days, you become responsible for contributing to the kitchen that feeds the poor; three months, to the fund for charity; six months, to the fund for clothing; nine months, to the fund for the burial society; and twelve months, to the fund for the repair of community walls.

—*Talmud*

[Descending levels on giving charity:]
The person who gives to the poor before being asked.
The person who gives to the poor after being asked.
The person who gracefully gives less than he should.
The person who gives with resentment.

—*Maimonides*

If what you want is to help someone rise from the mud and filth, don't think it is enough to stand on top and offer a hand by reaching down.

You must go down yourself, down into the mud and filth itself. Then take the person with your strong grip and pull both of you out into the light.

—*Rabbi Solomon ben Meir ha-Levi of Karlin*

[Descending ethical scale on giving charity:]
That the giver and the receiver are unknown to each other.
That the giver knows who is receiving, but the receiver does not know who is giving.
That the giver does not know who is receiving, but the receiver knows who is giving.

—*Maimonides*

Those who donate a great deal to charity become richer as a result because you open a wide channel for God's blessings to reach you.

—*Zohar*

The reward you receive for your charity is entirely dependent on the kindness in your giving.

—*Talmud*

It happened that a beggar came to Rabbi Schmelke's home when the rabbi had no money to give, and his wife was not at home. Desiring to respond to the beggar, the rabbi began searching through his wife's drawers for something to give and came upon a ring.

When his wife returned home, she discovered her bureau open and her treasured ring missing. She began to shout and was only quieted when the rabbi explained what he had done. The wife requested the rabbi to find the beggar as the ring was extremely valuable.

Hearing this, the rabbi left, quickly chasing the beggar. When the rabbi found him, he explained to the man: "I am so glad to have found you. I have just been told by my wife that the ring I gave you is of great value. When you sell it, be sure you do not allow anyone to cheat you by giving you any less than it is worth."

—Adapted legend of Rabbi Schmelke of Nikolsburg

We have been taught by our rabbis: We lend support to the poor who are not Jewish as well as to those who are Jewish; and visit the sick who are not Jewish as well as the sick who are Jewish; and bury the poor who are not Jewish as well as the poor who are Jewish; in the interests of peace.

—Talmud

A certain righteous man lived in a certain community and had an incredible capacity to get even those who would never give to give to others.

Another sage came to the collector of charities and asked if he didn't think it was below him to have to bend, and bow, and beg for the sake of charity.

"My friend," the righteous man answered, "let us see if we can find an answer to your question by observing nature. In nature, man is God's most excellent creation. We certainly are much higher than the lowly cow. But, no matter how high we hold ourselves, we must bend before a cow if we would milk her."

—Adapted Hasidic folktale

A man who is a miser and a fat cow are useful only after they're dead.

—Shalom Aleichem

Take care that the doors of your home are not shut against the needy.

—Zuta

There are ten strong things in the world: Rock, but iron cuts it. Fire [which melts iron], but water puts it out. Water, but clouds carry it. Clouds, but the wind blows them. Wind, but the body bends with

it. The body, but fear controls it. Fear, but wine chases it. Wine, but
sleep clears it. [So] Death [the long sleep] is stronger than anything,
but charity saves one from death [Proverbs 10:2].

—*Judah ben Ilai, Talmud*

. . . Do not harden your heart or close your hand to those who are
in need. Instead, open your hand and lend whatever is necessary. . . .

Give without hesitation and without regret, and as a consequence,
the Lord your God will bless your efforts and work in life. There will
never be a time without those who will need in your land, so again, I
command you: open your hand to the poor and those in need.

—*Bible, Deuteronomy 15:7–11*

CHAPTER 28

Luck, Opportunity

The harder I work, the luckier I get.

—Samuel Goldwyn

When fortune calls, offer her a place to sit.

—Yiddish folk saying

Next to knowing when to seize an opportunity, the most important thing in life is to know when to forgo an advantage.

—Benjamin Disraeli

Those who do not depend on luck have less bad luck.

—Yiddish folk saying

All beginnings are difficult.

—Ishmael ben Elisha, Mekilta

Opportunities are usually disguised as hard work, so most people don't recognize them.

—Ann Landers

Opportunity falls into the hands of those who are prepared to receive it.

—Yalkut Shimoni

Entrepreneurs are simply those who understand that there is little difference between obstacle and opportunity and are able to turn both to their advantage.

—Victor Kiam

When the price drops, buy.

—Eleazar Bar Kappara, Talmud

PART NINE

Without Doubt There

Can Be No Certainty

TO UNDERSTAND JUDAISM'S HIGH REGARD FOR LEARNING, ONE MUST remember that the Talmud directs every Jew to find both a teacher and someone with whom to study. And while the Talmud also states that a school is not allowed to be turned into a synagogue, the word *rabbi* itself means "teacher." In Judaism we are all students; the great sage Hillel, in the talmudic Ethics of the Fathers, directs us to remember, "He who does not increase [his knowledge] decreases it."

Jews have often been referred to as "the people of the book." Indeed, according to our tradition the entire world was brought into existence by the Word of God. Consequently this makes language, both written and spoken, sacred. And if language is sacred, silence is the sacred canvas (the first letter in the Hebrew alphabet, aleph, is silent) on which all language is painted. The central prayer in Judaism is the *Shma,* which begins: "Hear, O Israel . . ." The lesson is clear. We cannot learn, nor can we be transformed by learning, until we quiet ourselves. Learning begins with listening—if only to our own ignorance.

To the Jew the classroom is no smaller than the world which God created. Just as God's handiwork can be seen everywhere, school is always in session. The only question is whether we are paying attention.

CHAPTER 29

Knowledge, School, Learning,

Ignorance, Study, Teachers,

Scholars, Students

Think and thank.

—*Moses Montefiore*

One of the "wise men" of Chelm said to his wife, "If I were the czar, I would be even richer than the czar."

"How is that possible?" asked his wife.

"Well," said the "sage," "if I were the czar, I would do a little teaching on the side."

—*Yiddish folk tradition*

There is no education like adversity.

—*Benjamin Disraeli*

A great deal of intelligence can be invested in ignorance when the need for illusion is great.

—*Saul Bellow*

Included among the "sages" of Chelm was one Lemach ben Lekish, who, when people who could not find an answer to a particularly difficult question, would answer with his own wit.

For example:

"Why does the hair on a man's head turn gray sooner than the hair in his beard?"

"This is because the hair on the man's head is twenty years older than his beard."

"Why is the sea water so salty?"

"Why? Of course, because hundreds of thousands of herring live in the sea."

—*Yiddish folk tradition*

Above all we take pride in the education of our children.

—*Josephus*

Woman was bequeathed more intelligence than man.

—*Judah ha-Nasi, Talmud*

Let your house be a meeting place for the sages, and sit amid the dust at their feet, and drink in their words with thirst.

—*Jose ben Joezer of Zeredah, Pirke Avot*

The sages said, "I have learned a great deal from my teachers, more from other teachers, but most of all from my students."

Even a small piece of wood can kindle a large log.

—*Maimonides*

A little light is precious, but too much is blinding.

—*Joseph Solomon Delmedigo*

No person can give a better example of his skill and inclination than for the people he is teaching to arrive and live, at the very least, in a state of their own reason.

—*Baruch Spinoza*

Rabbi Abbahu sent his son Hanina to study in Tiberias. Later he was informed that Hanina was doing community work, and he wrote him: "My son, was there no good to be done in Caesarea, your native town, that I sent you to Tiberias? Haven't we decided that learning takes precedence?"

The other rabbis of Caesarea said: "Learning comes first only if there are others to do the works of kindness; but if there is no one else, doing comes first."

—*Talmud*

Those who truly guard the state are the teachers.

—*Jerusalem Talmud*

Don't live in a city run by scholars.

—*Rabbi Akiba, Talmud*

Education is that which remains when one has forgotten everything he learned in school.

—*Albert Einstein*

Teachers learn from the discussions of their students.

—*Rashi*

To know the taste of the wine, it is not necessary to drink the whole barrel.

—*Hayyim Nachman Bialik*

Provide yourself with a teacher, find someone to study with, and judge all men favorably.

—*Joshua ben Perahia, Mishneh Torah*

There are four types of those who sit before the Sages: the sponge, the funnel, the strainer, and the sieve. The sponge, which soaks up everything; the funnel, which takes in one end and lets out at the other; the strainer, which lets out the wine and retains the lees; the sieve, which lets out the bran and retains the fine flour.

—*The Sages, Pirke Avot*

Most mistakes in philosophy and logic occur because the human mind is apt to take the symbol for the reality.

—*Albert Einstein*

Only the learning that is enjoyed will be learned well.

—*Judah ha-Nasi, Talmud*

Those who do not add to their learning, diminish it.

—*Talmud*

Constant study is not study all day, but each day.

—*Israel Salanter Lipkin*

If a scholar engages in business and is not successful, it is a good omen for him. It means God loves his learning and does not wish to enrich him.

—*Midrash Samuel*

When all think alike, then no one is thinking.

—*Walter Lippmann*

Why should society feel responsible only for the education of children, and not for the education of all adults of every age?

—*Erich Fromm*

Morality has more importance than learning.

—*Abba Saul, Talmud*

. . . Knowledge alters what we seek as well as what we find.

—*Freda Adler*

If you lack knowledge, what have you acquired?
If you acquire knowledge, what do you lack?

—*Midrash Rabbah*

Happy is the one whose deeds are greater than his learning.

—*Midrash Rabbah*

I will not close myself off in the house of study when there is no bread in my home.

—*Talmud*

Creative minds have always been known to survive any kind of bad training.

—*Anna Freud*

Everybody calls "clear" those ideas that have the same degree of confusion as their own.

—*Marcel Proust*

Those who learn for the purpose of teaching receive inspiration.

—*Midrash Rabbah*

He who learns receives but one fifth of the reward that goes to one who teaches.

—*Midrash Song of Songs*

Fill your time to whatever extent you can by learning about things that are divine, not simply to know them but also to do them; and when you shut your book, observe around you, see within you, to know if by your own hand you can make into a deed something that has been learning.

—*Moses of Evreux*

Raba said: "If there are more than twenty-five children in a class for elementary learning, an assistant should be appointed.

"If there are fifty children in a class, two capable teachers should be hired to supervise."

—*Talmud*

A person can forget in two years what took twenty to learn.

—*Rabbi Nathan, Pirke Avot*

Rabbi Abbahu and Rabbi Hiyya ben Abba came to the same town at the same time.

Rabbi Hiyya delivered a scholarly discourse on the Law, while Rabbi Abbahu delivered a midrashic sermon. Afterward all the people left Rabbi Hiyya and came to Rabbi Abbahu.

Rabbi Hiyya was seriously discouraged, but his colleague said to him, "I will tell you a parable. Two men entered the same village, the one offering to sell precious gems and pearls, the other costume jewelry.

"To whom do you think the people rushed? Of course it was the man selling the costume jewelry, for that was what the people could afford to purchase."

—*Talmud*

A deeply religious person sought the advice of the Ba'al Shem Tov: "I have worked many years in the fields of the Lord, but I am no better than when I began my efforts. I remain common and unlearned."

The Ba'al Shem Tov answered: "For any of us to come to the

understanding that we are common and unlearned is the
accomplishment of a lifetime."

—*Ba'al Shem Tov*

None of us are poor but those of us who are without knowledge.

—*Talmud*

A follower approached Rabbi Isaac Meyer of Ger.

"Rebbe, no matter how hard I try, I inevitably forget what I have
just learned."

"And do you forget," asked the rebbe, "how to slip the spoon into
your mouth when you eat?"

"Of course not," said the disciple, "it would be impossible for me
to survive without eating."

"And you will not survive without learning," said the rebbe. "If
you remember this, you will not forget what you learn."

—*Rabbi Isaac Meyer of Ger, the Gerer Rebbe*

The school is the most original institution created by post-biblical
Judaism.

—*Louis Ginzberg*

One who will not support a scholar will not see a blessing.

—*Eleazar ben Pedat, Talmud*

What we do is more important than what we study.

—*Judah ha-Nasi, Talmud*

Above all we take pride in the education of our children.

—*Josephus*

We must try to teach even those who are not intelligent.

—*Rashi*

An industrious student will study on his own, and if another pupil is
not paying attention, place him beside the one who is directed.

—*Talmud*

No one has yet fully realized the wealth of sympathy and kindness
and generosity hidden in the soul of the child. The effort of every true

educator should be to unlock that treasure—to stimulate the child's impulses and call forth the best and noblest tendencies.

—*Emma Goldman*

Rabbi Jose ben Halafta said, "There is nothing more fruitless than to learn and not to teach."

—*Midrash Rabbah*

Study directs you to correctness, correctness directs you to ardor, ardor directs you to chasteness, chasteness directs you to moderation, moderation directs you to righteousness, righteousness directs you to spirituality, spirituality directs you to humility, humility directs you to the avoidance of sin, the avoidance of sin directs you to saintliness, saintliness directs you to embracing the sacred spirit, the sacred spirit directs you to life forever.

—*Talmud*

The trouble with most men of learning is that their learning goes to their head.

—*Isaac Goldberg*

Man learns and learns and dies a fool.

—*Jacob Lazarus*

The children arrived after school. They folded their bodies onto the flour sacks.

. . . A boy found his courage and asked Jacob, "Why do you say, 'A child sees what I only understand'?"

Jacob paused a moment before answering, letting the silence draw the boy's face upward.

When Jacob spoke, his voice had a long-ago quality.

"Imagine a boy, sitting on a hill, looking out through his innocence on the beauty of the world.

"Slowly, the child begins to learn. He does this by collecting small stones of knowledge, placing one on top of the other.

"Over time, his learning becomes a wall, a wall he has built in front of himself.

"Now, when he looks out, he can see his learning, but he has lost his view.

"This makes the man, who was once the boy, both proud and sad.

"The man, looking at his predicament, decides to take down the wall. But to take down a wall also takes time, and when he accomplishes this task, he has become an old man.

"The old man rests on the hill and looks out through his experience on the beauty of the world.

"He understands what has happened to him. He understands what he sees. But he does not see, and will never see the world again, the way he saw it as a child on that first, clear morning."

"Yes . . . but," interjected a little girl unable to contain herself, "the old man can remember what he once saw!"

Jacob's head swiveled toward the child.

"You are right. Experience matures to memory. But memory is the gentlest of truths."

"Are you afraid of growing old, Jacob?" asked a child, giggling while she spoke.

"What grows never grows old," said Jacob.

—*Noah benShea*

Ask and learn.

—*Apocrypha, I Maccabees*

A school is not allowed to be turned into a synagogue.

—*Pappi, Talmud*

You are not allowed to go into a house of learning with weapons.

—*Talmud*

Explaining his success, an official answered:
"I kept my mind awake and my desire asleep."

—*Moses ibn Ezra*

Learn to unlearn.

—*Benjamin Disraeli*

CHAPTER 30

Wisdom, Genius, Fools,
Understanding, Logic, Will,
Reason, Experience,
Common Sense

Who is wise? He who learns from all men.
—*Ben Zoma, Pirke Avot*

Wisdom is cognizance of self.
—*Maimonides*

Without doubt, there can be no certainty.
—*Elias Levita*

A wise word is not a substitute for a piece of herring.
—*Shalom Aleichem*

A sage's question is half of his wisdom; an open manner to others is half of intelligence . . .

What sort of person is prepared to be king? Either a sage who has achieved power or a king who pursues wisdom.

I am not looking, said Aristotle, for wisdom with the anticipation of coming to its final borders or grasping it fully; instead I am searching for wisdom with the hope that I might not be a fool, and any intelligent person should find this motive enough.

Aristotle was asked, "Why are you wiser than your companions?" He answered, "Because I spend more on oil to study at night than they spend on wine."

People are only wise while they are searching for wisdom; when they feel they have achieved it completely, they are fools.

Kings may find themselves the judges on earth, but wise people are the judges of kings.

The worth of every person is marked against what they know.

The great wise man Diogenes, when asked to answer, "Who is more, the wise or the rich?" replied, "The wise." "But," contested those around him, "why then are there more people of wisdom at the gates of the rich than wealthy at the gates of the wise?" And Diogenes answered, "That is because the wise value the advantage of riches, but the rich do not value the advantage of wisdom."

. . . The finest quality in a person is that they should be an explorer, a person of questions . . . Wisdom that is not questioned is like a buried treasure from which nothing can be taken.

. . . It is the habit of fools, when they do wrong, to blame others; it is the habit of someone who is truly seeking knowledge to hold himself liable; but it is the habit of the sincere sage . . . to hold himself and others harmless.

Those who think they can act like sages, without achieving the wisdom, are like asses working at the millstone—they travel around and around all day but get nowhere.

. . . Be cautious of the fool who is pious, and of a sage who is a sinner.

. . . To any fool silence is always the best reply.

—*Solomon ibn Gabirol*

An expert is a person who avoids the small errors as he sweeps on to the grand fallacy.

—*Benjamin Stolberg*

The core of a person is his mind's understanding. Therefore we are where our thoughts are.

—*Nachman of Bratslav*

Humor is a gift given not by the mind but by the heart.

—*Ludwig Boerne*

Pessimism is a luxury that a Jew can never allow himself.

—*Golda Meir*

Anyone who understands his foolishness is already a little wiser.
—Yiddish folk saying

Only relatively civilized people have a sense of humor.
—Abraham Arden Brill

Wine helps open the heart to reason.
—Yiddish folk saying

Reason explains the darkness, but it is not a light.
—Noah benShea

Experience is more convincing than logic.
—Isaac Abravanel

There is more hope for a fool than for a man wise in his own eyes.
—Bible, Proverbs 29:20

If one person says, "You're a donkey," don't mind; if two say this, be worried; if three say so, get a saddle.
—Adapted from Midrash Rabbah

To make a mistake is not a dishonor.
—Aaron Al-Rabi

Not to answer is an answer.
—Yiddish folk saying

Every woman has her own mind.
—Talmud

Every production of genius must be a production of enthusiasm.
—Isaac D'Israeli

Every village has its idiot.
—Yiddish folk saying

A fool inevitably informs others that he is a fool.
—Yiddish folk saying

Rabbi Johanan said, "The Holy One, blessed be He, gives wisdom only to those who have wisdom."

—Talmud

You can teach a fool but you can't make him think.

—Yiddish folk saying

It takes a clever man to turn cynic, and a wise man not to.

—Fannie Hurst

When a fool holds his tongue, he, too, is thought clever.

—Bible, Proverbs 17:28

Beware of the fool who is pious.

—Solomon ibn Gabirol

A fool thinks everyone else is a fool.

—Midrash Rabbah

A fool says what he knows, a sage knows what he says.

—Yiddish folk saying

When a wise person has a conversation with a fool, two fools are talking.

—Yiddish folk saying

. . . We see more than we understand.

—Wisdom of Ben Sira

A fool who is ashamed of being a fool and hides it is wiser than the clever who constantly parade their wisdom.

—Yiddish folk saying

The most incomprehensible thing about the world is that it is comprehensible.

—Albert Einstein

Understanding is bread, which is filling; wit is spice, which makes the bread appetizing.

—Ludwig Boerne

Wise men think out their thoughts; fools proclaim them.
—*Heinrich Heine*

If you will it, it is no dream.
—*Theodor Herzl*

It is possible to be a sage in some things and a child in others, to be at once ferocious and retarded, shrewd and foolish, serene and irritable.
—*Walter Lippmann*

Doing well in business does not necessarily make you wise.
—*Hillel the Elder*

Fools follow rules, wise men precede them.
—*Israel Zangwill*

One fool is an expert on another.
—*Yiddish folk saying*

Man is only wise while he is seeking wisdom; when he thinks he's grabbed it, he's a fool.
—*Solomon ibn Gabirol*

He whose deeds exceed his wisdom, his wisdom endures; but he whose wisdom exceeds his deeds, his wisdom does not endure.
—*Rabbi Hanina ben Dosa, Pirke Avot*

Come and see: Everything has secret wisdom.
—*Rabbi Shim'on, Zohar*

Mind is the foundation of man.
—*Ba'al Shem Tov*

Everything changes but change.
—*Israel Zangwill*

. . . the highest mental achievement that is possible in a man [is] that of struggling against an inward passion for the sake of a cause to which he has devoted himself.
—*Sigmund Freud*

We feel in one world, we think and name in another. Between the two we can set up a system of references, but we cannot fill the gap.

—*Marcel Proust*

A fool is his own informer.

—*Yiddish folk saying*

"For example" is not proof.

—*Yiddish folk saying*

Woe unto them that are wise in their own eyes.

—*Bible, Isaiah 5:21*

It is only a fool who has never felt like one.

—*Noah benShea*

To be conscious that you are ignorant is a great step to knowledge.

—*Benjamin Disraeli*

The profound thinker always suspects that he is superficial.

—*Benjamin Disraeli*

The wise turn their vices into virtues; the fool, virtues into vices.

—*Orhot Tzaddikim*

Behind every argument is someone's ignorance.

—*Louis D. Brandeis*

There is no wisdom like frankness.

—*Benjamin Disraeli*

Consistency requires you to be as ignorant today as you were a year ago.

—*Bernard Berenson*

Great men are not always wise.

—*Bible, Job 32:9*

The more gifted we are, the more we owe to God.

—*Joseph L. Baron*

Get wisdom: and with all thy getting get understanding.

—*Bible, Proverbs 4:7*

The only interesting answers are those which destroy the questions.

—*Susan Sontag*

A quotation at the right moment is like bread in a famine.

—*Talmud*

The principal mark of genius is not perfection but originality, the opening of new frontiers.

—*Arthur Koestler*

One fool can pose a question that a thousand sages cannot answer.

—*Jacob Emden*

The fool wonders, the wise man asks.

—*Benjamin Disraeli*

He who feels it below his dignity to ask when he is in doubt is unwise.

—*Ben Azzai, Tosefta*

The Talmud says a measured amount of wine opens the mind of a person: Someone who never drinks usually does not have great wisdom.

—*The Koretser Rabbi*

The business of the philosopher is well done if he succeeds in raising genuine doubts.

—*Morris Raphael Cohen*

Who is wise? Those who hold on to their learning.

—*Sifrei*

If you understand the old lessons, you will understand the new.

—*Talmud*

Happy is the person who finds wisdom,
And the person who obtains understanding.
For this merchandise is better than silver,
And the gain is better than fine gold.

—*Bible, Proverbs 3:13–14*

When a wise soul dies, everyone is a member of his family, and should mourn for this person.

—*Talmud*

Common sense is enhanced by joy.

—*Nachman of Bratslav*

When you welcome wisdom to enter you,
And knowledge is something from which you draw pleasure,
Discretion will watch over you,
Discernment will guard you,
And you will be saved from the influence of evil people.

—*Bible, Proverbs 2:10–11*

It happened that a Roman lady put a question to Rabbi Jose ben Halafta:

"Is it true that all of God's praise consists in His 'giving wisdom to the wise'? Shouldn't He instead be giving wisdom to the fools?"

Rabbi Jose said to her, "Do you have any jewels?"

"Of course," answered the lady.

"And if someone came to you and wished to borrow them, would you lend your jewels to that person?"

"Well, that depends," she said, "on whether the person asking to borrow the jewels was responsible."

"In this way," said Rabbi Jose, "as you would not lend your jewels to someone who was not worthy, shall God give His wisdom to fools?"

—*Talmud*

Fortune has rarely condescended to be the companion of genius.
—*Isaac D'Israeli*

On the whole, those with a sharp wit are not wise. Nor are the wise necessarily clever of wit, they are innocent.
—*Jacob Klatzkin*

Common sense is not so common.
—*Edith Cohen Schwartz*

Doubts make people wise.
—*Samuel Uceda*

The wise are pleased when they come upon the truth, fools when they discover lies.
—*Solomon ibn Gabirol*

Nothing is so sure of itself as ignorance.
—*Ludwig Lewisohn*

Arrogance guards ignorance.
—*Noah benShea*

Surely this is . . . a wise and understanding people.
—*Bible, Deuteronomy 4:6*

Those who have understanding have everything.
—*Talmud*

To remember much is not necessarily to be wise.
—*Samuel David Luzzatto*

The emperor's daughter once said to Rabbi Joshua ben Hanania [who was homely]: "How is it that your God saw fit to put such glorious wisdom in so hideous a vessel!"
The rabbi replied, "Why does your father keep his wine in an earthen vessel?"
"How else should we have it kept?" she asked.

"Well," said the rabbi, "people of your position should keep their wine in containers of gold or silver."

On hearing this, the empress convinced her father to pour his wine from earthen to gold and silver containers. Soon, however, the wine turned sour.

The emperor had the rabbi brought to the palace and asked why he had given such poor advice.

Rabbi Joshua said, "I said what I did to teach your daughter that wisdom, like wine, is best kept in a plain vessel."

"But," contested the empress, "it is true that there are handsome scholars!"

"Yes," agreed the rabbi, "but they might have been greater scholars had they been ugly."

—*Talmud*

. . . Humanity is in the highest degree irrational, so that there is no prospect of influencing it by reasonable arguments.

—*Sigmund Freud*

Do not judge something proved because you have found it written in a book; as a liar will lie with spoken words, a liar will not hesitate to do similarly with written words.

There are many fools who accept a truth as proved only because it is written.

—*Maimonides*

To lament nothing is the beginning of all wisdom.

—*Ludwig Boerne*

We should take care not to make the intellect our god; it has, of course, powerful muscles, but no personality.

—*Albert Einstein*

If not for the light, there would be no shadow.

—*Yiddish folk saying*

If two people discover each other's blindness, it is already growing light.

—*Noah benShea*

A person's wisdom makes his face shine.

—*Bible, Ecclesiastes 8:1*

Better a combative sage than a friendly fool.

—*Joseph Zabara*

I have made an unending effort not to ridicule, not to bewail, not to scorn human actions, but to understand them.

—*Baruch Spinoza*

Give your heart to learning.

—*Bible, Proverbs 23:12*

CHAPTER 31

Information, Science, Progress, Imagination

[Scientists] are Peeping Toms at the keyhole of eternity.
—*Arthur Koestler*

Thought is a cosmos of freedom.
—*Yiddish folk saying*

Wonder, rather than doubt, is the root of knowledge.
—*Abraham Joshua Heschel*

As far as the laws of mathematics refer to reality, they are not certain, and as far as they are certain, they do not refer to reality.
—*Albert Einstein*

All the sciences are gates that the Creator has opened to rational beings.
—*Bahya ben Joseph ibn Pakuda*

The supreme task of the physicist is to arrive at those universal elementary laws from which the cosmos can be built up by pure deduction. There is no logical path to these laws; only intuition, resting on sympathetic understanding of experience, can reach them.
—*Albert Einstein*

There are children playing in the street who could solve some of my top problems in physics, because they have modes of sensory perception that I lost long ago.

—*J. Robert Oppenheimer*

What the world needs is a fusion of the sciences and the humanities. The humanities express the symbolic, poetic, and prophetic qualities of the human spirit. Without them we would not be conscious of our history; we would lose our aspirations and the graces of expression that move men's hearts. The sciences express the creative urge in man to construct a universe which is comprehensible in terms of the human intellect. Without them, mankind would find itself bewildered in a world of natural forces beyond comprehension, victims of ignorance, superstition and fear.

—*Isidor Isaac Rabi*

Science without religion is lame; religion without science is blind.

—*Albert Einstein*

. . . The essence of science: ask an impertinent question and you're on the way to the pertinent answer.

—*Jacob Bronowski*

We are free in our imagination, but restricted by reason.

—*Israel Salanter Lipkin*

Everything should be made as simple as possible, but not simpler.

—*Albert Einstein*

The pursuit of science in itself is never materialistic. It is a search for the principles of law and order in the universe, and as such an essentially religious endeavor.

—*Arthur Koestler*

Infinity converts that which is possible into the inevitable.

—*Norman Cousins*

A theory can be proved by experiment; but no path leads from experiment to the birth of a theory.

—*Albert Einstein*

Generally the theories we believe we call facts, and the facts we disbelieve we call theories.

—*Felix Cohen*

The essential . . . is not to find truth but to investigate and pursue it.

—*Max Nordau*

All things in the world follow thought.

—*Sifrei*

Reality always will remain unknowable.

—*Sigmund Freud*

The power of thinking has two servants: the power of memory and the power of imagination.

—*Zohar*

In Sadgora was a rebbe who told his Hasidim, "Something can be observed and learned from anything. And we may learn not only from the things that God has made. The creations of man can also serve as a teacher."

"Then tell us, rebbe," said one of the Hasids, smiling, "what does a train teach us?"

"A train can teach us," said the rebbe, "that if a person is sometimes even one second late, he can miss everything."

"And, rebbe," asked another Hasid, "what possibly can a telegram teach us?"

"From a telegram," said the rebbe, "we learn that in life every word is counted and we are charged for every word."

"And, rebbe," asked another Hasid, sure he had caught his teacher, "what in the slightest can a telephone teach us?"

"Ahh," came the answer. "From the telephone we learn that everything we say *here* is heard *there*," said the rebbe, pointing to the heavens.

—*Adapted from a story by Hasidic rabbi Abraham Jacob of Sadgora*

The sciences are pearls strung on a cord of faith.

—*Joshua Steinberg*

Reason and regret come too late.

—*Shalom Aleichem*

CHAPTER 32

Torah, Bible, Talmud

Every living soul is a letter of the Torah, and therefore all the souls taken together make up the Torah.

—*Nathan of Nemirov*

The study of Torah gives you an extra soul.

—*Zohar*

I owe my entire enlightenment to a very old and plain book . . . a book that welcomes us with the assuring intimacy and blessed loving . . . of an old grandmother. . . . This [book] is properly called the Holy Scripture. Those who have lost God will find Him again in this book, and those who have never known Him will [in this book] draw in the word of God's breath. The Jews . . . knew very well what they were doing when, during the utter destruction of the Second Temple, they let be the gold and silver elements used for the sacrifice, the elaborate candlesticks and lamps, even the astounding jewel-encrusted breastplate worn by the high priest, and saved only the Bible. This was the Temple's real treasure.

—*Heinrich Heine*

On the first day that a child begins to learn Hebrew, a drop of honey should be placed on the letter aleph, the first letter in the alphabet. Then the child should move the tip of his forefinger from

the letter to his lips so that the taste of the sweetness and the Holy
Tongue should be forever mingled.

—*From the tradition*

It happened that Rabbi Abba declared once in a speech that
everyone who studies Torah obtains wealth. Among those in
attendance was a young man named Jose who took the rabbi's words
to mean material riches. Therefore, he came to Rabbi Abba and said,
"I want to study so I may have this wealth."

Time passed, and now Rabbi Jose wanted to know when the riches
would come to him. Rabbi Abba was concerned that this excellent
student was driven by worldly considerations. Rabbi Abba said to his
student, "You continue to study, and if you must have this worldly
wealth, I will do what I can to get this for you."

Then a youth from a wealthy family entered the academy and asked
to see Rabbi Abba. The youth said, "I have inherited significant
riches. I also appreciate the value in the study of Torah and want to
give a container of pure gold to an excellent student on the condition
I shall have a share in the honor of his Torah study." Rabbi Abba, on
hearing this, called forth Rabbi Jose and said to him, "Here is the first
part of your worldly wealth."

Shortly after this, Rabbi Jose began to perceive the real spiritual
wealth of the Torah, and he came crying to Rabbi Abba.

"Why are you weeping?" asked his teacher. Rabbi Jose answered,
"Because I have sold the truth for false wealth."

Rabbi Abba's heart smiled. He called the rich student back and said
to him, "My student is sorry for having taken your gold. Take back
the vessel and give the money among the poor and orphans, and you
will be given credit as if you had studied as much Torah as the rest of
us."

Rabbi Jose was greatly joyed to see the "pure gold" [Paz] given
away in this manner, and Rabbi Jose was henceforth called "Ben
Pazi," meaning the "Son of Pure Gold."

—*Zohar*

Open my heart to your Torah.

—*Amidah, Hebrew prayer*

[The purpose of what we are commanded in the Torah is] to advance compassion, loving-kindness, and peace in the world.

—*Maimonides*

The essence of the Torah is intellectual creativity.

—*Joseph B. Soloveitchik*

The more the study of Torah, the more life.

—*Hillel the Elder, Pirke Avot*

If you have studied much of the Torah, claim not merit for yourself, for to this end were you created.

—*Johanan ben Zakkai, Pirke Avot*

Simchat Torah means "the Torah's joy," and implies that it is not sufficient for a Jew to discover joy in the Torah, but the Torah should also discover joy in the Jew.

—*Joseph B. Soloveitchik*

The Talmud preserved and promoted the religious and moral life of Judaism; it held out a banner to the communities scattered in all corners of the planet, and protected them from schism and sectarian divisions; it acquainted later generations with the history of their nation; finally it produced a deep intellectual life which kept the enslaved free and not subject to stagnation and lit for them the torch of science.

—*Heinrich Graetz*

The absolute premise of Talmud study is that the Torah must be fully understood.

. . . The search for truth is its own justification.

—*Adin Steinsaltz*

It was the Holy Book, and the study of it, which kept the scattered people together.

—*Sigmund Freud*

For everyone who engages Torah days and nights occupies two worlds: the higher world and the lower world.

—*Rabbi El'azar, Zohar*

The Talmudic dialectic can be compared to an inquiry in pure science, particularly in the sphere most closely resembling Talmudic study—that of mathematics.

—*Adin Steinsaltz*

The very incoherence of the Talmud, its confusion of voices, is an index of free thinking.

—*Israel Zangwill*

When you walk, it [the Torah] shall lead you; when you sleep, it will watch over you, and when you wake, it will talk with you.

—*Bible, Proverbs 6:22*

In the whole realm of the Divine Law, not one single truth is revealed to us that is only of theoretical interest.

—*Samson Raphael Hirsch*

When an evil side approaches to seduce a human being, he should pull it toward Torah and it will leave him.

—*Rabbi El'azar, Zohar*

When a Jew finds himself being assaulted, he should not keep the Torah in front of him as a shield; rather, he should keep himself as a shield in front of the Torah.

—*Franz Rosenzweig*

If an angel were to show me all the mysteries of the Torah, it would give me little pleasure, because study is more important than knowledge. Only what we achieve through effort is dear to us.

—*Rabbi Elijah ben Solomon, the Vilna Gaon*

Talmudic scholars would gather together at fixed times of the year, or might meet by chance. Their conversations, their teachings and their conduct were committed to memory [and sometimes recorded in writing in brief notes]. This material makes up the Talmud. An eminent scholar had to be completely proficient in the Written Torah and equally knowledgeable about the entire Mishnah. Only a scholar who had mastered these two areas was considered sufficiently advanced to enter the deeper area of Torah study—the Talmud.

—Adin Steinsaltz

The Song of Songs is Wisdom, the Book of Ecclesiastes is Understanding, and the Book of Proverbs is Knowledge.

—Zohar

The Torah is described in the words: "Her paths are peace" [Proverbs 3:17].

—Midrash Rabbah

Torah is excellent when it is joined to a worldly occupation.

—Ishmael ben Elisha, Talmud

Rabbi Abbahu said, "For forty days Moses was taught the details of the Torah and forgot them with as much speed as he learned them. On the fortieth day the Torah was given to Moses by God and Moses no longer had any trouble remembering it.

"In this same way, students who put in effort need not worry because they forget what they have just learned. At the right time knowledge will be reliably placed in their memory."

—Talmud

Every time a student of Torah discovers something original a new heaven is created.

—Zohar

A man from Persia came to the Rav and said, "Will you teach me the Torah?"

He agreed and showed him the letter aleph [the silent letter A].

The Persian said, "How will you prove to me that this is really the letter aleph?"

Next the Persian went to Samuel and tried the same argument with him.

Samuel took hold of the man's ear and pulled. The Persian shouted, "Owww, my ear, my ear!"

"And how will you prove to me that this is your ear?"

"Everyone knows that this is my ear."

"In the same way everyone knows that this is an aleph," was the teacher's reply.

—*Midrash Rabbah*

The letters of the Torah Scroll must not be gilded.

—*Talmud*

The whole Torah was inscribed on the altar in seventy languages.

—*Talmud*

Torah is peace.

—*Zohar*

All souls stood at Sinai, each accepting their share in Torah.

—*Moses Alshek*

The road to Heaven has signposts based upon insights in the Torah. Those who study the Torah will be able to find their way to Heaven.

—*Zohar*

The Torah is meant to be a commandment lasting forever, without change, deduction, or addition.

—*Maimonides*

Do not use the Torah as a crown to make yourself appear more important.

—*Hillel the Elder, Pirke Avot*

Those who neglect the study of Torah have neglected God, for Torah is one of the supreme manifestations of God.

—*Zohar*

The Torah is a tree of life for those who will cling to it.

—*Ben Zoma, Pirke Avot*

The laws of the Torah were given so human beings should live by them, not that they should die by them.

—*Talmud*

A man came to the great teacher Shammai and asked him, "Can you teach me everything there is to know about Judaism while I stand on one foot?"

Shammai threw the man out.

Next the man went to the great teacher Hillel and asked him: "Can you teach me everything there is to know about Judaism while I stand on one foot?"

And Hillel answered, "Do not do to others what you would not do to yourself. All the rest is commentary. Go and study."

—*Talmud*

A person cannot understand Torah until he has stumbled in it.

—*Talmud*

No bread, no Torah; no Torah, no bread.

—*Mishneh Torah*

The Fathers said:

"Build a fence around the Torah" [Pirke Avot 1:1], because a vineyard with a fence is safer than one without a fence.

But a person should guard against building the fence too high, for then it may fall in and crush the plants it is supposed to guard.

—*Rabbi Nathan, Pirke Avot*

The whole Torah exists only for the sake of peace.

—*Joseph ben Hiyya, Talmud*

Do what the Torah says for the sake of the doing, speak of the Law to others singularly for the sake of it.

Do not say to yourself, "I will learn Torah so that I may be called wise, or be appointed to sit in a college, or achieve long days in the world to come."

—*Sifrei*

The general aim of the Torah is twofold: the well-being of the soul and the well-being of the body.

—*Maimonides*

Don't divest lines from the Bible from their literal meaning.

—*Talmud*

If Torah is here, wisdom is here.

—*Yiddish folk saying*

The laws of the Torah are not a burden, but a way of insuring mercy, kindness, and peace in the world.

—*Maimonides*

The Gerer Rebbe brought one of the younger students close and asked him, "Have you learned any Torah?"

"Just a little," answered the boy.

The rebbe nodded warmly. "That is all any of us have ever learned."

—*Rabbi Isaac Meyer of Ger, the Gerer Rebbe*

Ben Azzai said, "A man is obligated to teach his daughter Torah."

—*Mishneh Torah*

A person who takes a friend's child and teaches him Torah is thought of in the Scriptures as having given birth to this child.

—*Talmud*

When God gave the Torah, no bird put forth their song, no bird took wing, no ox gave bawl, no angel moved a feather. The angels did not say, "Holy, Holy," the sea did not release its roar, and no creature said a word.

The entire planet stood absent of sound in an unbreathing quiet, and the Voice went out and exclaimed, "I am the Lord your God."

—*Midrash Rabbah*

As King Solomon said, "He who loves silver will never get enough of it" [Ecclesiastes 5:9]. Rashi commented, "He who loves Torah will never get his fill of it."

—*Rashi*

The Torah is the map of the world.

—*Zadok HaCohen Rabinowitz*

Rashi, commenting on another's Talmud interpretation, said, "It is very deep, but it is not defensible."

—*Rashi*

The priestly caste did not support the Ark; the Ark supported those who carried it.

—*Benectiate ben Natronai tia-Nakdan*

The true Torah . . . has as its first purpose to build good mutual relations among people by removing injustice and creating the noblest of feelings.

—*Maimonides*

The early Hebrews had created the Bible out of their lives; their descendants created their lives out of the Bible.

—*Abram Leon Sachar*

The stories in the Bible are only the external cover of the Torah, and what a sadness it is to those who think this is the actual Torah.

—*Zohar*

Rabbi Johanan said, "The words of the Torah live only with those who regard themselves as nothing."

—*Talmud*

Every one of the 613 commandments [mitzvoth in the Torah] can be found in the Ten Commandments.

—*Rashi*

When a passenger on the deck of a ship falls into the sea, the captain throws the person a line to cling to, shouting, "Hold on to it tightly and do not let go or you will die."

In this same way, in the middle of life's troubled seas on our earthly voyage, we should hold tightly to principles of Torah and in this way remain attached to God. By doing this we will save our life.

—*Tanhuma Buber*

Study of Torah leads to exactness, exactness to ardor, ardor to morality, morality to restraint, restraint to purity, purity to holiness, holiness to mildness, mildness to fear of sin, fear of sin to saintliness, saintliness to the holy spirit, and the holy spirit to life eternal.

—*Phineas ben Yair, Talmud*

The Torah begins with kindness and ends with kindness.

—*Talmud*

CHAPTER 33

Language, Books, Reading, Talking, Silence

Set a guard, O Lord, to my mouth.

—*Bible, Psalms 141:3*

I am not a man of words.

—*Bible, Exodus 4:10*

The world would be much happier if men were as fully able to keep silent as they are able to speak.

—*Baruch Spinoza*

To those who curse me, let my soul be silent.

—*Hebrew Prayer, Amidah*

Quiet streams wear away the shores.

—*Yiddish folk saying*

Words . . . conceal one's thought as much as they reveal it; and the uttered words of philosophers, at their best and fullest, are nothing but the floating buoys which signal the presence of submerged unuttered thoughts.

—*Harry Austryn Wolfson*

It is unwise to wish everything explained.

—*Benjamin Disraeli*

Often what is easy to say is difficult to bear.
                                    —*Yiddish folk saying*

Fewer words. Fewer mistakes.
                                    —*Solomon ibn Gabirol*

Say little and do much.
                                    —*Rabbai Shammai, Pirke Avot*

Speech is a gift God has given only to man, and must not be used
for that which is degrading.
                                    —*Maimonides*

A man's tongue is often his worst foe.
                                    —*Yiddish folk saying*

Satire is moral outrage transformed into comic art.
                                    —*Philip Roth*

One voice can enter ten ears, but ten voices can't enter one ear.
                                    —*Pesikta Rabbati*

For an extended period the Tzartkover Rebbe gave no sermons or
talks.
    His followers, confused, finally pleaded with him to offer an
explanation.
    "There are seventy ways to teach Torah," said the rebbe. "And one
of the paths is through silence."
                                    —*The Tzartkover Rebbe*

All translation is commentary.
                                    —*Leo Baeck*

Those who never quote in return are seldom quoted.
                                    —*Isaac D'Israeli*

. . . In those days, people had convictions; we, who hold ourselves
as modern, have opinions.
                                    —*Heinrich Heine*

To have more than the sense of a donkey, you must do more than carry books.

—*Bahya ben Joseph ibn Pakuda*

If you should happen to spill even a single drop of ink at the same moment on your book and on your jacket, clean the book first.

—*Sefer Hasidim*

When you reread a classic you do not see more in the book than you did before; you see more in you than there was before.

—*Clifton Fadiman*

If you keep on talking, you will end up saying what you didn't intend to say.

—*Yiddish folk saying*

If everyone involved in good work, or desiring to teach the correct and proper way, were to be quiet and wait until his purpose had been completely realized, not a single word would be spoken by anyone after the Prophets who God chose as His messengers and gave strength with His Divine aid.

—*Bahya ben Joseph ibn Pakuda*

If a horse with four legs can sometimes stumble, how much more a man with only one tongue.

—*Shalom Aleichem*

It's not what you say, it's how you say it—personality always wins the day.

—*Arthur Miller*

Only suppressed language is dangerous.

—*Ludwig Boerne*

If silence is wise for the wise, how much better for the fools.

—*Talmud*

Teach your tongue to say, "I do not know," otherwise you will invent something and be trapped.

—*Talmud*

It is beneath us to repress books or stifle teachers.

—*Judah Low*

Don't let the simple parable appear insignificant. Through the simple parable one can achieve insight on the most complex Law.

—*Midrash Rabbah*

When there is a difficult situation facing me—when I discover my path narrowing, and can discover no alternative for sharing an honest but unattractive truth that will please one person of wisdom and displease ten thousand fools—I choose to speak to the one, and ignore altogether the negation of the mass.

—*Maimonides*

Just as I have been rewarded for what I have explained, I have also been rewarded for what I have not explained.

—*Nahum of Gimzo, Talmud*

Not everything that is thought should be spoken, not everything that is spoken should be written, and not everything that is written should be printed.

—*Israel Salanter Lipkin*

Nothing can be said so correctly that it cannot be twisted into being wrong.

—*Baruch Spinoza*

The question is whether a man who speaks many languages has anything to say.

—*Noah benShea*

Languages are spiritual organisms, vital works of art, each of them having its measure of creative power, splendor, depth, logic to explore and to construct the world of nature in life.

—*Nahman Syrkin*

Men can rule anything easier than their tongues.
— *Baruch Spinoza*

Do what you say, but don't talk about what you do.
— *Rabbi Elijah de Veali*

The wise knows what he says, the fool says what he knows.
— *Judah Leib Lazerov*

I like people who refuse to speak until they are ready to speak.
— *Lillian Hellman*

The library is not a shrine for the worship of books. It is not a temple where literary incense must be burned or where one's devotion to the bound book is expressed in ritual. A library, to modify the famous metaphor of Socrates, should be the delivery room for the birth of ideas—a place where history comes to life.
— *Norman Cousins*

Do not the most moving moments of our lives find us all without words?
— *Marcel Marceau*

The less you talk, the more you're listened to.
— *Abigail Van Buren*

Dreams, Superstition

I [God] do speak . . . in a dream.

—*Bible, Numbers 12:6*

All the things one has forgotten scream for help in dreams.

—*Elias Canetti*

A follower of the Parsischarer Rebbe came to the rebbe and told him about a vivid dream.

In the dream, the man's father appeared and told the follower that he should become a great tzaddik.

Throughout the dream recollection the rebbe said nothing. When the man had finished, he asked the rebbe, "So what do you think I should do?"

The rebbe answered, "The next time your father comes to you in a dream and tells you to become a blessed tzaddik, ask your father to appear in the dream of many others and tell them they should wake and become your disciples."

—*Simcha Bunam (the Tzaddik of Parsischa)*

What is in a good dream or a bad dream is never altogether brought into being. . . .

It is impossible to harvest wheat without straw, and there cannot be dreams that do not contain some senselessness.

. . . A person discovers in his dreams what is implied by his own mind.

—Talmud

I was not looking for my dreams to interpret my life, but rather for my life to interpret my dreams.

—Susan Sontag

A dream that is not interpreted is like a letter that is left unread.

—Talmud

. . . Superstition's most significant victims are those people . . . believing the ghosts of fantasy, dreams, and . . . absurdities to be in themselves voices of Heaven. Do they think that God has turned away from the wise and penned His orders . . . in the intestines of animals . . . and birds?

This lack of reason can only be understood as stark terror's capacity to manipulate people.

Superstition is at its source, and in its preservation, parented by fear.

—Baruch Spinoza

Every thing man believes in was once a dream.

—Theodor Herzl

CHAPTER 35

Nature, Environment

What has been is that which will be,
What has been done is that which will be done,
There is nothing new under the sun.
—*Bible, Ecclesiastes 1:9*

Everything in nature is a cause from which there flows some effect.
—*Baruch Spinoza*

Everyone should be taught not to be wasteful.
—*Talmud*

Only we who have erected the objectivity of a world of our own from what nature gives us, who have built it into the environment of nature so that we are protected from her, can look upon nature as something "objective." Without a world between man and nature, there is eternal movement but no objectivity.
—*Hannah Arendt*

Nature uses only the longest threads to weave her patterns, so each small piece of her fabric reveals the organization of the entire tapestry.
—*Richard Feynman*

Man masters nature not by force but by understanding.
—*Jacob Bronowski*

Only a fool grows without rain.

—*Yiddish folk saying*

Even the things that we may think are not necessary on the planet, like fleas, gnats, and flies, even these are included in what has been created for this world.

God conducts His plan through all his creations, including using a snake, including using a gnat, including using a frog.

—*Midrash Rabbah*

The Law of Moses does not include philosophical theories, or investigations of logic, or proofs involving high inquiries. For the success of man is above Reason and beyond Nature.

—*Isaac Abravanel*

There is no difference . . . between the pain a human experiences and the pain of anything else that is alive, as the love and care of a mother for her children is not created by reasoning.

—*Maimonides*

Man is a complex being: he makes deserts bloom—and lakes die.

—*Gil Stern*

To expect us to feel "humble" in the presence of astronomical dimensions merely because they are big, is a kind of cosmic snobbery. . . . What is significant is mind.

—*Viscount Herbert Samuel*

Two forces rule the universe: light and gravity.

—*Simone Weil*

The words "There is yet much work to be done" mean that the process of the world's creation is only in its infancy.

—*Pesikta Rabbati*

All rivers run to the sea, But the sea is never full.

—*Bible, Ecclesiastes 1:7*

"Do not take the mother together with her young"—the Bible does not allow something destructive that causes the extinction of any species even if it has allowed for the ritual slaughtering of that species. And anyone who kills a mother and her children on the same day, or takes them when they are capable of flying, is thought of as if they had destroyed the species.

—Nachmanides on Deuteronomy 22:6

The person who chops down a tree that can bear fruit is like a person who commits murder.

—Nachman of Bratslav

It came to pass that Rav traveled to a particular community and had the people of that community both fast and pray in the hope of bringing rain. But there was no rain.

Then the person who read in the synagogue went to the Holy Ark and repeated words from the book of prayers.

"He causes the wind to blow," and suddenly the wind stirred.

"He makes the rain to come down," and rain poured from the heavens.

Rav turned to the Reader, "What have you done by merit to cause your prayers to be so speedily answered?"

The Reader replied, "I am a teacher for the younger children, some of whose parents are rich and some poor. I request no money from those who cannot afford to offer any. In addition, I have a pond filled with fish, and if a youth cannot bring himself to study, I take him fishing and soon he sees the way of learning."

—Talmud

The morning stars sang together.

—Bible, Job 38:7

. . . He who has no need to make a living from [hunting], that is, his hunting has nothing to do with his work, then [his hunting] is cruelty.

—Ezekiel Landau

There is no vacuum in nature.

—Baruch Spinoza

One incredible chain of love, of giving and receiving, unites all creation; nothing exists singularly by or for itself, but everything is born into an ongoing reciprocal state of action.

—*Samson Raphael Hirsch*

When you are laying siege to a city for a long time, in the process of making war against the city, you are not allowed to take an axe to the surrounding trees and make war on them. You are allowed to eat the fruit of the trees but you are not allowed to cut down the trees. Are the trees capable of fleeing from you when you lay siege?

—*Bible, Deuteronomy 20:19*

Every river has its own course.

—*Joseph ben Hiyya, Talmud*

Wisdom's work is to investigate everything that nature has to show.

—*Philo*

Thought is invisible nature; nature, visible thought.

—*Heinrich Heine*

. . . Those who chop down fruit trees, those who destroy things in a home, rip clothes, damage a building, block a water spring, or waste sustenance in a destructive manner break the commandment "You shall not destroy."

—*Maimonides*

Truth and nature can never be obsolete.

—*Isaac D'Israeli*

It is forbidden to reside in a community that does not have a green garden.

—*Jerusalem Talmud*

The splendor of the world is always in accordance with the splendor of the mind that contemplates it.

—*Heinrich Heine*

For the Lord thy God bringeth you into a good land, a land of brooks of water, of fountains and depths that spring out of valleys and hills; a land of wheat, and barley, and vines, and fig trees, and pomegranates; a land of olive oil, and honey;

a land wherein you shalt eat bread without scarceness, you shalt not lack any thing in it; a land whose stones are iron, and out of whose hills you mayest dig brass.

When you have eaten and are full, then you shalt bless the Lord your God for the good land which he has given you.

—Bible, Deuteronomy 8:7–10

After God had created the first man, He led him on a path through the trees in the Garden of Eden.

God then said to the man, "Observe what I have done, see how beautiful and worthy of appreciation they are. Everything I have done has been for your sake. Take this to heart and do not do evil or harm My creation; because if you hurt it, there will be no one to fix it after you."

—Midrash Rabbah

PART TEN

*Nobody Tries to
Steal Your Troubles,
and No One Can Take
Your Good Deeds*

AS JEWS MOVED INTO MAINSTREAM SOCIETY IN THE 19TH AND 20TH CEN-
turies many were no longer ritually observant. While orthodox custom
is to offer prayers three times daily, by the late 20th century less than
10 percent of the American Jewish community attended synagogue services once a week. Nevertheless, members of the broad Jewish community still continue to live what they consider ethically centered Jewish
lives. And Jews who have long ceased attending *shachrit,* morning prayer
services, still can be heard weighing the quality of another Jew, or non-
Jew, with the fundamental question: "Is he a mensch?"

In Yiddish, *mensch* means "person." But to be a mensch also means to
be a person of integrity. Decidedly different from the German *Über-
mensch* (a superman), a mensch is not someone who holds himself above
others but one who fulfills ethical obligations. The test of whether one's
integrity is intact is in how one answers the question "Am I conducting
myself like a mensch?" The test of whether the broader society has
retained its integrity is in whether it allows others to live like *menschen.*

To the Jew the world is not beyond repair. Furthermore, to the Jew
one's own actions must not, in the main, wait for the world to right
itself. Indeed, in the Jewish mind, conducting oneself like a mensch is a
significant first act in Tikkun Olam, healing the world.

CHAPTER 36

Ethics, Virtue, Honor, Loyalty, Integrity, Evil

Nobody tries to steal your troubles, and no one can take your good deeds.

—Yiddish folk saying

It is integrity that involves man with immortality and places upon him the privilege of direct communication with God.

—Bahya ben Asher

Be the master of your will, and the slave of your conscience.

—Hasidic folk saying

If you're going to do something wrong, at least enjoy it.

—Yiddish folk saying

What gives you pleasure today will give you tears tomorrow.

—Rabbi Elijah ben Solomon, the Vilna Gaon

It's better to be embarrassed than ashamed.

—Yiddish folk saying

Who wins through evil loses.

—Solomon ibn Gabirol

Say little and do much.

> —*Rabbi Shammai, Pirke Avot*

If your life has been blessed, the way to say *thank you* is by conducting yourself responsibly.

> —*Noah benShea*

Moral action is the meeting-place between the human and the divine.

> —*Leon Roth*

Men makes mistakes not because they think they know when they do not know, but because they think others do not know.

> —*Shalom Aleichem*

It is not what a person does, but how he does it, which is either profane or sacred.

> —*Heymann Steinthal*

It is easier to abandon evil traits today than tomorrow.

> —*Hasidic folk saying*

The greater the man the greater his potential for evil, too.

> —*Talmud*

The urge to evil enters as a guest and soon becomes the host.

> —*Midrash Rabbah*

Feel no sadness because of evil thoughts: it only strengthens them.

> —*Nachman of Bratslav*

When we die and appear to answer for our lives in heaven, God will not ask "Did you believe in Me?" but "How have you dealt with those around you?"

> —*Talmud*

Life is unfair.

> —*Milton Friedman*

Good deeds are better than wise sayings.

—*Pirke Avot*

Even virtue in excess becomes negative.

—*Joseph Ezobi*

Small sins are great when great people commit them.

—*Abraham ibn Ezra*

A person of virtue among the wicked is better than a person of virtue among the righteous; a person who sins among the righteous is worse than a person who sins among the wicked.

—*Sefer Hasidim*

When we repeat our sins we feel permitted.

—*Talmud*

A worm can enter a fruit only after it has begun to rot.

—*Solomon Ansky*

Never waste good agony.

—*Viscount Herbert Samuel*

It is easier to fight for principles than to live up to them.

—*Alfred Adler*

Life is too short to be small.

—*Benjamin Disraeli*

If you can't do as you wish, do as you can.

—*Yiddish folk saying*

When you always drink vinegar you don't know anything sweeter exists.

—*Yiddish folk saying*

Honor is measured by those who give it, not by those who receive it.

—*Yiddish folk saying*

The finest virtue in man is that of which he is unaware.

—*Moses ibn Ezra*

In virtue is the art of one's entire life.

—*Philo*

If it is done at the right time, it is no sin.

—*Yiddish folk saying*

Life is an effort that deserves a better cause.

—*Karl Kraus*

Some men are born mediocre, some men achieve mediocrity, and some men have mediocrity thrust upon them.

—*Joseph Heller*

Evil does not prevail until it is given power.

—*Rabbi El'azar, Zohar*

A good intention is added as a good deed.

—*Zohar*

There is no worldly pleasure that does not have some sin following it.

—*Moses Luzzatto*

He who repays good for evil will live many years.

—*Nachman of Bratslav*

One good deed has many claimants.

—*Yiddish folk saying*

To be sure, the dog is loyal. But why, on that account, should we take him as an example? He is loyal to men, not to other dogs.

—*Karl Kraus*

So long as a man's power is bound to the goal, the work, the calling, it is, in itself, neither good nor evil, only a suitable or unsuitable instrument. But as soon as this bond with the goal is broken off or loosened, and the man ceases to think of power as the capacity to do something, but thinks of it as a possession, then his power, being cut off and self-satisfied, is evil and corrupts the history of the world.

—*Martin Buber*

A precedent embalms a principle.

—*Benjamin Disraeli*

Commit a sin twice and it will not seem like a crime.

—*Rabbinical saying*

Advice is what we ask for when we already know the answer but wish we didn't.

—*Erica Jong*

It is much easier to be critical than to be correct.

—*Benjamin Disraeli*

. . . Take the gold from the dust, and the roses from the middle of the thorns.

—*Immanuel of Rome*

If err we must, let us err on the side of tolerance.

—*Felix Frankfurter*

I cannot and will not cut my conscience to fit this year's fashions.

—*Lillian Hellman*

There are people who dress on the inside also as fashion dictates.

—*Berthold Auerbach*

There is perhaps no phenomenon which contains so much destructive feelings as moral indignation, which permits envy or hate to be acted out under the guise of virtue.

—*Erich Fromm*

Unless the reformer can invent something which substitutes attractive virtues for attractive vices, he will fail.

—*Walter Lippmann*

We who are liberal and progressive know that the poor are our equals in every sense except that of being equal to us.

—*Lionel Trilling*

How wonderful it is that nobody need wait a single moment before starting to improve the world.

—*Anne Frank*

Racism is . . . the maximum of hatred for a minimum of reason.

—*Abraham Joshua Heschel*

The difference is no less real because it is of degree.

—*Benjamin N. Cardozo*

Honor wears different coats to different eyes.

—*Barbara Tuchman*

Life engenders life. Energy creates energy. It is by spending oneself that one becomes rich.

—*Sarah Bernhardt*

Nurture gentleness.

—*Talmud*

When the poor man, the rich man, and the evil man stand in Judgment, the poor man will be asked, "Why have you not learned and obeyed the Torah?"

If he says, "I was forced to earn a living," he is asked, "Were you poorer than Hillel, who studied in the middle of the deepest poverty?"

If the rich man answers the same question by saying, "I was too caught up in business affairs," he is told, "Were you richer than Rabbi Eliezer ben Harson, who owned a thousand villages but left the management to others so he could study day and night?"

If the evil man in reply to the question says, "My passions were too strong for me," they say to him, "Were they stronger in you than in a lonely young boy named Joseph, the son of Jacob? If one human being can conquer the excuses of his life and achieve goodness, others can do so, for Joseph was a human like the rest of us."

—Talmud

There is no absolute good without some evil in its midst.

—Tanhuma

The essence of goodness is good intent.

—Talmud

Man is coated with an extremely thin layer of culture. Scratch in the slightest—and the beast will be made visible.

—Wilhelm Stekel

I have come to understand that although people have a sincere urge to achieve evil, they are less purposeful of the path toward that which is high and good.

People are always late in their attempt toward good but linger on the ways of the insignificant and pleasurable. If a lustful picture appears before them and motions to them, they lie so they can head in that direction.

People create reasons to make what is slanted appear straight, what is shaky appear solid, what is unanchored appear pulled together.

Although the light of truth beckons people, they create reason after reason to explain why they refuse to turn toward it. They construct arguments against the truth, say its paths are lost and confusing, challenge the premises to make the truth look contradictory and thus offer themselves an excuse to stay another course.

In this way, every person's foe is in his own chest.

—Bahya ben Joseph ibn Pakuda

Exaggerated respect for athletics, an excess of coarse impressions brought about by the technical discoveries of recent years, the increased severity of the struggle for existence due to the economic crisis, the brutalization of political life: all these factors are hostile to the ripening of the character and desire for real culture, and stamp our age as barbarous, materialistic, and superficial.

—Albert Einstein

He may be called a man who restrains his desire to do evil.

—*Zohar*

A person who walks his path in life without regard to ethical standards is like a blind man who does not know his journey is along the bank of a river.

The person can at any moment succumb to the dangers of a wrong step and the odds are more certainly toward his being hurt than escaping harm.

—*Moses Luzzatto*

Living life in this world is like drinking salt water—while quenching our thirst we thirst for more.

—*Rabbi Elijah ben Solomon, the Vilna Gaon*

The Riziner Rebbe lived an openly luxurious life. When a follower asked the rebbe how he came to live like this, the rebbe answered:

"Money is collected by three different categories. The first is contributed by the truly righteous and that covers my barest needs. The second comes from the heads of different families that are sort of religious. These funds I give to charity for those who have less. And lastly, the third fund is established by the ones who sin over and over again. This fund is used for extravagant expenditures. But if the number of people who sin over and over again is the largest group, and this fund is the largest, am I to blame?"

—*Adapted from a story about the Riziner Rebbe*

Now, more than any time previous in human history, we must arm ourselves with an ethical code so that each of us will be aware that he is protecting the moral merchandise absent of which life is not worth living.

—*Sholem Asch*

Deed, not Creed.

—*Felix Adler*

We are taught by our rabbis that the children of Noah were handed seven commandments:

To set up a legal system, and to abstain from blasphemy, idolatry, sexual immorality, bloodshed, theft, and eating the flesh from a living animal.

—*Talmud*

There is nothing which at first sight seems more puzzling than the wickedness of good people.

—*Israel Zangwill*

When what is good is missing is the only time we see it.

—*Moses Gentili*

A poor man in the community came to the Kobriner Rebbe complaining that the urge to do evil constantly threw him off course in his life. "What am I to do?" asked the poor soul.

"Excuse me," said the rebbe, "but do you know how to ride a horse?"

"Absolutely," said the man, not understanding the connection to his problem.

"And how do you respond when you happen to fall off your horse?" asked the rebbe.

"Well, I get back on. What else is a man to do?"

"So," said the Rebbe. "Think of the Evil Force as your horse. When you fall off, get back on. As you have said, 'What else is a man to do?' Soon you will be the horse's master."

—*The Kobriner Rebbe*

In morals, Jew and non-Jew stand under the same law.

—*Sifrei*

The great happiness in life is not to donate but to serve.

—*Louis D. Brandeis*

Virtue, not blessedness, is the reward of virtue.

—*Baruch Spinoza*

I feel that the greatest reward for doing is the opportunity to do more.

—*Jonas Salk*

. . . the reward for a good deed is another good deed.

—*Ben Azzai, Pirke Avot*

Better to be good than to be pious.

—*Yiddish folk saying*

If a person tries to show you how to keep evil thoughts from upsetting your prayers and learning, do not take this person seriously. For this is our work in the world to the moment we die: to struggle again and again with what is of little value, and again and again to raise up what is of no importance and find its place in the nature of the Divine Name.

—*Ba'al Shem Tov*

CHAPTER 37

Law, Justice, Truth, Honor, Forgiveness, Mercy, Patience, Consideration, Vengeance, Covetousness, Hypocrisy

. . . One should accept the truth from whatever source it proceeds.
—*Maimonides*

Truth is what stands the test of experience.
—*Albert Einstein*

The truth is often a terrible weapon of aggression. It is possible to lie, and even to murder with the truth.
—*Alfred Adler*

Better to suffer an injustice than to commit one.
—*Yiddish folk saying*

A man who makes arrows is often slain by one of them.
—*Talmud*

If someone comes to murder you, move first to kill him.
—*Talmud*

When a crook kisses you, count your teeth.
—*Yiddish folk saying*

The meek do prematurely inherit the earth—six or more feet of it.
—*Abraham Myerson*

The man who covets is guilty of robbery in thought.

—*Nachman of Bratslav*

The truth is the safest lie.

—*Yiddish folk saying*

The Lord will judge His people.

—*Bible, Deuteronomy 32:36*

A judge is required to keep in mind that when he tries a case he is himself on trial.

—*Philo*

What begins as flattery matures into falsehood.

—*Yiddish folk saying*

There is nothing like desire for preventing the things we say from having any resemblance to the things in our mind.

—*Marcel Proust*

While Moses was feeding his father-in-law's sheep in the wilderness, a young kid left the others.

Moses followed the kid until it reached the edge of a ravine, where it found water to drink.

On reaching the animal, Moses said, "I did not know that you ran away because you wanted water. Now you must be tired."

He lifted the kid and carried it back in his arms.

Then God said, "Because you have shown compassion in bringing back one of the sheep belonging to man, you will lead My flock, Israel."

—*Midrash Rabbah*

A man is not allowed to eat before he has fed his animal, because it is written: "I will provide grass in the fields for your cattle," and then says: "that you shall eat your fill" [Deuteronomy 11:15].

—*Talmud*

Drive your horse not with a whip but with oats.

—*Yiddish folk saying*

The guilty run when no one is chasing them.

—*Yiddish folk saying*

Not to have had a chance to lie does not mean one has been honest.

—*Arthur Schnitzler*

To avoid insulting someone, you may tell a white lie.

—*Sefer Hasidim*

There is no true justice unless mercy is part of it.

—*Zohar*

In all the communities which the LORD your God is giving you, you are to appoint judges and officials for your different tribes, to judge the people properly.

You must not prevent justice; you must show no partiality; nor take a bribe. . . .

Justice, and justice only must you strive for.

—*Bible, Deuteronomy 16:18–20*

The Torah states, *"Tzedek, tzedek* [Justice, justice] you shall pursue" (Deuteronomy 16:20). Why should the Torah repeat the term *tzedek?*

Rabbenu Bachaye . . . interprets that the Torah intimates how the same standard of justice and righteousness that is applied toward Jewish brothers is also to be applied toward all Gentiles.

—*Ahron Soloveichik*

Listen fully to what those around you say and make just decisions between any person and another Jew or a stranger.

You will not be biased in your judgment: listen to those who are important and unimportant. Fear no man, for judgment is God's.

—*Bible, Deuteronomy 1:16–17*

Joseph . . . cried out . . . to his brothers . . . Do not be worried or angry with yourselves because you sold me into slavery; the purpose was to save life. . . .

God sent me ahead of you to make sure you survived on earth and to save your lives in a remarkable deliverance.

—*Bible, Genesis 45:1–7*

. . . Eye for eye, tooth for tooth.

—Bible, Leviticus 24:19

One would think that when an individual puts out the eye of another, the offender should lose his eye . . . or when he breaks another's limb, the offender should have his limb broken. But this is not so. . . .

In the Bible it is said: "A murderer who is guilty of a capital crime may not ransom his life; he must pay with his life" [Numbers 35:31].

From this we understand, money may not be substituted only when murder has occurred, but you may take compensation. . . .

Rabbi Dostai ben Judah said . . . if one person had a large eye and the other person had a small eye, how could you then equally impact the theory of an "eye for an eye"? . . .

Rabbi Simeon bar Yohai said . . . how could one deal with the case in which a blind person puts out someone else's eye . . . or a cripple breaks another person's leg? . . .

Abbaye said: . . . if you understand it that the Bible in fact meant retaliation, you might by mistake take an eye and a person's life as compensation for an eye because in the violence of losing an eye the person might die.

—Talmud

Those who take revenge destroy their own house.

—Talmud

Thou shalt not take vengeance, nor bear a grudge.

—Bible, Leviticus 19:18

If you don't help a neighbor because he has been unkind to you, you are guilty of revenge; if you respond to his request for help and remind him of his [earlier] unkindness, you are guilty of holding a grudge.

—Sifrei

Every judge who judges truthfully, even for a single hour, is credited as though he had become a partner with God in the creation of the world.

—Talmud

Vengeance is Mine.

—*Bible, Deuteronomy 32:35*

Warning must precede punishment.

—*Talmud*

You may not condemn a criminal to death unless, prior to the crime, he had been warned against doing such a thing by at least two people willing to give witness.

—*Jose ben Halafta*

A man should not act as a judge either for someone he loves or for someone he hates. For no man can see the guilt of someone he loves or the good qualities in someone he hates.

—*Talmud*

The deepest truth blooms only from the deepest love.

—*Heinrich Heine*

Since when do you have to agree with people to defend them from injustice?

—*Lillian Hellman*

Before a thief steals, he has learned to lie.

—*Isaac Friedman*

You are not responsible when you are being tortured.

—*Rav, Talmud*

Hypocrites are excluded from the presence of God.

—*Talmud*

As soon as one is unhappy one becomes moral.

—*Marcel Proust*

There was a king who had several empty goblets. The king said, "If I put hot water in them, they will break. If I put cold water in them, they will crack." So the king mixed the cold and hot water together, poured the water into the goblets, and the goblets were not injured.

In this same way, God said, "If I create the world with mercy at its foundation, sin will flourish; if I create the world with justice as the foundation, how will the world endure?

"So I will create the world with both mercy and justice, so the world will flourish and endure."

—Adapted from Midrash Rabbah

Cease to do evil, and learn to do good! See justice, and relieve the oppressed . . .

—Bible, Isaiah 1:17

God loves the persecuted and hates the persecutors.

—Pesikta Rabbati

A liar never believes anyone else.

—Yiddish folk saying

In a distant land, a king traveled to a jail and spoke with the prisoners.

Each of the men behind bars told the king of their innocence, except one.

This man admitted he was a thief.

Looking at all who proclaimed their innocence as a chorus against the one who confessed, the king pointed to the one and said, "Release this man from jail! He will pervert the innocent."

—Adapted from a Hasidic folktale

Now and then even a liar tells the truth.

—Moses ibn Ezra

If you desire to make a lie believable, stir in a little of the truth.

—Zohar

The worst libel is the truth.

—Yiddish folk saying

A hint hits harder than the truth.

—*Yiddish folk saying*

With lies you can go far, but not back again.

—*Yiddish folk saying*

Antonius spoke to the rabbi, saying:

"Both the body and the soul have the ability to free themselves from judgment. The body can say, 'The soul has committed the sin,' and the soul can say, 'The body has committed the sin.' "

The rabbi replied, "I will tell you a parable that replies to your question: Once there was a king who owned an incredible orchard with the finest figs. The king appointed two men to watch over the orchard. One of the men was lame and the other blind.

"One day, the lame watchman said to the blind watchman, 'I can see that there are beautiful figs in the orchard. Lift me up onto your shoulders so we can pluck and enjoy them.'

"Then the lame man moved onto the shoulders of the blind man, grabbed some figs, and they both devoured them. When the king came into the orchard to check on his fruit, he asked what had happened to his figs. The lame man asked, 'Do I have legs to reach the figs?' And the blind man asked, 'Do I have eyes to see the figs?'

"So, what did the king do? He put the lame man on the blind man's shoulders and put them on trial as one. In this way, God will put the soul in the body and judge them as one."

—*Talmud*

Do not judge someone else until you have been put in their position.

—*Hillel the Elder, Pirke Avot*

A person may not accuse himself of a crime.

—*Talmud*

The Lord has appointed me to bring good tidings to the humble. He has sent me to proclaim liberty to the captives . . . to comfort all that mourn.

—*Bible, Isaiah 61:1–2*

[Hypocrisy] is like a woman who is in the apartment of her lover, and swears by the life of her husband.

—*Tanhuma*

Secrecy necessarily breeds suspicion.

—*Louis D. Brandeis*

Happy are the Righteous who turn judgment into mercy.

—*Midrash Rabbah*

Justice is truth in action.

—*Benjamin Disraeli*

Truth is not compatible with dogma.

—*Samuel Max Melamed*

All His ways are justice.

—*Bible, Deuteronomy 32:4*

PART ELEVEN

The Meaning of
Life Is That It Stops

WHEN JEWS RAISE THEIR GLASSES IN A TRADITIONAL TOAST, THEY SAY *l'chaim,* to life. From life all things are possible. And although Jews have been forced through a history of adversity to often live under inhumane conditions, the biblical message has remained constant and clear: *choose life.* In Judaism, death's significance is in its relationship to God's gift of life.

Across the millennia Jewish bravery has found less opportunity to express itself in military might than in its courage to transcend justified fears and anxieties and to find joy in what has been afforded. This experience of refusing to hold life in abeyance while living under real affliction redefines heroism. A Jew with no chicken for the Sabbath meal gives thanks for the bread. Although tragedy is part of life, Jewish mettle has birthed both a uniquely Jewish sense of humor, its own medicinal courage, and a conviction that reminds any of us in anguish that this pain will pass.

Rabbinic sermons seldom use the threat of hell as a set of religious reins for controlling the acts of Jews. Human suffering, as all people, including Jews, have witnessed, is not necessarily an event postponed until death. Talmudic dictum makes it very clear that any Jew who does a good deed with the thought of what it will get him, including a place in heaven, loses whatever the act may have earned by expecting a reward. Heaven, in Jewish understanding, is not a place limited to Jews.

In Judaism we are all God's children. For Jews to get to heaven we must conduct ourselves responsibly as Jews—here and now. Our conduct is not to be conditional on its recompense in the hereafter. Day-to-day acts that make life a little less like hell for others inevitably draw us closer to heaven.

CHAPTER 38

Death

Life is an incurable disease from which everyone has so far died, and the only ones who survive are those who have never been born.

—*Moritz Gottlieb Saphir*

Dying while you are young is of great advantage when you are old.

—*Yiddish folk saying*

Once there was a student who was with a teacher for many years. And when the teacher felt he was going to die, he wanted to make even his death a lesson.

That night, the teacher took a torch, called his student, and set off with him through the forest.

Soon they reached the middle of the woods, where the teacher extinguished the torch, without explanation.

"What is the matter?" asked the student.

"This torch has gone out," the teacher answered and walked on.

"But," shouted the student, his voice plucking his fear, "will you leave me here in the dark?"

"No! I will not leave you in the dark," returned the teacher's voice from the surrounding blackness. "I will leave you searching for the light."

—*Noah benShea*

For each one of us the moment comes when the great nurse, death, takes man, the child, by the hand and quietly says, "It is time to go home. Night is coming. It is our bedtime, child of earth. Come; you're tired. Lie down at last in the quiet nursery of nature and sleep. Sleep well. The day is gone. Stars shine in the canopy of eternity."

—*Joshua Loth Liebman*

The cause of death is life.

—*Joseph Zabara*

Death is time when it is frozen. Time is melted death.

—*Franz Werfel*

If the rich could employ the poor to die for them, the poor would prosper.

—*Yiddish folk saying*

Make plans in this world as if you hoped to live forever, but make plans for the world to come as if you expected to die tomorrow.

—*Solomon ibn Gabirol*

At the moment of his death the Ba'al Shem Tov said, "Now I know why I was created."

—*Ba'al Shem Tov*

Some who live are dead, and some who are dead still live.

—*Philo*

There are no bad mothers and no good death.

—*Yiddish folk saying*

Sleep is lovely, death is better still, not to have been born is of course the miracle.

—*Heinrich Heine*

He decided to live forever or die in the attempt.

—*Joseph Heller*

Sleep is death without the responsibility.

—*Fran Lebowitz*

While Rabbi Meir was giving his weekly lecture during the Sabbath afternoon, his two most loved sons suddenly died at home. The boys' mother covered them with a sheet, and as it was the Sabbath forbade anyone from mourning on a day sacred for its peace and joy.

After the evening services, Rabbi Meir returned home and asked for his sons, who had not come to the synagogue. The rabbi's wife ignored the request, brought him the evening meal, and asked the rabbi to say the Havdalah prayer concluding the Sabbath.

Then the wife said to her husband, "I have a question for you. A friend once gave me two incredible jewels to hold for him; now he wants them back. Shall I return them?"

"Without doubt," said Rabbi Meir.

The rabbi's wife took him by the hand, led him to the bedroom, and drew back the sheet. Tears burst forth in a bitter torrent from the saddened couple. "You see," said the wife, "these jewels were entrusted to us by God to hold for Him and now He has taken back what is His."

—*Midrash*

Set your house in order.

—*Bible, II Kings 20:1*

Previously, they would bring food to the house of mourning, the rich would transport the food in baskets of silver and gold, and poor people in baskets of willow twigs; consequently the poor felt belittled. On this account, a law went into effect that out of consideration for the poor, everyone should use baskets of willow twigs. . . .

. . . Previously, they used to bring the dead for burial, the wealthy on a huge bed with rich covers, the poor in a simple box; and the poor felt belittled. On this account, a law went into effect that out of consideration for the poor all those who had died should be carried in a plain box. . . .

. . . Previously, the cost of burying the dead sometimes became a more dreadful burden than the loss . . . Rabbi Gamaliel required himself to be buried in a plain linen shroud instead of a costly garment, and since then people have been buried in this way.

—*Talmud*

Funeral shrouds have no pockets.

—*Yiddish folk saying*

On the day he dies every man feels he has lived only a single day.

—*Zohar*

Death doesn't take the time to knock on the door.

—*Yiddish folk saying*

It is forbidden to pray that a wicked man should die. Had Terah [Abraham's father] died while he worshipped idols, Abraham would not have come into the world.

—*Midrash*

Better a noble death than a terrible life.

—*Yiddish folk saying*

An ancient saying goes: "Many an old ass carries a load of hides from young foals."

As Moses and Aaron led the tribes of Israel into the desert, Aaron's two ambitious sons, Nadab and Abihu, said to each other: "When the old leaders pass away, we shall take control of the leadership."

But God said, "Let us first see who buries whom."

—*Talmud*

The Tzaddik of Parsischa lay on his death bed. His wife perched beside, crying terribly.

"Why are you weeping?" asked the rabbi. "I have been given an entire life simply so I might be taught to die."

—*Simcha Bunam*

Two groups of Hasidim were approaching each other in the market place.

The first, on seeing the second, said, "Ha, here are the Hasidim who even though their rebbe has died have kept him as their rebbe."

And the second group replied, "You are right. We have kept our rebbe as our rebbe, even though he has passed away, may he rest in peace."

"And how do you explain doing this?" asked the first group, mocking while they asked.

"It is our opinion, in all modesty," said the second group of

Hasidim, "that it is better to have a dead rebbe who is alive than a live rebbe who is dead."

—Hasidic folk tradition

The basis of wisdom is not in the reflection on death but in the reflection on life.

—Baruch Spinoza

In the flood of death it is the flood which supports the ark of life.

—Noah benShea

People are incapable of seeing God when they are alive, but they can see Him at their death.

—Midrash Rabbah

If you would prevail in life, be prepared for death.

—Sigmund Freud

The meaning of life is that it stops.

—Franz Kafka

CHAPTER 39

Sorrow, Mourning, Fear,

Despair, Danger, Worry

I don't think of all the misery, but of all the beauty that still remains.
—*Anne Frank*

Don't let worry enter your heart, because worry has killed person after person.

—*Talmud*

Have no concern for trouble that is to arrive tomorrow, for you cannot be sure what the day will bring. If tomorrow arrives and we have left, we will have been worried about a world that is not ours.
—*Talmud*

Death is not the greatest loss in life. The greatest loss is what dies inside us while we live.

—*Norman Cousins*

Everyone worries: some because they don't have enough pearls, others because they don't have enough beans in their soup.
—*Yiddish folk saying*

The art of living lies less in eliminating our troubles than in growing with them.

—*Bernard M. Baruch*

If we are afraid of anything but God, we are in some way worshipping idols. Because to fear is to worship what you fear. And we are to worship only God.

—Rabbi Isaac Meyer of Ger, the Gerer Rebbe

Be strong and of good courage, fear not.

—Bible, Deuteronomy 31:6

In life, be careful. Ask God questions and He may insist you come up to hear the answers.

—Yiddish folk saying

There is no hope not mixed with fear, and no fear not mixed with hope.

—Baruch Spinoza

Fear is hate's father.

—Yiddish folk saying

Whoever fears the Lord is afraid of nothing.

—Wisdom of Ben Sira

The source of most lies is fear of others.

—Nachman of Bratslav

The greatest worries don't pay the smallest debts.

—Yiddish folk saying

Only fools never fear.

—Heinrich Heine

This life is a very narrow bridge. . . . But you shall not be afraid.

—Talmud

Despair is the conclusion of fools.

—Benjamin Disraeli

Show up for your inheritance and you may have to pay for the funeral.

—*Yiddish folk saying*

[Those] who are not patient in concluding their mourning extend their grief.

—*Solomon ibn Gabirol*

Weeping may endure for a night, but joy cometh in the morning.

—*Bible, Psalms 30:5*

We cannot banish dangers, but we can banish fears. We must not demean life by standing in awe of death.

—*David Sarnoff*

When the dead are at rest, let their memory rest too; take comfort as soon as they have released their last breath.

—*Wisdom of Ben Sira*

Nothing is more sad than the death of an illusion.

—*Arthur Koestler*

Fear of what could happen is often worse than what could happen.

—*Hasidic folk saying*

Fear is the pain before the wound.

—*Noah benShea*

Have fear for only two: God and those who have no fear of God.

—*Hasidic folk saying*

If God didn't hide from all people the date of their death, nobody would build a home, nobody would plant a vineyard, because everyone would say, "I'm going to die tomorrow, so of what purpose is it for me to work today?"

For this reason, God denies us knowing the day of our death, in the hope we will build and plant.

. . . [If not us,] others will benefit from our labor.

—*Yalkut Shimoni*

If any linking has the strength to manacle heaven to earth, it is this prayer.

—Leopold Kompert, on Kaddish

Glorified and sanctified be God's great name throughout the world which He has created according to His will. May He establish His kingdom in your lifetime and during your days, and within the life of the entire house of Israel, speedily and soon; and say, Amen.

May His great name be blessed forever and to all eternity.

Blessed and praised, glorified and exalted, extolled and honored, adored and lauded be the name of the Holy One, blessed be He, whose glory is beyond all the blessings and hymns, praises and consolations that are ever spoken in the world; and say, Amen.

May there be abundant peace from heaven and life, for us and for all Israel; and say, Amen.

May He who creates peace in His high places create peace for us and for all Israel; and say, Amen.

—Kaddish, traditional prayer in memory of the dead

Anybody who comes upon a person who went into mourning a year ago and at meeting now offers words of consolation, to whom can this person be compared?

This kind of person can be compared to a doctor who meets somebody who had broken his leg a year ago and now that the leg has healed offers: "Let me break your leg again, and set it again, so I may be able to convince you of what a good doctor I am."

—Rabbi Meir, Talmud

From the day a man comes out of his mother's womb, until the day he returns to the mother of all that is alive . . . [he is filled with] preoccupation and anxiety and concern for the future . . . [both] he who sits . . . on a throne . . . [and] he who is dressed in dust and ashes.

—Wisdom of Ben Sira

Drink poison rather than worrying.

—Solomon ibn Gabirol

If you keep on saying things are going to be bad, you have a good chance of being a prophet.

—Isaac Bashevis Singer

CHAPTER 40

Afterlife, Judgment, Heaven, Hell

For dust thou art, and unto dust thou shalt return.

            —Bible, Genesis 3:19

Naked I came from my mother's womb and naked shall I return there.

              —Bible, Job 1:21

Hide me in the shadow of Your wings.

             —Bible, Psalms 17:8

A wandering soul was being shown around both Paradise and Hell by an angel. In both Paradise and Hell the soul could see huge tables filled with wonderful things to eat. Men and women were seated lining both sides of the tables. The soul then had something pointed out to him by the angel. "You will notice that in both places neither the men nor women can bend their elbows," said the angel.

"Well then," asked the soul, "can you tell what makes Paradise different from Hell?"

"Certainly," said the angel. "The difference between the two is that in Hell everyone is trying to feed himself, but because their elbows cannot bend, they are tempted but cannot eat. But in Heaven, all the souls, whose arms cannot bend, reach across the table, each person feeding the person on the opposite side."

          —Adapted from Hebrew legend

Through our soul is our contact with heaven.

—*Sholem Asch*

Rabbi Eliezer ben Hyrcanus said, "Repent one day before your death."

His disciples asked him, "How is it possible for a person to repent one day before they die, since one does not know when one will pass away?"

The rabbi answered, "It is for this reason that you should reflect on your life every day in case you die the next day. In this way all our days are a source of reflection, penance."

—*Rabbi Nathan, Pirke Avot*

Some of us achieve eternity after a lifetime of struggle, others in a moment.

—*Judah ha-Nasi, Talmud*

Only our concept of time makes it possible for us to speak of the Day of Judgment by that name; in reality it is a constant court in perpetual session.

—*Franz Kafka*

A clown may be the first in God's heaven, if he has helped to diminish the sadness of human life.

—*Talmud*

We feel and we know that we are eternal.

—*Baruch Spinoza*

What a man does now and here with sacred intent . . . is no less important [than what he does] in the world to come.

—*Martin Buber*

This world is like an entrance hall leading to the world to come.

—*Rabbi Jacob, Pirke Avot*

Jerusalem, like Heaven, is more a state of mind than a place.

—*Israel Zangwill*

It is said in *The Book of the Pious* . . . we are not allowed to raise our voices and cry loudly at the moment when a soul is leaving so we will not make the soul come back and experience further pain.

—*Hayyim Palaggi*

I believe in heaven and hell—on earth.

—*Abraham L. Feinberg*

The spirit, which lives forever, is not born after death, but is, like God, always with us.

—*Moses Hess*

When the hour of death is near, the soul is very afraid and refuses to leave the body.

Then the Shekinah [God's presence] comes to the soul and gestures to it. The soul, filled with a deep urge to join with the Shekinah, does by its own decision exit the body.

—*Zohar*

Afterlife is felt to be a reunion and all of life a preparation for it.

—*Abraham Joshua Heschel*

The mystics saw the body as a weighted garment that falls away at death and leaves the true person free to rise into heavenly light.

—*Zohar*

The paper burns, but the words fly away.

—*Rabbi Akiba*

In the world to come . . . the virtuous rise to a knowledge and reality of the truth concerning God unknown to them in this world, because they were restricted to a stained and lowly body.

—*Maimonides*

Our exit from the world as compared to our entry is offered by Rabbi Levi in this way: Imagine two great sailing ships. One arrives in port and one prepares to leave. Clearly the one that arrives in port is a source of great joy. In this way, we should see our departure from this world without sorrow or fear, because at death we have already entered the harbor—a haven of rest in the World-to-Come.

—*Midrash Rabbah*

Two creatures are blended in man—one intended for this life and the other for the life hereafter.

—*Midrash Rabbah*

Rabbi Simeon ben Lakish and two others were once both companions and robbers in their youth. However, Rabbi Simeon did penance and became a man of deep religious character and understanding. His companions, however, did not change their ways.

As it happened, all three died on the same day. Rabbi Simeon was taken to Paradise, but his former friends were sent to Gehenna. There the men complained: "How does this happen. Rabbi Simeon was with us in our robberies." The answer given to the men was, "But Simeon repented and you didn't."

"Now we are ready to repent," they said. And the answer told the men was this: "Those who travel in the desert must take along food or they will starve. Those who travel across huge seas must take along provisions or they will go hungry. The Life-After-Death is like both the desert and seas and no supplies can be purchased there."

—*Pirke de Rabbi Eliezer*

This world is a hotel. The World-to-Come is your home.

—*Talmud*

I am exiting through one door, and I am entering through another.

—*Ba'al Shem Tov*

Death is a change of cosmic address.

—*Bob Toben*

This world is on a wheel that never stops turning. Those who are rich today may not be so tomorrow, and those who are poor today may not be so tomorrow.

—*Midrash Rabbah*

The righteous among the Gentiles will have a share in the World-to-Come.

—*Yalkut Shimoni*

It was said by Rabbi Elimelech of Lyzhansk:

When I pass away and am standing in the court of justice, I will be asked if I was as just a person as I should have been.

I will say no.

After this, I will be asked if I have been as giving to charity as I should have been.

I will say no.

And after this, I will be asked if I studied as much as I should have studied.

I will say no.

And after this, I will be asked if I prayed as much as I should have prayed.

I will say no.

Then the Judge of all judges will offer me a smile and say, "Elimelech, because you said what was true, On this alone you merit a share of the world to come."

—*Adapted legend about Hasidic rabbi Elimelech of Lyzhansk*

PART TWELVE

Imagination Is More Important than Knowledge

THE ARTIST AFFORDS SOCIETY A PERSPECTIVE ON ITSELF. THE ARTIST comes to this perspective either by stepping back or by being set apart. And while all Jews are certainly not artists, seeing life from such a viewpoint is an experience the children of Israel have, across time, shared, by choice and circumstance, with artists.

In the second of the Ten Commandments the children of Israel are told, "Thou shall not make unto thee a graven image, nor any manner of likeness, of any thing that is in heaven above, or that is in the earth beneath, or that is in the water under the earth." Distanced by commandment from the visual arts, Jewish craft artists nevertheless used their talents to form treasured ritual objects, such as menorahs, spice boxes, and illuminated texts. Records of craftsmanship as a divine calling can be found as early as the redemption from Egypt, when Bezalel is chosen by God to construct the Holy Ark in the wilderness of Sinai.

Approximately three thousand years ago, a young shepherd in the Judean hills plucked his harp and sang his psalms; the music was heard in heaven. Today, whether in painting, sculpture, literature, music, dance, drama, or film, King David's great-grandchildren continue within the tradition of making art by lending craft to the soul.

CHAPTER 41

Art, Creation

Imagination is more important than knowledge.

—*Albert Einstein*

While it is not possible for every human being to be an author, it is possible for every author to be a human being.

—*Moritz Gottlieb Saphir*

The lash may force men to physical labor; it cannot force them to spiritual creativity.

—*Sholem Asch*

I cannot tell you how much I love to play for people. Would you believe it—sometimes when I sit down to practice and there is no one else in the room, I have to stifle an impulse to ring for the elevator man and offer him money to come in and hear me.

—*Arthur Rubinstein*

Practice creates the artist.

—*Solomon Hanau*

Writing comes more easily if you have something to say.

—*Sholem Asch*

Writing is one of the easiest things; but erasing is one of the most difficult.

—*Israel Salanter Lipkin*

He who has found poetry has found God.

—*Alter Esselin*

Jacob took a thick pencil from his back pocket and began to write. But it really wasn't Jacob writing.

Jacob was a reed, and the breath of God blew through Jacob, made music of him.

—*Noah benShea*

If a composer doesn't write from the heart, he simply can't compose good music.

—*Arnold Schoenberg*

Make music unto the Lord . . .

—*Bible, Psalms 30:5*

Artisans look after the fabric of the world, and in the handwork of their craft is their prayer.

—*Wisdom of Ben Sira*

. . . In art, and in life, the hidden truth of happiness is in the beginning to move as far away as you can from home and then to return home: in this way, each piece of art is a kind of prodigal son, which treasures its set point in space, like in morality, by moving from it.

—*Nahum Sokolow*

Now the Lord said unto Abram, "Get thee out . . . from thy father's house. . . ."

—*Bible, Genesis 12:1*

Remarks are not literature.

—*Gertrude Stein*

Perfumes are the feelings of flowers.

—*Heinrich Heine*

A photograph is . . . something directly stenciled off the real, like a footprint, or a death mask.

—*Susan Sontag*

Sculpture is the art of thinking in shapes.

—*Viscount Herbert Samuel*

Originality is the only thing that counts.

—*George Gershwin*

Those who love art, and are truly susceptible to its spell, do die young in the sense that they remain young to their dying day.

—*Otto Kahn*

One who is able to write a book and does not is like one who has lost a child.

—*Nachman of Bratslav*

A writer is someone who can make a riddle out of an answer.

—*Karl Kraus*

Thou shalt not make unto thee a graven image, nor any manner of likeness, of anything that is in heaven above, or that is in the earth beneath, or that is in the water under the earth.

—*Bible, Exodus 20:4*

Every animal leaves traces of what it was; man alone leaves traces of what he created.

—*Jacob Bronowski*

Poets are the only people to whom love is not only a crucial, but an indispensable experience, which entitles them to mistake it for a universal one.

—*Hannah Arendt*

I lived in solitude in the country and noticed how the monotony of a quiet life stimulates the creative mind.

—*Albert Einstein*

Art is the unceasing effort to compete with the beauty of flowers and never succeeding.

—*Marc Chagall*

. . . It is impossible for the artist to find all the various types in nature, for the most incredible types are shown to the artist in his soul.

—*Heinrich Heine*

When I am finishing a picture I hold some God-made object up to it—a rock, a flower, the branch of a tree, or my hand—as a kind of final test. If the painting stands up beside a thing man cannot make, the painting is authentic. If there's a clash between the two, it is bad art.

—*Marc Chagall*

A work of art has an author and yet, when it's perfect, it has something that is essentially anonymous about it.

—*Simone Weil*

Idea and pathos are the two most prominent characteristics of the Jewish Muse.

—*Phillip Max Raskin*

[Those] who sing in the present world will also sing in the next.

—*Joshua ben Levi, Talmud*

Poetry . . . focuses what most often floods past us in a polite blur.

—*Diane Ackerman*

Intuition antedates all creation.

—*Hayyim Nachman Bialik*

Artists are not required to stand up from their work when a Sage passes by them.

—*Talmud*

Interpretation is the revenge of the intellect upon art.
—*Susan Sontag*

It is the silence between the notes that makes the music.
—*Noah benShea*

A WORD ABOUT THE
INDEX THAT FOLLOWS . . .

Words are vehicles of labor. They carry an idea and are never the idea. The sources referred to here are reeds. The wisdom of their message plays though them, makes music of them.

Fewer words following an individual or source do not imply lesser importance. Nor the reverse.

None of the descriptions are attempts to encapsulate.

This index is intended to offer you a handle of information that might afford you some grasp but will preferably allow you the capacity to turn an idea's source over and on your own discover more.

Words in boldface have entries elsewhere in this index.

In some cases, as my knowledge or research allowed or my curiosity dictated, I have tried by way of a detail, a story, or an obscure fact to provide a window. Peering through the words you might see the shadow of a sage, the outline of a wit, a mountain of wisdom, or an invisible truth that is the flesh and the bone of a people's spirit.

Here are lives that are wise, accomplished, and too often too long ignored. Here are scriptural sources that are left to you as a gift, yours for taking the time to open. Here are courageous souls, many of whom sailed across seas of poverty, doubt, and hate, and kept their souls intact, serving as a testimony to the rest of us that this can be done.

INDEX OF BIOGRAPHICAL AND SCRIPTURAL DESCRIPTIONS

Aaron Al-Rabi—15th-century Sicily. Kabbalist; see **Kabbala**.

Abba—a name often given to sages in the Talmud, it means "father" in Hebrew.

Abba Saul—1st- and 2nd-century Israel. *Tanna*.

Abin Halevi—4th-century Israel. Rabbi, sage, *amora*.

Abraham ibn Ezra—12th-century Spain. Hebrew poet, wrote biblical exegesis.

Israel Abrahams—19th- and 20th-century England. Scholar, writer.

Isaac Abravanel—15th- and 16th-century Portugal. Philosopher, scholar, biblical commentator, statesman. Served, like his father, Judah, before him, as treasurer to King Alfonso V of Portugal. Headed an effort to ransom Jewish captives from North Africa. Sentenced to death by the new king of Portugal, Isaac fled and was taken into the court of Ferdinand and Isabella. During the Spanish Inquisition he sailed to Naples, where he served in the court of the king of Naples, Ferrante I. There he continued writing his commentary throughout political intrigues. He died in Venice and was buried in Padua, but destruction of Jewish cemeteries during the wars of the early 16th century left the exact location of his grave unknown.

Diane Ackerman—20th-century America. Writer, poet.

Alfred Adler—19th- and 20th-century Austria. Psychologist, founding father of the psychological movement.

Felix Adler—19th- and 20th-century America. Social philosopher, writer, major force in school of Ethical Culture.

Freda Adler—20th-century America. Writer, educator.

Mortimer Adler—20th-century America. Philosopher, educator. On the board of editors of the *Encyclopaedia Britannica*. Opposed the educational notions of John Dewey and thought education should be centered instead around the reading and study of the Great Books of the Western World, of which he was co-editor, with Robert Maynard Hutchins.

Victor Adler—19th- and 20th-century Austria. Labor activist and leader in the international labor movement; took a prominent role in the Austrian Social-Democratic party.

Agada, Aggadic—See **Haggadah** and **Midrash**.

Agadat Shir ha-Shirim—9th- and 10th-century **Midrash** on the Song of Songs.

Samuel Joseph Agnon—19th- and 20th-century Galicia and Israel. Hebrew and Yiddish writer. Given name Samuel Josef Czackes, Hebrew name Shmuel Yosef (Shani) Agnon. A central figure in Hebrew fiction, his work often focused on the falling away of everyday life as we know it, current spiritual issues, and questions of faith and identity. Nobel Prize for Literature, 1966.

Ahad Ha-Am—19th- and 20th-century Russia, England, and Israel. Scholar, philosopher, Hebrew essayist, and Zionist. Given name Asher Hirsch Gihrsberg. His work and thinking remain a major influence.

Rabbi Akiba (Akiba ben Joseph)—1st- and 2nd-century Israel. Rabbi, patriot, martyr. A sage among the *tannaim*. A poor shepherd in his youth, he came to be considered the foremost scholar of his period, playing a major role in the growth and manner of **halakah**. Akiba's disciple Aquila was moved by his teacher to write the Greek translation of the Bible. Considered in the Jerusalem Talmud as "one of the fathers of the world," Akiba had a lifelong concern and care for the welfare of the poor and backed the revolution led by Bar Kochba against the Romans, by whom he was imprisoned and had the flesh torn from his body before death.

Joseph Albo—14th- and 15th-century Spain. Theologian.

Shalom Aleichem—19th- and 20th-century Russia and America. Yiddish writer and humorist, the best known of his genre, considered a "Yiddish Mark Twain." Born Shalom Rabinowitz. The pen name Shalom Aleichem means "peace on your path."

Moses Alshek—16th-century Israel. Rabbi.

amora (plural, *amoraim*)—Sages from the 2nd century to the 5th century whose thoughts make up the **Gemara**.

Amshinover Rebbe—19th-century Eastern Europe. Hasidic rabbi.

Jacob Anatoli—12th- and 13th-century France. Translated Arabic scientific research into Hebrew. Preacher.

Solomon Ansky—See **S. J. Rappaport**.

Mary Antin—19th- and 20th-century America. Writer.

Apocrypha—a term applied to a collection of books that have not been accepted into the Judeo-legal conception of the Bible although some are accepted into the Roman Catholic and Greek Orthodox canon. Of this collection only Ecclesiasticus (**Wisdom of Ben Sira**) is referred to in the literature of the Talmud.

Hannah Arendt—20th-century Germany and America. Philosopher, writer, sociologist.

Sholem Asch—20th-century Polish-American. Yiddish novelist, wit.

Asher ben Yehiel—13th- and 14th-century Germany and Spain. Scholar, Talmudist.

Berthold Auerbach—19th-century Germany. Writer, thinker.

Avot de Rabbi Nathan—Thought of as one of the more minor tractates in the Talmud, the work is a commentary on the **Pirke Avot**.

Azariah—4th-century Israel. *Amora*.

Ba'al Shem Tov—18th-century Podolia, southeast Poland/southwest Ukraine. Rabbi, founder of the Hasidic movement. The name Ba'al Shem Tov, often referred to by the shortened "BeShT," literally means "Master of the Good (Divine) Name." Although others, from the Middle Ages forward, had been known by this name, Israel ben Eliezer (his given name) is the one who is usually thought of and is the most famous. Those who took or were given the name supposedly had the knowledge of the Divine's sacred and secret holy names, which could then be used to exercise miracles and/or gain mystical power. Israel ben Eliezer was orphaned while a child, worked as a watchman, a teacher, and in a quarry, retreated to the Carpathian mountains in reflection, and, according to tradition, revealed himself on his thirty-sixth birthday as a charismatic leader of wisdom and caring and stories. Remarkable legends surrounded his character, including his ability to see both the past and future via dreams. "Faith," said the Ba'al Shem Tov, "is the adhesion of the soul to God."

Leo Baeck—19th- and 20th-century Germany. Rabbi, writer, scholar, philosopher. A central figure in German-Jewish life, he stayed with his community and was sent to a concentration camp by the Germans during World War II, which he survived.

Bahya ben Asher—13th- and 14th-century Spain. Writer of biblical commentary and interpretation.

Bahya ben Joseph ibn Pakuda—11th-century Spain. Philosopher and moralist.

Baraita (plural, Beraitot)—Aramaic for the Hebrew word meaning "outside," a Baraita is consequently an "outside **Mishna**," a **Mishna** that is outside the material initially collected and codified by **Judah ha-Nasi**. Beraitot are sometimes used to add to accepted **halakah** or **agada**, and other times as straw dogs whose lack of authority is used to defeat an argument posed in the literature by one scholar to another. A wide range of Beraitot types, by various scholars, can be found. *Perek ha-Shalom,* from the Hebrew, means "a chapter on peace."

Joseph L. Baron—19th- and 20th-century Poland/Lithuania and America. Rabbi, scholar, editor of Jewish literature.

Bernard M. Baruch—19th- and 20th-century America. Stock analyst, statesman. Member of a prominent American family that immigrated from Prussia in the mid-19th century. Chairman of the War Industries Board during World War I. Personal economic adviser to every American president from Wilson to Roosevelt.

Vicki Baum—19th- and 20th-century Austria and America. Novelist.

Ben Azzai—1st- and 2nd-century Israel. *Tanna*. Full name Simeon ben Azzai.

David Ben-Gurion—19th- and 20th-century Russian Poland and Israel. Ben-Gurion's father, Avigdor Gruen, was a dedicated Zionist. Ben-Gurion learned Hebrew as a child, and at fourteen he was already a leader in Zionist youth groups in Poland. Arrested by authorities and released (with the help of his father), he settled in Israel when he was twenty, and became a leader in the labor movement that played a commanding role in founding the modern state. He fought for independence, the ingathering of Jews, and Jewish security. He was both the first prime minister and the first defense minister of Israel. Repeatedly left and returned to office at the call of his people and his personality. With his shock of white hair and his unaffected manner and his belief that his people and the land were one, Ben-Gurion was, even with all the political infighting over the years, a symbol of 20th-century Israel. A lifelong student of the Bible, as well as of **Spinoza**, Buddhism, and Greek philosophy. His name in Hebrew means "son of the lion."

Noah benShea—20th-century Canada and America. Poet, philosopher, writer, teacher.

Ben Zoma—2nd-century Israel. *Tanna*. Full name Simeon ben Zoma.

Norman Bentwich—19th- and 20th-century England. Scholar. Attorney general of Mandated Palestine.

Berditschever Rebbe—18th- and 19th-century Eastern Europe. Hasidic rabbi.

Berechiah ben Natronai ha-Nakdan—12th- and 13th-century France. Writer, creator of fables.

Bernard Berenson—19th- and 20th-century Poland, America, and Italy. Art critic, writer.

Henri Bergson—19th- and 20th-century France. Philosopher.

Eliezer Berkovits—20th-century Transylvania, Germany, England, Australia, America, and Israel. Rabbi, modern orthodox theologian, philosopher, Zionist, author, and professor. Chairman of the department of Jewish philosophy at Hebrew Theological College in Chicago, he wrote extensively on modern-day issues of faith and the Holocaust. An inspiring teacher and scholar, Rabbi Berkovits influenced others as much by his character as by his learning.

Milton Berle—20th-century America. Comedian, entertainment personality. A major star in early television.

Irving Berlin—19th- and 20th-century Russia and America. Born Israel Baline. Composer and lyricist of popular songs. The son of a cantor, he first worked as a singing waiter. His initial big hit was "Alexander's Ragtime Band." He wrote for the stage and film, and was responsible for over a thousand songs, including "God Bless America." Berlin's song "White Christmas" is the all-time best-selling song in the world.

Sarah Bernhardt—19th- and 20th-century France. The most renowned actress in the world during her time, she was referred to as "the Divine Sarah" by the French writer Victor Hugo.

Bershider Rebbe—18th- and 19th-century Eastern Europe. Hasidic rabbi.

Hayyim Nachman Bialik—19th- and 20th-century Russia and Israel. Writer, editor, essayist, and translator. Thought to be the most significant Hebrew poet of the modern era. Bialik saw **Ahad Ha-Am** as his mentor. Wrote "On the Slaughter" in response to the Kishinev pogroms. Gave expression to his people, their plight, and their dreams.

Alexander Bloch—19th- and 20th-century America. Musician.

Léon Blum—19th- and 20th-century France. Poet, writer, philosopher, socialist, political figure. The first Jew and first socialist to become premier of France, a post he held three times. Played a major role in France's support of Israel during the UN vote in 1947.

Ludwig Boerne—19th- and 20th-century Germany. Writer, philosopher.

Louis D. Brandeis—19th- and 20th-century America. Jurist, philosopher, Supreme Court Justice.

Joseph Hayyim Brenner—19th- and 20th-century Ukraine and Israel. Hebrew writer, poet.

Isaac Breuer—19th- and 20th-century Germany. Rabbi.

Abraham Arden Brill—19th- and 20th-century America. Psychiatrist, writer.

Sidney Brody—20th-century America. Writer.

Jacob Bronowski—20th-century Poland, England, and America. Mathematician, philosopher, writer. An authority on the poet William Blake. Concerned with science and human values, was UNESCO's head of projects. Wrote and hosted a public-television series.

Lenny Bruce—20th-century America. Humorist.

Martin Buber—19th- and 20th-century Austria, Germany, and Israel. Leader in the Zionist movement, philosopher, and theologian. Began studying Hasidism when he was twenty-six. Retold the stories of **Nachman of Bratslav** in German. At the onset of World War I Buber founded the Jewish National Committee in Berlin, which worked, among other duties, to ease the burden of Jews in Eastern Europe under German occupation. In his Zionist activities he urged that the needs of Arabs should also be taken into consideration. In 1923 his basic work of philosophical dialogue concerning self and the surrounding world, *Ich und Du* [*I and Thou*], was published. He translated the Bible into German with **Franz Rosenzweig**. During the rise of the Nazi party Buber gave lectures and talks on Jewish issues until 1935, when he was forbidden to do so. In 1938 he moved to Israel and became a professor of social philosophy at Hebrew University in Jerusalem. In witnessing the ongoing conflict between Arabs and Jews, Buber felt that compromise was as necessary as a solution. He lectured widely around the world and was considered a sage and taken to heart by people of widely different religious backgrounds.

Simcha Bunam—18th- and 19th-century Eastern Europe. Hasidic rabbi, known as the *Tzaddik* of Parsischa and as the Parsischarer.

George Burns—20th-century America. Comedian, entertainer, writer.

Cabala—See **Kabbala**.

Edward N. Calisch—19th- and 20th-century North America. Rabbi.

Elias Canetti—20th-century Bulgaria and England. A highly regarded novelist and playwright, his work is serious, marked by the world's cruelty and the failures that allow evil to exist. His work is written in German. In 1981 he won the Nobel Prize in Literature.

Benjamin N. Cardozo—19th- and 20th-century America. Jurist, Supreme Court justice.

Joseph Caro—15th- and 16th-century Israel. Rabbi and mystic. In 1564 wrote the Shulhan Aruk, "The Prepared Table," the code of Jewish law that remains in use today as the authorized outline of behavior for observant Jews around the world.

Bennett Cerf—20th-century America. Publisher, ally of writers, major figure in the 20th-century publishing industry.

Marc Chagall—19th- and 20th-century Russia and France. Painter. Spotted as a talent early in his life, Chagall's mother prevailed, despite his father's reservations, and the boy was enrolled in an art school. Chagall's work has been exhibited at every major museum in the world, and is included in the collections of the Vatican and the Israeli Knesset. Chagall is considered among the rarest of 20th-century artistic giants. His work, much of which draws on the simple images of his youth and its people, is magical in its color and line, filled with lyricism and poetic grace. The family name was Segal and the spelling "Chagall" was later adopted by the artist himself.

Chelm—A city in the southeastern portion of Poland. Oldest Jewish community in Poland, dating from around the 11th century. In a multitude of folklore stories Chelm became the seat of simpletons called the Wise Men of Chelm. In a 20th-century tragedy, the Germans during World War II destroyed all the Jewish municipal buildings, including the seven-hundred-year-old synagogue, and shot, or sent to concentration camps, much of the Jewish community. On November 6, 1942, the entire remaining Jewish population was sent to the Sobibor death camp for extermination.

"The Chofetz Chaim"—19th- and 20th-century Poland. Rabbi. Given name Israel Meir Kagan, also known as "the Radiner Rebbe" and Israel Meir ha-Cohen.

Felix Cohen—19th- and 20th-century America. Lawyer. As assistant solicitor at the United States Department of the Interior he led a fight in 1937 for the rights of Jewish immigrants who were not being hired by big businesses due to anti-Semitism.

Hermann Cohen—19th- and 20th-century Germany. Philosopher, writer.

Morris Raphael Cohen—19th- and 20th-century America. Scholar, writer, naturalist philosopher.

Moses Cordovero—16th-century Israel. *Safed,* sage, mystic, kabbalist.

Norman Cousins—20th-century America. Writer. One of America's most influential editors. Also a social philosopher, his later work was on the mind's ability to influence health.

Joseph Solomon Delmedigo—16th- and 17th-century Italy. Physician, pupil of Galileo.

Derek Eretz—one of the minor tractates in the Talmud, its name means "the way of the world." In the main deals with morality and customs, but as a term used in the Talmud it generally speaks to how one should act to others, and the ethics of human behavior.

Benjamin Disraeli—19th-century England. Politician, prime minister of Britain, social commentator, novelist. In 19th-century England the two major political figures were the prime ministers Gladstone and Disraeli, of whom this story is told: If you were invited to dinner and spent the evening next to Gladstone, you felt as if you had just dined with the wisest man in the empire. But if you were invited to dinner and spent the evening next to Disraeli, you came away thinking *you* were the wisest man in the empire.

Isaac D'Israeli—18th- and 19th-century England. Writer, father of Benjamin Disraeli.

Bob Dylan—20th-century America. Singer, songwriter, musical social philosopher. A major influence on the 1960s and early 1970s, brought together folk music, social activism, and rebellion. Given name Robert Zimmerman.

Abba Eban—20th-century South Africa, England, and Israel. Statesman, diplomat, and writer. Studied oriental languages and classics at Cambridge; also lecturer in Arabic and president of the student union. He served as a major in World War II with the British representatives in Cairo. Trained volunteers in Israel, and became Israel's first representative to the United Nations. Deputy prime minister under Levi Eshkol, Israel's foreign minister. Records and tapes have been made of his brilliant oratory.

Marcus Ehrenpreis—19th- and 20th-century Galicia and Sweden. Rabbi.

Albert Einstein—19th- and 20th-century Germany and America. Scientist, physicist, discoverer of the Theory of Relativity, and winner of the Nobel Prize. Considered to be one of the greatest scientific minds of all time. A friend of **Chaim Weizmann**, Einstein was actively involved in the support of Israel. This was not a hollow gesture by a famous scientist but the act of a sincerely kind man who throughout his life did not forget that he was forced to flee for his life from Nazism. Einstein demonstrated his real concern for humanity in his letter to Roosevelt about the destructive potential of atomic energy and in his endless hours spent on behalf of refugees. Einstein appears to have been a soul as rare as he was wise.

Eleazar Bar Kappara—3rd-century Israel. *Tanna* and *amora*.

Eleazar ben Azariah—1st-century Israel. *Tanna*.

Eleazar ben Judah—12th- and 13th-century Germany. Rabbi, kabbalist, philosopher, Talmudist.

Eleazar ben Judah (of Bartota)—1st- and 2nd-century Israel. *Tanna*.

Eleazar ben Pedat—3rd-century Israel. Sage, *amora*.

Eleazar the Great—11th-century Germany. Rabbi, philosopher. His efforts as a teacher of the Talmud and Talmudic commentary caused him to be referred to as *Hagadol,* "the Great." He is supposed to have left the document quoted in this book for his son and his work is a fine example of the unaffected ethical writing found often in Jewish medieval life. His given name was Eleazar ben Isaac.

Elijah ben Solomon, the Vilner Gaon—18th-century Poland/Lithuania. The name implies the "Sage of Vilna." Given name Elijah ben Solomon. Rabbi, philosopher, thought to be the foremost Talmudist of his day. Broadly educated, he brought a new scientific approach to study, and was thought by some to be the founder of the "modernist" movement in Orthodox Judaism. Given to asceticism and refusing of honors, because of his actions the term *Gaon* sometimes also implies "saint." See **Gaon**.

Elijah de Veali—18th-century Italy. Rabbi, poet, kabbalist. Full name Elijah ben Raphael de Veali.

Elimelech of Lyzhansk—18th-century Galicia. Hasidic rabbi, ethicist. His community also known as Lizhensk of Lezajsk.

Jacob Emden—18th-century Germany. Rabbi, Talmudist.

Levi Eshkol—19th- and 20th-century Russia and Israel. Labor leader, statesman. Born to a wealthy Hasidic family, he went to Israel when he was nineteen, worked in the agricultural fields, and fought in the Jewish Legion in World War I. He was arrested in Europe while trying to arrange arms for Israel. He played a vital role in the establishment of the Jewish defense forces and national water sources, and became minister of defense and prime minister of the state of Israel. Although at one time accused of hesitating in leadership roles, his capacity to work even with those with whom he disagreed is now seen as one of his great strengths. Birth name Levi Shkolnik.

Alter Esselin—20th-century Ukraine and America. Yiddish poet. Esselin emigrated at the age of sixteen and later prided himself on having spent his days as a "working man," living far from Yiddish centers in towns such as Milwaukee, where he finally settled. This gave him both poetic distance and melancholy, and he described his life as poet as one in which he drank the poison of songs mixed both with honey and arsenic. Born Ore Serebrenik.

Joseph Ezobi—13th-century France/Provence. Rabbi, poet, and scholar. A highly regarded writer, best known for his poem "Silver Plate," which makes reference to the offering of the princes of Israel to God and is a moving reminder to Ezobi's son to follow the ways of the Torah. Full name Jehoseph ben Hanan ben Nathan.

Emile Ludwig Fackenheim—20th-century Germany, Canada, America, and

Israel. Rabbi, scholar, philosopher, writer, and teacher. Fackenheim is a thinker who is sometimes referred to as a theological existentialist. A premise included in Fackenheim's work is the belief that the Divine is Israel's central issue.

Clifton Fadiman—20th-century America. Writer, radio show host, social philosopher. Editor, *Encyclopaedia Britannica*.

Jules Feiffer—20th-century America. Social cartoonist, dramatist, social critic, humorist.

Abraham L. Feinberg—20th-century America and Canada. Rabbi, writer, liberal social and political peace activist. Radio singing star under the name Anthony Frome.

Dianne Feinstein—20th-century America. Politician, mayor of San Francisco, United States senator from California.

Edna Ferber—19th- and 20th-century America. Writer, novelist.

Richard Feynman—20th-century America. Physicist, Nobel Prize winner, thinker, writer.

Louis Finkelstein—20th-century America. Rabbi.

Edmond Fleg—19th- and 20th-century France. Poet, playwright, essayist. A highly regarded French writer, much of whose work deals with Jews and Judaism. He took an active role with international Jewish organizations. A forest in Israel has been named in honor of him. Born Edmond Flegenheimer.

Abe Fortas—20th-century America. Lawyer, jurist. Son of a furniture woodworker from Tennessee. Adviser to the commission that laid the foundations for the United Nations. Fortas argued against the House Un-American Activities Committee. He was a lifelong friend of President Lyndon Baines Johnson. A justice of the United States Supreme Court, he was considered a first-rate legal scholar with a concern for individual rights. Bowing to pressure, Fortas resigned from the Supreme Court after being nominated for chief justice but denied confirmation under the accusation of financial impropriety, which he fully denied and which was never proved.

Anne Frank—20th-century Holland. Writer. After hiding with her family in Holland during the Nazi occupation, she was discovered and murdered by the Germans while still a child. Her *Diary* has provided global testimony to her tragedy, the larger horror, and the human spirit.

Felix Frankfurter—19th- and 20th-century Austria and America. Jurist, legal philosopher. He was brought to the United States by his parents when he was twelve, and subsequently went to Harvard. As an undergraduate he was a leading member of his class. He went to Harvard Law School, then went to work for United States Attorney, and later Secretary of War, Henry L. Stimson. In Washington he became friends with Justice Oliver Wendell Holmes. He was appointed professor at Harvard Law School, a post he held for twenty-five years until appointed a member of the United States Supreme Court. Held a close relationship with **Louis D. Brandeis**. Referring to himself as a Jew, Frankfurter said he was "a believing non-believer."

Viktor E. Frankl—20th-century Austria. Psychiatrist. Founder of existential psychotherapy, called "logotherapy."

Anna Freud—19th- and 20th-century Austria. Psychoanalyst. She did much of her work in the field of children's psychology. The youngest daughter of **Sigmund Freud**, she was a noted scientist in her own right.

Sigmund Freud—19th- and 20th-century Austria. Physician, father of psychoanalysis and its Freudian school, his role in comprehending the psychology of human beings and human psychological unrest has no equal. His theory of personality structure created the metaphors of the id, the ego, and the superego. After fleeing from the Nazis he died in London.

Betty Friedan—20th-century America. Writer, social philosopher, essayist, feminist.

Isaac Friedman—19th- and 20th-century Lithuania. Rabbi.

Milton Friedman—20th-century America. Economist, philosopher, writer. Professor of economics at the University of Chicago, and an adviser to President Richard M. Nixon. As a leader of the "Chicago school" of economic theory—as opposed to those who followed the thinking of John Maynard Keynes—he argued that controlling the money supply rather than taxes was the best way for the government to influence the economy. He wanted to do away with the welfare system and replace it with a "negative income tax" to provide available dollars for those below the poverty line to pay for their basic requirements. Among his many books, *A Monetary History of the United States,* written with Anna Schwarz, is considered among the major writings on the history of economics.

Erich Fromm—20th-century Germany and America. Psychologist.

Gastininer Rebbe—19th-century Eastern Europe. Hasidic rabbi.

Gaon (plural, Geonim)—the director of an academy of learning in post-talmudic times, particularly in Babylonia. Later a term for a rabbi or anyone whose learning was held in extremely high esteem.

Abraham Geiger—19th-century Germany. Rabbi.

Lionel Morris Gelber—20th-century America. Political scientist.

Gemara—This is the section of the Talmud in which the **amoraim** offer explanation, interpretation, and additional insights to the **Mishna**. The word *gemara* comes from the Aramaic and its literal translation means "tradition" or "completion."

Moses Gentili—17th- and 18th-century Italy. Rabbinical scholar, poet. Wrote significant religio-philosophic commentary on the Pentateuch. Given Italian name rendered in Hebrew is Moses Heifetz.

Gerer Rebbe—18th- and 19th-century Eastern Europe. Hasidic rabbi, greatly admired as both a sage and a saintly soul, often referred to as "the Gerer." Given name was Isaac Meyer of Ger.

Jonah ben Abraham Gerondi—13th-century Spain/Catalonia. Sage, theologian.

George Gershwin—19th- and 20th-century America. Composer, wrote "Swanee," recorded by Al Jolson. Composed a jazz symphony for Paul Whiteman called *Rhapsody in Blue,* which translated jazz to the concert stage (and which was first performed in New York with Gershwin at the piano). He wrote *An American in Paris,* considered by many to be among the finest contributions to 20th-century American composition. His incredible volume of work for movies and Broadway included *Strike Up the Band, Of Thee I Sing,* and *Porgy and Bess.* The lyricist on much of Gershwin's work was his brother Ira.

Allen Ginsberg—20th-century America. Poet. A central figure in articulating the "Beat Generation," and a senior figure in 20th-century poetry. His two best-known works are *Howl* and *Kaddish.* Known as a gentle iconoclast.

Louis Ginzberg—20th-century America. Poet, scholar.

Seligman Ulman Ginzberger—15th-century Germany. Moralist.

Natalia Ginzburg—20th-century Italy. Playwright, novelist. Her first husband, Leon Ginzburg, was imprisoned and murdered by the Nazis in Rome. Her work is marked by pessimism against hope and an unusual use of language, which draws upon her family's background, including German, Spanish, and Jewish expressions. Her work has been produced in London by the National Theatre.

Glueckel of Hameln—17th- and 18th-century Germany. Writer, Yiddish memoirist. Mother of twelve children. Wrote her famous *Memoirs* so that her children and grandchildren might know more about their family. Often used parables and fables as metaphors to give moral examples.

Isaac Goldberg—19th- and 20th-century America. Writer.

Emma Goldman—19th- and 20th-century Lithuania and America. Anarchist, lecturer, philosopher, and writer. Advocated birth control before World War I. Her opposition to conscription in that war led to imprisonment and deportation to Russia. She fled Bolshevism to fight in the Spanish Civil War. Saw the state as a destructive force in the face of individual freedom.

Samuel Goldwyn—20th-century America. Motion picture producer.

Ellen Goodman—20th-century America. Writer, journalist, syndicated columnist. A social philosopher who writes with humor and intelligence.

Judah Leib (Leon) Gordon—19th-century Russia. Hebrew poet, thinker.

Heinrich Graetz—19th-century Germany. Historian.

Hannah Green—20th-century America. Writer, novelist.

Moritz Gudemann—19th- and 20th-century Austria. Rabbi.

Richard H. Guggenheimer—20th-century America. Painter, critic.

Haggadah—The root of this word is from the Hebrew, meaning "story/tale" or "the telling." Examples include the Haggadah that is read during the Passover Seder, telling the story of the Exodus from Egypt, and the collections of stories, metaphors, parables, folklore, and anecdotes that can be found throughout talmudic literature.

halakah—The root of this word is from the Hebrew, meaning "guidance" or "step," as in "this should be your guide in the way that you walk." Halakah is the legal aspect of Jewish law that encompasses and structures every act of an observant Jew's life as distinguished from understanding derived from the metaphors, ethics, or anecdotes that make up **Haggadah**.

Aaron Halevi—13th-century Barcelona. Talmudic commentator, writer.

Judah Halevi—4th-century Palestine. *Amora*. Full name Judah Halevi ben Shalom.

Judah Halevi—11th- and 12th-century Spain and Israel. Renowned Hebrew poet and philosopher. Although much of his poetry deals with love, the most significant number focus on friendship and eulogy. The best known of his poems are "The Poems of Zion."

Solomon Hanau—17th- and 18th-century Germany. Writer, scholar of language.

Hanina ben Dosa—1st-century Israel. *Tanna*.

Abraham Hasdai—13th-century Spain. Hebrew translator, writer, scholar.

Hasid (plural, Hasidim)—18th- and 20th-century Russia. The worldwide term for a follower of the Hasidic movement begun by the **Ba'al Shem Tov**. The root of the word *hasid* means "pious." The movement has broken into several main branches over time. Many of its teachers have taken the names of the communities in which they lived or taught. Hasidic belief, engendered by the Ba'al Shem Tov, was that joy and fervent, almost ecstatic, prayer (including through music and dance) was the high road to the Divine. A central role in Hasidic communities was the position of the *rebbe*. The *rebbe*, while a rabbi, was seen as more than a teacher, as a patriarchal figure of esteem who influenced every aspect of his followers' lives.

Hayyim ben Leibush of Zans—See **Hayyim Halberstram of Zans**.

Hayyim Halberstram of Zans—19th-century Galicia. Hasidic rabbi.

Ben Hecht—19th- and 20th-century America. Journalist, playwright, novelist, screenwriter. Quoted as saying: "When I came to Hollywood, I took off my mind and put on a sport coat."

Jascha Heifetz—20th-century Lithuania and America. Virtuoso concert violinist who played with the Berlin Philharmonic Orchestra when he was eleven. At the outbreak of the Russian Revolution his family emigrated to the United States via Siberia and Japan. Also a rare and talented pianist.

Heinrich Heine—19th-century Germany and France. Poet, philosopher, essayist. Considered among the greatest German lyric poets, and certainly the greatest Jewish writer who ever wrote in German, Heine was both prolific and extremely popular as a writer. He focused his pen and satirical wit on religious hate and reactionary politics. Attacked for this by anti-Semites, and fearing police arrest as well as the prohibition of sales of his writing, Heine left for France after the liberating July Revolution of 1848. He never returned for any prolonged period to Germany. Knew **Karl Marx** as an acquaintance. Heine suffered from spinal illness and paralyzing disease as he grew older, assigning him, as he put it, to a "mattress grave." Anti-Semitic attitudes fueled many of the German "literary" attacks on Heine. The municipality of Dusseldorf once refused a statue of him (it has since been relocated to New York); another statue, once in the possession of the empress of Austria, became the focal point of a riot in Hamburg, was later used by the Nazis for target practice, and is now in Toulon, France. His first name was originally Hayyim or Harry. Heine, although sometimes ambivalent or antagonistic to his Judaism, said: "I make no secret of my Judaism, to which I have not returned, because I have never left it."

Joseph Heller—20th-century America. Novelist. Best known for his study of the absurdity and tragedy of the military in *Catch-22*.

Lillian Hellman—20th-century America. Writer, dramatist, social philosopher.

Theodor Herzl—19th- and 20th-century Hungary and Austria. Journalist, social philosopher, founder of political Zionism. Herzl received a doctorate in law from the University of Vienna, where he experienced anti-Semitism. Later left law to write short stories and plays. His work displays a keen sense of observation of the human condition and an air of sadness about the destiny of his characters. He traveled throughout Europe, became a correspondent for the Vienna *Neue Freie Presse,* and witnessed the growth of anti-Semitism in France. He wrote a play, *Das Ghetto,* in 1894 and tried to put the "Jewish" issue on the stage. Herzl was present during the hysteria of the Dreyfus case in Paris and, hearing the cries of French mobs yelling "Death to the Jews," became convinced that henceforth his life, which was only to last another ten years, would be dedicated to the return of Jews to their own state. He was often disappointed by the response of philanthropists and political figures.

Abraham Joshua Heschel—20th-century America. Rabbi, writer, philosopher, social activist, inspiring soul, caring teacher.

Moses Hess—19th-century Germany. Philosopher, socialist.

Hillel the Elder—1st century B.C.E. and 1st century C.E. Babylonia. Considered the greatest sage during the time of the Second Temple. The title *Elder (Zaken)* was usually awarded to someone who was a member of the Supreme Bet Din (Supreme Court). A sage known for his humility, ethics, and pursuit of peace. A school of sages who followed in the tenor of his teachings was called *Bet Hillel,* House of Hillel.

Sidney Hillman—19th- and 20th-century America. Labor leader.

Samson Raphael Hirsch—19th-century Germany. Writer and rabbi. The most important leader of Orthodox Judaism in Germany in the 19th century. His two most important works were *Nineteen Letters on Judaism* and *Essays on Israel's Duties in the Diaspora.* Hirsch thought that the study of Torah needed to be joined with a worldly occupation and that the ideal, the "Israel-Man," was an enlightened Jew who followed the requirements of his religion. He thought of sincere Judaism as a manifestation of the Divine which could be observed in the Torah and nature. He brilliantly translated the Penateuch into German, and this, further translated into English, remains a central text in English-speaking Orthodox homes and synagogues.

Samuel Hoffman—20th-century America. Writer.

Huna—3rd-century Babylonia. ***Amora***.

Fannie Hurst—19th- and 20th-century America. Novelist, playwright.

Isachar Hurwitz—19th-century Poland. Hebrew author. Full name Isachar Dov Ha-Levi Hurwitz.

Ilai—2nd-century Israel. ***Tanna***.

Immanuel of Rome—13th- and 14th-century Italy. Hebrew poet, scholar. Forced to flee Rome when the pope issued a decree against the Jewish community in 1321. His work, laced with wit and exhibiting a clear control of language, is similar to that of **Solomon ibn Gabirol** and **Judah Halevi**. Full name Immanuel ben Solomon of Rome. In Italian he is referred to as Manoello Giudeo—"Immanuel the Jew."

Ishmael ben Elisha—1st- and 2nd-century Israel. *Tanna.*

Israel ben Joseph Al-Nakawa—14th-century Spain. Philosopher, writer. Dealt with moral issues.

Israel Meir ha-Cohen—See "**The Chofetz Chaim**."

Vladimir Jabotinsky—19th- and 20th-century Russia and Israel. Poet, writer, lecturer, linguist, soldier, political activist, and Zionist leader. Although often philosophically and violently opposed to other early Jewish leaders in Israel, especially as regarded Germany, Arabs, and the English, Jabotinsky was an inspiring leader who gave generously of his life so that Jews could protect themselves in Israel and beyond. A political giant in the modern history of the Jewish people, Jabotinsky, who wrote novels and plays, spoke seven languages and translated Edgar Allan Poe's "The Raven" into Hebrew, could have as easily spent his life as a scholar, writer, and teacher had not circumstances otherwise dictated.

Jacob—2nd-century Israel. *Tanna*, rabbi. Student of **Rabbi Meir** and teacher of Rabbi **Judah Ha-Nasi**. Full name Jacob ben Korshai.

Joseph Jacobs—19th- and 20th-century England. Historian, social commentator and critic, scholar of folklore.

Jedadiah ben Abraham Bedersi—See **Jedaiah of Béziers**.

Jedaiah of Béziers—13th- and 14th-century France. Physician, poet, philosopher. Given name Jedadiah ben Abraham Bedersi. A rationalist, his work was significantly influenced by Maimonides.

Johanan ben Nappha—3rd-century Palestine. *Amora.*

Johanan ben Zakkai—1st-century Israel. Rabbi, sage, a leader of sages. Often referred to as *Rabban,* "our master." A follower of **Hillel**, and his appointed successor to be "the father of next generations." He established the academy in Javneh, Judah, and fought the "temple cult" in Jerusalem. Among his students was **Rabbi Akiba**, the towering sage in the years to come. Many stories surround Zakkai's life.

Jonathan ben Joseph—2nd-century Israel. *Tanna.*

Erica Jong—20th-century America. Writer.

Jose ben Halafta—2nd-century Israel. *Tanna.*

Jose ben Hanina—3rd-century Israel. *Amora.*

Jose ben Joezer of Zeredah—2nd-century B.C.E. Israel. Sage.

Jose ben Judah—2nd-century Israel. *Tanna*.

Jose-Ber of Brisk—see **Joseph Baer Soloveichik**.

Joseph ben Hiyya—3rd-century Babylonia. *Amora*.

Joseph ibn Shem Tov—15th-century Spain. Writer, scholar.

Josephus—1st-century Israel. A central figure in Jewish-Hellenistic letters and an important Jewish historian. General, commander of the Galilee at the beginning of the Jewish War in 66 C.E., he accompanied Titus during the conquest of Jerusalem. As a participant in and recorder of historical events Josephus offers the most fascinating window on his period. Also known as Josephus Flavius.

Joshua ben Hanania—2nd-century Israel. *Tanna*.

Joshua ben Karha—2nd-century Israel. *Tanna*.

Joshua ben Levi—3rd-century Israel. *Amora*.

Joshua ben Perahia—2nd-century B.C.E. Jerusalem.

Judah Al-Harizi—13th-century Spain. Hebrew poet, translator, and scholar.

Judah ben Asher—13th- and 14th-century Germany and Spain. Talmudist.

Judah ben Samuel ha-Hasid—11th- and 12th-century Germany. Rabbi, philosopher, and mystic. His name means "Judah the Pious." Sometimes referred to as "Rabbi Judah of Regensburg." His most significant work in literary ethics was the *Sefer Hasidim,* "Book of the Pious," which he authored.

Judah ben Tema—2nd-century Israel. *Tanna*.

Judah ha-Nasi—2nd- and 3rd-century Judea. A sage of the highest order, editor of the **Mishna**, referred to as *"rabbenu ha-kodosh"* ("our holy teacher") or "rabbi," supposedly born on the day **Rabbi Akiba** died. Considered a savior of Israel.

Judah ibn Tibbon—12th-century Spain and France. Writer, Hebrew scholar, translator.

Kabbala—Jewish mystical lore. Kabbalists believed that there was a truth beyond reason and only by penetrating this mystery could one come to be with the One. While there is a tradition of religiously centered mysticism over thousands of years in Judaism there is also a ruling that a student should not study Kabbala until after the foundation of Torah and Talmud and until one is no less than forty years of age. The word *Kabbala* itself, and its entire substructure of spiritual arenas, is but one of many terms used to describe the mystical consciousness in Judaism.

Kaddish—Hebrew prayer (a) recited for those who have passed away, though it has no reference to death, and (b) glorifying the Lord and recited at regular transitional intervals in the Hebrew prayer service. Kaddish is taken from the Aramaic with the word root meaning "holy" and "consecration" in Hebrew. Aramaic was the language spoken by the Jews at the time of the Second Temple and during exile in Babylonia (see Time Chart).

Franz Kafka—19th- and 20th-century Prague. Czech-German novelist. Kafka's works left a significant philosophical and psychological impact on 20th-century thinking and literature. The term "Kafkaesque," a word used around the world, reflects the individual caught in a bizarre and contorted world.

Israel Meir Kagan—See **"The Chofetz Chaim."**

Leib Kagan—Circa 20th-century Russia. Rabbi.

Otto Kahn—19th- and 20th-century Germany and America. Banker, philanthropist, patron of the arts. Born into a historic banking family, served in a German elite cavalry unit, rose through talent, family, and marriage in banking-industry positions in Germany, London, and New York. By the age of thirty was one of the most highly regarded banking minds in the United States. He opposed the manner in which foreign war debts burdened Europe after World War I, wanting instead to extract observable commitments to peace. He gave significant financial support to schools, minorities, and the arts. As chairman of the Metropolitan Opera, was key to the success in bringing Toscanini to New York.

Kallah—One of the minor tractates in the Talmud. A student is considered learned when he can answer a question concerning **halakah** even from the section of Kallah. Also used as a term for the Hebrew months of Elul and Adar when, during the talmudic period, large numbers of students and sages would come together to learn Torah in Babylonia—the **rav** of the academy would announce what would be learned during the next "Kallah" and that would be the "Kallah tractate," which various sages and scholars would use as their focus in the interim period. *Kallah* means "bride" in Hebrew.

Mordecai M. Kaplan—19th- and 20th-century America. Rabbi, professor, founder of the Reconstructionist movement.

Kariver Rebbe—18th- and 19th-century Eastern Europe. Hasidic rabbi.

Joseph Karo—See **Joseph Caro**.

Gustav Karpeles—19th-century Germany. Literary historian.

Nahman Kasovir—18th-century Galicia. Rabbi. Known as Nahman of Kasovir, or Kasover.

Moses R. Kaufman—20th-century America. Thinker.

Walter Kaufmann—20th-century Germany and America. Professor of philosophy of religion, social philosophy, and history of ideas.

Victor Kiam—20th-century America. Businessman, entrepreneur.

Henry Kissinger—20th-century Germany and America. Professor of political science, foreign policy adviser to statesmen, U.S. secretary of state, author, political philosopher, winner of the Nobel Peace Prize.

Jacob Klatzkin—19th- and 20th-century Russia, Germany, America, and Switzerland. Writer, philosopher, brilliant Hebrew essayist. He and lifelong friend Nahum Goldmann served as the initiating force of the *Encyclopedia Judaica,* for which Klatzkin later served as editor in chief.

Kobriner Rebbe—18th- and 19th-century Poland. Hasidic rabbi, **tzaddik**, remembered for his honesty and his caring for his disciples (he would write them long letters of support and encouragement), his simple sayings, his leadership in ethics by example, and his insistence on deeds of caring rather than lengthy fasts or extreme asceticism. The last of his direct descendants, his great-grandson, was murdered in the Holocaust. His name is taken from the town of Kobrin, formerly in Poland and later in the USSR. His full name was Moses ben Israel Polier of Kobrin.

Arthur Koestler—20th-century Hungary and England. Novelist, philosopher, journalist. Changed from writing in Hungarian to German when he was seventeen, then from German to English when he was thirty-five. Participated, fought, and in some cases was imprisoned for activities in the USSR and the Spanish Civil War. Bitterly disenchanted with politics, he sought to understand the human role in modern society.

Abraham Kohn—19th-century Austria. Rabbi.

Leopold Kompert—19th-century Austria. Writer.

Abraham Isaac Kook—19th- and 20th-century Russia/Latvia and Israel. Renowned rabbi, rabbinic authority, mystic, and philosopher. First Ashkenazi chief rabbi of the modern state of Israel. Felt the return to the land of Israel stood for the beginning of divine redemption.

Zvi Judah Kook—20th-century Russia/Latvia and Israel. Rabbi, scholar, *rosh yeshiva.* The sole son of **Abraham Isaac Kook**, he had great impact on thousands of yeshiva students and brought not only Torah learning but also a respect for the state of Israel to centers of wisdom.

Koretser Rabbi—18th-century Lithuania. Traditionalist who was greatly influenced by the **Ba'al Shem Tov** and became a Hasidic rabbi. His teaching was premised on humility and the sanctity of the Divine. Given name Phineas ben Abraham of Korets.

Kotzker Rebbe—See **Menahem Mendel of Kotsk**.

Karl Kraus—19th- and 20th-century Bohemia and Austria. Social critic, satirist, poet, and writer. One of the supreme stylists of the German language.

Nahman Krochmal—18th- and 19th-century Galicia. Philosopher, writer, historian. One of the prime movers in the Haskalah (the urge toward "enlightenment") movement in Eastern Europe, and one of the early thinkers in what came to be known as "the science of Judaism."

Louis Kronenberger—20th-century America. Writer, editor, critic.

Maurice Lamm—20th-century America. Rabbi, scholar, writer. Widely known for his text presenting Orthodox Judaism's stance on death and dying.

Norman Lamm—20th-century America. Rabbi, scholar, writer, and educator. President of Yeshiva University. Regarded as a major thinker and force in modern Jewish Orthodoxy.

Ezekiel Landau—18th-century Poland. Rabbi.

Ann Landers—20th-century America. Widely syndicated advice columnist. Born Esther Friedman. Sister of **Abigail Van Buren**.

Bernard Lazare—19th- and 20th-century France. Writer, social philosopher.

Emma Lazarus—19th-century America. Poet. Best known for her sonnet inscribed on the base of the Statue of Liberty in 1903. Her early writing drew the notice of Ralph Waldo Emerson. The pogroms in Russia in the 1880s and the condition of immigrant Jews in whose cause and care she was active influenced the direction of her work. Wrote "The New Colossus" in 1883 with the hope that this sonnet would reflect the caring and needed shoulder America might offer those teeming to her shore.

Jacob Lazarus—19th- and 20th-century Rumania and Canada. Tinsmith.

Judah Leib Lazerov—19th- and 20th-century America. In the tradition of **Maggidim** he preached in Yiddish.

Fran Lebowitz—20th-century America. Writer, humorist, wit.

Herbert H. Lehman—19th- and 20th-century America. Banker, statesman, politician, governor of New York, senator from New York. Helped found the American Jewish Joint Distribution Committee; headed the United Nations Relief and Rehabilitation Administration. As a senator fought the House Un-American Activities Committee and Senator McCarthy. A supporter of Israel.

Moshe Leib—18th- and 19th-century Galicia. Hasidic rabbi. Known as Moshe Leib of Sasov.

Noah Lekhivitzer—18th- and 19th-century Eastern Europe. Hasidic rabbi.

Max Lerner—20th-century Russia and America. Journalist, author, editor, and academic. Edited *The Nation*. Took an approach that was both scholarly and journalistic in his writing on society and government. An intelligent, caring social commentator.

Oscar Levant—20th-century America. Writer, composer, wit, pianist, film and television personality.

Levi—3rd-century Israel. *Amora.*

Levi ben Gerson—13th- and 14th-century France. Philosopher, physician, writer.

Levi Isaac ben Meir of Berdichev—18th- and 19th-century Galicia. Hasidic rabbi, known as a true **tzaddik**. A renowned Torah scholar, he influenced and was truly loved by many who followed him. He felt that joy and oneness with God were central to spiritual elevation, and that a person should pray "with their entire heart and soul because then a person's spirit is so joyous it rises from the physical world." He brought Yiddish to both prayer and song. Became the subject of poems and stories. Also known as Levi Yitzhok.

Shemarya Levin—19th- and 20th-century Russia. Zionist, preacher.

Sam Levinson—20th-century America. Humorist, writer, entertainer.

Elias (Elijah) Levita—15th- and 16th-century Germany and Italy. Hebrew philologist and grammarian, poet.

Kurt Zadek Lewin—19th- and 20th-century Germany and America. Psychologist, author, professor. Left Germany with the rise of the Nazi party. Professor at Stanford. Directed research at Massachusetts Institute of Technology. A founding intellect in the study of group dynamics, he saw Zionism as a requirement for Jews who, as a people without their own land, were lacking their sociological center. Considered among the most original thinkers in the field of psychology.

Ludwig Lewisohn—19th- and 20th-century America. Critic.

Joshua Loth Liebman—20th-century America. Rabbi.

Max Lilenthal—19th-century America. Rabbi, writer.

Israel Salanter Lipkin—19th-century Lithuania. Renowned rabbi, philosopher, and moralist, who was the guiding figure and founder of Musar, a moralist movement.

Walter Lippmann—19th- and 20th-century America. Writer, journalist. Served as an assistant to the philosopher George Santayana. His work had significant influence on American public policy. A founder of *The New Republic*. Won two Pulitzer Prizes. His writing was syndicated to over 250 publications in 25 countries.

Solomon Loeb—19th- and 20th-century Germany and America. Prominent banker.

Herbert M. J. Loewe—19th- and 20th-century England. Philosopher, scholar.

Meyer London—19th- and 20th-century America. Political activist, socialist. Member of United States Congress.

Judah Low—16th-century Prague. Rabbi, talmudist, moralist, and mathematician. An esteemed sage known for his pious manner and ascetic ways, held in lofty regard by Jews and Gentiles. His reputation as the rabbi who brought the Prague golem to life is completely without any historical evidence except to the contrary. His ideas have seen new light in the twentieth century through the efforts in Israel of Rabbi **Abraham Isaac Kook**. Full name Judah Loew ben Bezalel.

Ernst Lubitsch—19th- and 20th-century Germany and America. Film director and producer. Played comic roles in Max Reinhardt's troupe in Germany. Produced early films that brought, among other European stars, Pola Negri to the attention of audiences. Came to America and directed Mary Pickford. Had a comic lightheartedness that was considered the "Lubitsch touch." Directed Greta Garbo in *Ninotchka*.

Lubliner Rebbe—18th- and 19th-century Poland. Hasidic rabbi.

Moses Hayyim Luzzatto—18th-century Italy. Hebrew poet, mystic, kabbalist, writer, ethicist, and philosopher.

Samuel David Luzzatto—19th-century Italy. Scholar, biblical commentator and translator, philosopher, writer.

I Maccabees—Historical work covering 175–135 B.C.E. The only historical source for the period. Covers the conquest of Alexander the Great and the Revolt of the Maccabees. The first leader of the revolt of the Hasmoneans (a family title) against Antiochus IV Epiphanes in 167 B.C.E. was Mattathias, a priest, sometimes referred to as a "high priest," who came from the village Modi'in. Mattathias headed the forces for a year before he died, leaving two of his five sons to take his lead: Judah Maccabee headed the military aspect and Simeon the Hasmonean was designated as the counselor.

Maggid (plural, Maggidim)—A Hebrew term for "preacher" or "teacher," a wandering storyteller or preacher who played a particularly significant role in 18th- and 19th-century Eastern European Jewish life. Maggidim were often learned, and even those who weren't were very often more effective in speaking to the common man than the great local scholar or rabbi who was "supposed" to study and not expected to give sermons. Most spoke Yiddish, and while some screamed against sin, most told fabulous stories and tales.

Norman Mailer—20th-century America. Writer, essayist.

Maimonides—12th-century Spain. Renowned rabbi, sage, physician, writer, philosopher, and theologian. Traveled from the Iberian penninsula to Egypt, where he died. Wrote and compiled *Guide for the Perplexed* c. 1190, and the *Thirteen Principles of Faith,* which can be found in virtually every prayer book. Known in rabbinic literature as "Rambam," derived from Rabbi Moses ben Maimon. (See **Mishneh Torah** for further commentary on Maimonides and this central work of Jewish scholarship and faith.) Given name Moses ben Maimon.

Bernard Malamud—20th-century America. Writer. His books *The Natural* and *The Fixer,* for which he won the National Book Award and the Pulitzer Prize, were made into motion pictures. His novels and short stories offer a unique view of the longing and isolation of the human experience and an even more particular view of the Eastern European Jew's sense of America.

Benjamin Mandelstamm—19th-century Russia. Writer, Hebrew author.

Louis L. Mann—20th-century America. Rabbi, philosopher.

Marcel Marceau—20th-century France. Mime artist known around the world. Described his work as "the art of expressing feelings by attitudes and not a means of expressing words through gestures." His father was murdered by the Nazis. Marceau worked for the underground in France during the war and participated in the smuggling of children out of occupied France and into Switzerland.

Groucho Marx—19th- and 20th-century America. Comedian, star of vaudeville, stage, radio, television, and screen. Groucho (Julius) was one of the famed Marx Brothers with his siblings Chico (Leonard), Harpo (Adolph), Gummo (Milton), and Zeppo (Herbert).

Karl Marx—19th-century Germany. Writer, socialist, political philosopher. Father of Communist theory.

Masada—King Herod's fortress tower located on the rocky heights between the valley of the Dead Sea and the Judean desert, the location of the final stand of the Jewish Zealots in the War on Rome in the first century. When the Romans finally took the fortress they discovered that the Jews had committed mass suicide rather than submit. Today it is the location where new members of the Israeli Defense Forces are taken for the final swearing in, both for the memory and for the promise of "never again."

André Maurois—19th- and 20th-century France. Writer, philosopher, renowned biographer. His work gave incredible attention to the psychological development of his characters. Elected to the French Academy. Given name Emile Herzog.

Milton Mayer—20th-century America. Journalist, writer, social philosopher.

Golda Meir—20th-century Russia, America, and Israel. Zionist, labor and political leader. Born at the very end of the 19th century into extreme poverty, she witnessed as a young child the pogroms against the Jews in Russia. Emigrated with her family to America in 1906. Graduated from high school in Milwaukee and attended a teachers' college. Turned to Zionism as her own memories were influenced by the slaughter of Jews during the Russian Revolution. Her own experiences of poverty and the conditions of the poor had already made her a political socialist. She became an effective and demanding speaker both in Yiddish and in English whether on Milwaukee street corners or in large halls. Moved to Israel with her husband when she was twenty-three and settled on a kibbutz. She was soon drawn into political activism and played a significant role in labor and foreign affairs, rising to secretary of labor and foreign minister before she eventually became prime minister of the state of Israel. Golda Meir survived wars in politics and against her country on the battlefield, and gave of her life until there was no more to give. Those who knew her admired her incredible strength of character and the gentle soul within. Born Golda Mabovitch, her married name was Golda Myerson.

Rabbi Meir—2nd-century Israel. Sage, ***tanna***.

Mekilta—An Aramaic word meaning "a measure," applied by the *amoraim* to signify a collection of halakic material, often midrashic in nature.

Mekilta of Rabbi Ishmael—3rd-century halakic Midrash on the Book of Exodus offering exegesis by chapter and verse. The language is mainly Hebrew, with some Latin and Greek terms. It is more the product of Rabbi Ishmael's school of learning than of Rabbi Ishmael himself. First printed in Constantinople and then Venice in the 16th century.

Samuel Max Melamed—19th- and 20th-century Lithuania, Germany, and America. Writer, editor, scholar.

Menachem ben Solomon ha-Meiri—13th- and 14th-century France. Scholar, talmudic commentator.

Menahem Mendel of Kotsk—18th- and 19th-century Poland. Hasidic rabbi, one of the Hasidic movement's most original leaders, sought "truth" in all things. Active in Polish revolution against the czars. Lived the last twenty years of his life in complete solitude.

Mendele (Moscher Sforim)—19th- and 20th-century Russia. Writer, satirist in both Hebrew and Yiddish. Full given name Mendele Moscher Sforim; pen name Sholom Jacob Abramowitz.

Moses Mendelssohn—18th-century Germany. Philosopher, writer, scholar.

Isaac Meyer of Ger—See the **Gerer Rebbe**.

Bette Midler—20th-century America. Singer, comedian, motion picture actress.

Midrash (plural, Midrashim)—A particular kind of rabbinic literature employing homilies, biblical interpretation, stories, and sermons meant to enlighten. There are many works of Midrash which speak to halakah, the legal aspect of rabbinic literature, but far and away the majority of Midrashim address Haggadah, the nonlegal aspects of rabbinic literature and stories. The name *Midrash* comes from the Hebrew root *drsh,* which in the main can be translated to mean "to seek," "to investigate," and "to examine."

Midrash Asseret ha-Diberot—7th- to 11th-century work more narrative than midrashic, primarily composed of stories. The name means "Midrash of the Ten Commandments."

Midrash ha-Gadol—13th-century Yemenite rabbinic text focusing on the Bible, anonymous in its origin but that scholars now attribute to David Ben Amram Adani (from Aden). A mainly older work by rabbis from talmudic times, it is very helpful in studying **Maimonides**, as it helps to discover sources to which Maimonides had access. The name means "the large Midrash."

Midrash Rabbah—5th- to 10th-century Palestine. A compilation of sayings, stories, sermons, and other *haggadic* material offered in response to the Pentateuch, the Song of Songs, Lamentations, Ecclesiastes, Ruth, and Esther. See **Midrash**.

Midrash Samuel—Midrashic exegesis and commentary on the Book of Samuel.

Midrash Shoher Tob—See **Shoher Tob**.

Midrash Tehillim I—circa 9th–12th century. Exegetical midrashic material on the Book of Psalms. (*Tehillim* means "psalms" in Hebrew.)

Arthur Miller—20th-century America. Playwright. Winner of two Pulitzer Prizes, considered to be one of the foremost dramatists of his age. At one time married to the actress Marilyn Monroe.

Mishna—The earliest major compilation of the Oral Law of the sages, *tannaim.* The editor of this code was Judah ha-Nasi (The Prince), circa 200 C.E. The word *Mishna* is drawn from the Hebrew root verb *shanah,* which means "to repeat," as it was in this way that one studied, and took to heart, the Oral Law—by verbally repeating the historic learning prior to this effort by ha-Nasi. All aspects of the Oral Law, *midrash, halakhot,* and *haggadot* are included in the Mishna.

Mishneh Torah—12th-century effort by **Maimonides**, taking ten years to write. In Maimonides' own words, "In our days . . . the wisest of our wise have disappeared . . . the laws . . . which they sought to make understandable . . . are now only comprehended by a few. . . . this regards the Talmud, Babylonian and Jerusalem, and the Sifra, Sifrei, and Tosefta, all requiring a wide mind, a wise soul, and a great deal of study. . . . [Therefore, so] one might learn . . . the proper way regarding what is permitted and what is not . . . I, Moses, the son of Maimon the Sephardi, have turned to this and relying on God's assistance, blessed be He, studied diligently all these works . . . so the entire Oral Law might become . . . known to all." The Mishneh Torah classifies by subject the complete talmudic and post-talmudic halakic material using an organized approach that had never previously been tried in Jewish scholarship. The work is set into fourteen books, each dealing with a different section in Jewish legal prudence. As each Hebrew letter has a numerical function, the number fourteen translates into the Hebrew word *yad,* which means "hand," and the Mishneh Torah is consequently often referred to by the alternative name *Yad ha-Hazakah,* "the strong hand."

Claude G. Montefiore—19th- and 20th-century England. Scholar.

Moses Montefiore—18th- and 19th-century England. Philanthropist. Sheriff of London, knighted. Made seven trips to Israel; initiated and supported a scheme to buy land in Israel for Jews to use in agricultural endeavors. Considered best-known English Jew of the 19th century.

Moses ben Maimon—See **Maimonides**.

Moses ben Nahman—See **Nachmanides**.

Moses ibn Ezra—11th- and 12th-century Spain. Philosopher, scholar, poet.

Moses of Evreux—13th-century France. Tosafist. He and his brothers Isaac and Samuel were known as "the scholars of Evreux." Students from afar came to study with the brothers, including **Jonah ben Abraham Gerondi**, who was to be a sage in the following generation. Those who studied with "the scholars of Evreux" were offered more opportunity for independent study and questioning of the teacher than usually allowed in these communities of scholarship.

Paul Muni—19th- and 20th-century America. Stage and screen actor. Began as an actor in Yiddish theater. Won an Academy Award. Born Muni Weisenfreund.

Abraham Myerson—19th- and 20th-century America. Psychiatrist.

Nachman of Bratslav—18th- and 19th-century Podolia. Hasidic rabbi and **tzaddik**. A great-grandson of the **Ba'al Shem Tov**, he felt obstacles blocked the human path but completely denied despair. He felt the divine was always present everywhere, even in evil, and that we hold on in life through faith and prayer, both of which are buoyed through music, dance, joy, and consistent and critical self-observation. Nachman of Bratslav was followed by a school of thinking and faith that remains to this day as the Bratzlaver Hasidim. Full name was Nachman ben Simha, the Bratzlaver.

Nachmanides—12th- and 13th-century Spain and Israel. Rabbi, physician, poet, philosopher, kabbalist. One of the most renowned Talmudists throughout the Middle Ages, he wrote extensive commentary on the Bible. Additionally known as Nahamani and Ramban, which was an acronym for *Rabbi Moses ben Nachman*. An adviser to King James I, he was forced by James to publicly present and defend Jewish views against spokespeople for the Church. Nachmanides was brilliant, but under constant pressure to recant he emigrated to Israel. His commentary on the Torah was begun in Spain but concluded in Israel and was a significant effort of his old age. Many of his writings on halakah are considered classics in rabbinic literature and have significantly influenced the work of those who followed. A significant aspect of his genius was his emphasis on those who study to see the "theme," both internal and integrated, without losing the "detail" in comprehending the halakah of Talmud.

Nahman ben Jacob—1st-century Israel. ***Tanna***.

Nahum of Gimzo—1st-century Israel. ***Tanna***.

Isaac Nappaha—3rd- and 4th-century Israel. ***Amora***. Given name Isaac ben Eleazar.

Nathan—2nd-century Israel. ***Tanna***.

Nathan of Nemirov—18th- and 19th-century Russia. Hasidic writer, author, philosopher.

George Jean Nathan—19th- and 20th-century America. Writer. The foremost drama critic of his period. Founder, along with H. L. Mencken, of *The American Mercury;* founder, with Theodore Dreiser, Eugene O'Neill, and others, of *The American Spectator.* A man of knowledge, vital insight, and personal courage.

Paul Nathan—19th- and 20th-century Germany. Caring leader of his community.

Louis Nizer—20th-century England and America. Attorney, author.

Max Nordau—19th- and 20th-century Hungary and France. Critic, physician, philosopher, Zionist. By the sheer weight of his intellect and capacity he had huge influence on many other thinkers around the world.

Raphael Norzi—16th-century Italy. Philosopher, moralist.

J. Robert Oppenheimer—20th-century America. Physicist, child prodigy, brilliant teacher. Headed the international team of scientists in construction of the first atomic bomb at Los Alamos, New Mexico. Director of the Institute for Advanced Studies at Princeton. Fought the further development of the H-bomb and the spread of nuclear warfare.

Orhot Tzaddikim—15th-century Germany. Anonymously written in Hebrew. The title means "The Ways of the Righteous." A very important Hebrew work concerning ethics and ethical behavior, it may have been purposely left anonymous on the advice of **Judah ben Samuel ha-Hasid**, who warned against descendants taking pride in the accomplishments of their ancestors. The first title of this work was probably not as shown here but instead *Sefer ha-Middot,* "The Book of Ethical Qualities."

Otzar Midrashim—*Otzar* is from the Hebrew meaning "treasury" and the work is a treasury of **Midrashim**, written in the 20th century by Judah David Eisenstein (19th- and 20th-century Poland and America), who after emigrating to America became a successful coat manufacturer. Eisenstein was also an encyclopedist, anthologist, and author. A number of his anthologies were called *Otzar,* including his own autobiography, translated literally as a *Treasury of My Memories.*

Cynthia Ozick—20th-century America. Writer, essayist, social philosopher.

Hayyim Palaggi—18th- and 19th-century Smyrna. Rabbi, scholar, writer, appointed *rav kolel,* "chief of the rabbis," of the surrounding communities, his son Abraham was also a rabbinic scholar. The distinguished family name was also written Palache.

Pappi [Papi]—3rd- and 4th-century Babylonia. *Amora.*

Alexander H. Pekelis—20th-century Russia. Philosopher, legal sociologist.

S. J. Perelman—20th-century America. Humorist, writer, screenwriter, essayist.

Isaac Leibush Peretz—19th- and 20th-century Poland. Hebrew and Yiddish poet, novelist, dramatist, short story writer, and critic. Considered one of the central figures in modern Yiddish literature. His work, which helped bring the form of the modern short story into the Yiddish and Hebrew, is known for its caring and sensitive tones for the human condition and particularly toward those who were put upon by others. He caught on paper a period and a people with great art and gave his readers a view that otherwise might have been lost forever.

pesikta—a homiletic Midrash on a particular section of religious literature, the word *pesikta* itself means "the section" or "the portion."

Pesikta Buber—See *pesikta* and **Tanhuma Buber**.

Pesikta Kahana—Of the homiletic Midrashim, this is thought to be among the oldest. Using the language, rabbinic names, and place-names, the work is now determined to be from Israel and probably from the 5th century.

This *pesikta* contains teachings on sections of readings for particular Sabbaths and the festivals.

Pesikta Rabbati—This *pesikta* is a Midrash written during the medieval period. It is a compilation of lectures and moral teachings on the yearly festivals.

Philo—1st-century B.C.E.–1st-century C.E. Egypt. Jewish philosopher from the most aristocratic Jewish family in Alexandria, his work is basically Stoicism with Platonic inclinations. Philo felt that although man comes to know God usually in two manners, through fear and through love, fear is the lesser of the two and often wrong. As a Stoic he felt fear was something for man to rise above in life. A great deal of Philo's writings have been preserved in the original Greek by the Christian Church. Full name Philo Judaeus.

Phineas ben Yair—2nd-century Israel. *Tanna*.

Arthur Wing Pinero—19th- and 20th-century England. Playwright.

Leo Pinsker—19th-century Russia. Physician.

Pirke Avot—One of the briefest tractates of the Talmud, in subject a collection of ethical maxims. The name means "Ethics of the Fathers."

Pirke de Rabbi Eliezer—8th-century Israel. Anecdotes using stories from the Bible as their foundation.

Belva Plain—20th-century America. Writer.

Chaim Potok—20th-century America. Rabbi, author, scholar.

Aaron Leib Premislaner—19th-century Eastern Europe. Hasidic rabbi, known as the Premislaner Rebbe.

Marcel Proust—19th- and 20th-century France. Novelist, philosopher.

Pseudo-Phocylides—Circa 100 B.C.E. Israel. A poem of moral aphorisms and adages teaching a moral code for all rather than the teachings of a particular religion, although the Jewish sense can be seen. Written by a Hellenized Jew. Initially attributed to the 6th-century poet Phocylides, the work is clearly not his and hence the name.

Rabban Gamaliel—3rd-century Israel. *Tanna*. A member of the last generation of *tannaim*. Also known as Gamaliel III; was the son of Rabbi Judah ha-Nasi.

Rabbi—Hebrew for "my teacher."

Isidor Isaac Rabi—20th-century Austria-Hungary and America. Physicist, Nobel Prize winner. Opposed military control of atomic energy development. Chairman of the general advisory committee of the Atomic Energy Commission, member of the board of governors of the Weizmann Institute in Israel.

Rabina ben Huna—3rd- and 4th-century Babylonia. Rabbi, sage, *amora*.

Solomon ha-Kohen Rabinowich of Radamsko—19th-century Poland. Hasidic rabbi, philosopher, considered a true **tzaddik**, the last of the Hasidic rabbis of Radomsk. He was murdered in the Warsaw Ghetto.

Zadok ha-Cohen Rabinowitz—19th-century Poland. Hasidic rabbi.

Gilda Radner—20th-century America. Comedian, entertainer.

Rambam—See **Maimonides**.

Ramban—See **Nachmanides**.

Ram Dass—20th-century America. Professor of psychology at Harvard University, writer, philosopher, humanitarian. Given name Richard Alpert.

S. J. Rappaport—19th- and 20th-century Russia. Yiddish writer, author of *The Dybbuk,* named for a haunting spirit in Yiddish folklore. Given name Solomon Ansky (Anski).

Rashbam—See **Samuel ben Meir**.

Rashi—11th- and 12th-century France. Born Solomon ben Isaac. Rabbi, writer, philosopher, Talmudist. Often considered the foremost commentator on the Bible and Talmud, meticulously analyzing the language of the text, his own language is concise and direct. The height of his work is his commentary on the Babylonian Talmud. He experienced the devastating massacres of Jews by the First Crusade. The name Rashi is drawn from the fuller name Rabbi Shlomo Yitzhaqi. An intellectual giant and remarkable human being.

Phillip Max Raskin—19th- and 20th-century America. Poet.

Rav—The term, the Babylonian form of "rabbi," means "Master." Rav in particular was an important 3rd-century Babylonian *amora* and one of the founders of the academy at Sura. His name was Abba ben Aivu, but he was in addition referred to as Abba Arikha ("Abba the Tall").

Theodor Reik—19th- and 20th-century Austria and America. Psychoanalyst and writer. In 1946 he was elected president of the National Association of Psychoanalytic Psychology.

Solomon Reinach—19th- and 20th-century France. Archeologist.

Simon H. Rifkind—20th-century America. Attorney and judge.

Riziner Rebbe—18th- and 19th-century Poland. Hasidic rabbi.

Julius Rosenwald—19th- and 20th-century America. Merchant and philanthropist. His parents were German immigrants. He worked in his uncle's men's clothing store, opened his own store, began manufacturing clothing, bought a quarter interest in a new mail-order company called Sears, Roebuck and Company, and became president and then chairman. Active in the American Jewish Committee; a major donor to the University of Chicago; served as adviser to the Council of National Defense during World War I.

Franz Rosenzweig—20th-century Germany. Philosopher, theologian, writer.

Henry Roth—20th-century Austria and America. Writer. Roth's novel *Call It Sleep,* 1934, concerns immigrant life on the Lower East Side of New York in the early 20th century. The work received high praise for the realism presented through the eyes of a wise child.

Leon Roth—20th-century England. Professor of philosophy, writer.

Philip Roth—20th-century America. Novelist and short-story writer.

Meir ben Baruch Rothenburg—13th-century Germany. Tosafist, rabbi, poet, scholar.

Ephraim Rottenberg—20th-century Hungary and America. Rabbi, scholar, philosopher.

Richard L. Rubenstein—20th-century America. Rabbi, writer, philosopher.

Solomon Rubin—19th- and 20th-century Galicia. Hebrew writer.

Arthur Rubinstein—19th- and 20th-century Poland and America. An internationally recognized piano virtuoso.

Arthur Ruppin—19th- and 20th-century Germany and Israel. Sociologist, Zionist, writer.

Sa'adia ben Joseph—10th-century Babylonia. Rabbi. Known as Sa'adia Gaon (see **Gaon**).

Abram Leon Sachar—20th-century America. Scholar, historian, educator, and writer. President of Brandeis University.

Abraham Jacob of Sadgora—19th-century Eastern Europe. Hasidic rabbi, talented teacher, and philosopher. Sadgora moved between Ukrainian, Polish, and Rumanian control but remained an important, and sometime competitive, center for Hasidic life until after WWII, when the Hasidic movement in Sadgora moved to Israel.

Mort Sahl—20th-century America. Humorist, social critic, entertainer.

Israel Salanter—See **Israel Salanter Lipkin**.

Jonas Salk—20th-century America. Epidemiologist. Helped in the development of a flu vaccine. Salk found the cure for polio and is honored for his impact on lives around the world. Founded the Salk Institute for Biological Studies in La Jolla, California.

Samuel ben Meir—11th- and 12th-century France. Sage, philosopher, commentator on the Bible and Talmud. Son of Meir ben Meir, one of the first tosafists and a major student, and son-in-law, of **Rashi**. Samuel learned from his father but mostly from his grandfather Rashi; sometimes Rashi would consider his grandson's answer to the extent that he would correct his own commentary on the issue. Samuel's commentary always worked with the literal meaning and his language is precise and clear. Considered perhaps the most important of the tosafists, often referred to as the Rashbam.

Herbert Louis Samuel—19th- and 20th-century England. Statesman, philosopher, Zionist. High commissioner of Palestine. Knighted and made a viscount.

Maurice Samuel—20th-century America. Author, wit.

Moritz Gottlieb Saphir—19th-century Hungary, Germany, and Austria. German satirist, writer, social wit.

David Sarnoff—19th- and 20th-century Russia and America. Pioneer in the electronics and media industry; business executive. Taught himself to use the telegraph and was on duty when the call came in from the sinking *Titanic*. Rose to become president of RCA, the Radio Corporation of America; founded NBC, the National Broadcasting Company, as a subsidary of RCA. Built RCA into the world's largest electronics company. A brigadier general in the U.S. Army Reserve.

Moshe Leib Sassover—18th- and 19th-century Eastern Europe. Hasidic rabbi, a sage of love and caring. Also known as the Sassover Rebbe.

Anatoly B. Scharansky—20th-century USSR and Israel. Zionist activist, writer, and philosopher. A computer technician, he came to consciousness as a Jew and sought to leave for Israel, but was tried on false charges of "treason" and "espionage." Sentenced and jailed, he refused to submit, and became a celebrated "prisoner of conscience" and international figure symbolizing the brutality of the Soviet Union. He was finally allowed to leave and reunite with his wife, Avital, and family in Israel. Active in Israel as a voice for other Soviet immigrants, those still imprisoned in what was the Soviet Union, and "prisoners of conscience" around the world.

Solomon Schechter—19th- and 20th-century Rumania, England, and America. Rabbi, rabbinic scholar, philosopher.

Schmelke of Nikolsburg—18th-century Eastern Europe. Hasidic rabbi, sometimes referred to as "the Nikolsburger."

Arthur Schnitzler—19th- and 20th-century Austria. Philosopher, novelist, playwright.

Arnold Schoenberg—19th- and 20th-century Austria and America. Composer. Influenced by Brahms and Wagner. Appointed director of master's school of musical composition at the Prussian Academy of Arts in Berlin, he was later removed from this position due to the Nazi "race" laws. He emigrated to America and taught at the University of Southern California and at the University of California at Los Angeles. Schoenberg created a new method of composition with twelve tones, each equal in relation to the others. His work progressed over time, as did his accolades and the questions of his critics. Considered one of the major composers of the 20th century.

Edith Cohen Schwartz—20th-century Poland and America. Social philosopher.

Sefer Hasidim—See **Judah ben Samuel ha-Hasid**.

Joseph Seligman—19th-century Bavaria and America. International banker. Began as a peddler, then was joined by brothers in running a store in Watertown, New York. He became friends with Ulysses S. Grant. Later made money on the California gold rush with the only brick building in San Francisco; ran a monopoly in clothing; sold U.S. government bonds in Europe at the outbreak of the Civil War, and became active in railroad financing. Headed the Panama Canal financing company, which developed into the Tri-Continental Corporation, among the largest investment trusts in America. Seligman was active in New York German-Jewish life, and a significant philanthropist to Jewish and non-Jewish charities.

Maurice Sendak—20th-century America. A highly honored and widely popular writer and illustrator of children's books.

Hannah Senesh—20th-century Hungary and Israel. Writer, poet. Made a heroic parachute return to Europe during World War II to save imperiled Jewish lives, but was murdered by the Germans.

Ben Shahn—20th-century America. Illustrator, painter, writer.

Shammai—1st century B.C.E. Israel. Rabbi, historic sage. His students and followers are referred to as "the House (or School) of Shammai." He stringently interpreted the law, often, though not always, in a contradictory spirit to **Hillel**.

Phineas (Pinhas) Shapiro—See **Koretser Rabbi**.

Shemaiah—See **Shammai**.

Joel ben Abraham Shemaria[h]—18th-century Lithuania. Rabbi, scholar. Excerpts from his last will and testament, a small portion of which can be found in the text, were later published by a friend who reminded the reader: ". . . so small in size, so great in worth." Sometimes referred to as Rabbi Joel.

Shoher Tob—The name given to a **Midrash** on the Psalms, also called **Agadat** and Tehillim (Psalms).

Shulhan Aruk—See **Joseph Caro**.

Sifra—from the Aramaic and Hebrew words for "book," *sifrah* and *sefer*, respectively. A halakic Midrash to the Book of Leviticus interpreting the work by chapter and verse, probably put together in Israel around the end of the 4th century C.E.

Sifrei—from the Aramaic and Hebrew words for "books," *sifray* and *saferim,* respectively. A halakic Midrash to the Book of Numbers and the Book of Leviticus. Here, as with *sifra,* the work explains and comments on Numbers and Leviticus by chapter and verse. This work is also thought to have been compiled not prior to the conclusion of the 4th century C.E.

Simone Signoret—20th-century France. Film actress.

Beverly Sills—20th-century America. Renowned opera singer, arts administrator.

Abba Hillel Silver—19th- and 20th-century Lithuania and America. Rabbi, author, Zionist leader, and scholar. Appreciated **Ahad Ha-Am,** but admired **Herzl.** At twenty-four he became rabbi at the prestigious reform Congregation Tifereth Israel in Cleveland, Ohio, where he remained his entire life. He was a powerful national speaker, perhaps the most highly regarded individual in Cleveland, a voice for the labor movement, liberal agendas, and the Zionist movement. One of the few national Jewish figures who was in fact aligned with the Republican party, he took the cause for the state of Israel to both the Democratic and Republican parties and got their backing. He was president of the Central Conference of American Rabbis, president of the Zionist Organization of America; at the latter's inception "made the argument" for the state of Israel before the United Nations.

Simeon ben Azzai—See **Ben Azzai.**

Simeon ben Eleazar—2nd- and 3rd-century Israel. *Tanna.*

Simeon ben Gamaliel—See **Simeon the Just.**

Simeon ben Lakish—3rd-century Palestine. *Amora,* Torah sage.

Simeon ben Yohai—2nd-century Israel. *Tanna,* student of **Rabbi Akiba.** When Akiba was arrested, Simeon continued to learn from him and take care of him. One of the five students who remained alive after Bar Kochba's revolt against the Romans, he is, with the four others, credited in the Talmud with keeping the Torah alive during this period. His continued opposition to the Romans brought him a death sentence, but Simeon and his son, Eleazar, fled for their lives and hid in a cave, where they continued their studies, for twelve years. He later went as a representative of the Sanhedrin, academy of sages, to Rome in the hope of alleviating some Roman legislation prohibiting Jews from following their commandments. A great many of the **Mishna** are attributed to Simeon ben Yohai, among them the Mishna of **Judah ha-Nasi.** In the mystical tradition it is Simeon ben Yohai who is considered the author of the **Zohar**, probably premised on his long seclusion and ascetic conditions. Also known as Simeon Bar Yohai.

Simeon the Just—3rd-century B.C.E. Israel. Rabbi, sage. High priest during the days of Alexander the Great. Earned his epithet "the Just" not only by his devotion to the Divine but also by his depth of caring for his people. Ben Sira characterized Simeon's emerging from the Second Temple as "the morning star radiating between the clouds."

Ernst Simon—20th-century Germany and Israel. Scholar, philosopher, writer.

Isaac Bashevis Singer—20th-century Poland and America. Yiddish novelist, winner of the Nobel Prize, his stories are filled not only with accurate portrayals of the passing "Old World" but also penetrating studies of people struggling and straining in the present.

Nahum Sokolow—19th- and 20th-century Poland. Hebrew editor and writer. A central figure in early modern Hebrew journalism, he also wrote in German, Polish, and Yiddish, and was the head of the Jewish delegation to the Paris Peace Conference at the conclusion of World War I. Also president of the World Zionist Organization.

Solomon ben Meir ha-Levi of Karlin—18th-century Russia. Hasidic rabbi. Sometimes known as Solomon of Karlin.

Solomon (ben Yehuda) ibn Gabirol—11th-century Spain. Renowned poet, philosopher, scholar of biblical Hebrew, ethicist.

Solomon ibn Verga—15th- and 16th-century Spain. Historian, physician.

Ahron [Aaron] Soloveichik—20th-century Russia and America. Orthodox rabbi, talmudist, scholar. Brother of **Joseph B. Soloveitchik**. A central and leading figure in Orthodox Judaism, *rosh yeshiva,* and dean of academics at Hebrew Theological College, Skokie, Illinois. He saw that the only path toward peace and uplifting of the human spirit depended on humankind's willingness to follow **halakah**.

Joseph Baer Soloveichik—19th-century Russia. Talmudist, *rosh yeshiva,* head of a center of higher learning. Devoted to the poor and the needs of the communities he served, he cared deeply even for those with whom he argued concerning Jewish law. Unable to bend his spirit to community committees, he gave up the rabbinate in the late 19th century and moved to Warsaw where he lived privately in great poverty, all the while continuing his studies. He later accepted an invitation to once again serve as a rabbi, this time in Brest-Litovsk (Brisk), under the condition that his decisions would be followed. Given name Joseph Baer Soloveichik (of Volozhin). A prime figure in the Soloveichik rabbinic dynasty.

Joseph B. Soloveitchik—20th-century Poland, Germany, Belorussia, Gemany.

Talmudist, rabbi, sage. Referred to reverentially as "the Rav." Ph.D. in philosophy from the University of Berlin. His early focus was entirely on Jewish learning. A brilliant orator in several languages, the Rav influenced thousands of scholars and students and was held by many in the United States and Canada to be the most important figure in contemporary Orthodoxy. *Halakhic Man* is generally considered his most important work.

Susan Sontag—20th-century America. Philosopher, critic, writer.

Baruch Spinoza—17th-century Holland. Philosopher. A major influence on philosophical thought in the following centuries, he was at one point excommunicated by the Jewish religious community for his ideas. Spinoza, who made a living as a lens grinder, was forced to wander and, though invited into European court and intellectual communities, lived an almost ascetic life of the mind. Spinoza remains a point of irritation for some theologians, but a source of pride and reflection for almost all serious thinkers. He has been characterized in contradiction by other philosophers as both a "God-intoxicated man" and a "systematic atheist."

Gertrude Stein—19th- and 20th-century America and France. Poet, surrealist, critic, innovator of poetic language, and essayist. A member of the artistic circle in Paris that included Hemingway, Picasso, and Matisse.

Leo Stein—19th- and 20th-century America. Writer.

Joshua Steinberg—19th- and 20th-century Poland. Thinker, Hebrew author.

Milton Steinberg—20th-century America. Rabbi, writer, thinker.

Gloria Steinem—20th-century America. Writer, social philosopher, feminist.

Adin Steinsaltz—20th-century Israel. Rabbi, teacher, talmudic scholar, scientist, mystic, and social critic. He has served as a resident scholar at both Yale and the Institute for Advanced Studies at Princeton. Won the Israel Prize. *Time* magazine has referred to him as "a once-in-a-millennium scholar."

Heymann [Herman] Steinthal—19th-century Germany. Psychologist, philosopher.

Wilhelm Stekel—19th- and 20th-century Austria. Psychiatrist.

Gil Stern—20th-century America. Social commentator.

Judith Stern—20th-century America. Social commentator.

Benjamin Stolberg—20th-century America. Writer.

Susan Strasberg—20th-century America. Actress, writer.

Barbra Streisand—20th-century America. Singer, actress, motion picture director and producer. Considered by many to be the best voice of her generation. Has enjoyed huge success over several decades.

Herbert Bayard Swope—19th- and 20th-century America. Journalist, writer.

Nahman Syrkin—19th- and 20th-century Russia and America. Zionist, socialist, Yiddish writer.

Talmud—Collection of rabbinic wisdom divided into six major "orders" and comprised of the **Mishna** and the **Gemara**. The word *talmud* actually means "the teaching" or "the learning." There are two different Talmuds: One is the Palestinian, or Jerusalem, Talmud and is dated at 400 C.E. The other, the more authoritative, is the Babylonian, which is dated at around 500 C.E. In this collection, unless Jerusalem Talmud is specifically noted, "Talmud" refers to the Babylonian Talmud.

Tanhuma, Tanhuma Buber—A collection of homilies on the Pentateuch drawn from rabbis over time. The edition edited in the 19th century by Solomon Buber, a sage in his own right, bears his name.

tanna (plural, *tannaim*)—A name for those teachers and scholars whose thoughts and decisions make up the **Mishna**.

Tarfon—1st-century Israel. *Tanna,* rabbi.

Bob Toben—20th-century America. Artist, social philosopher.

Michael (Mike) Todd—20th-century America. Major theatrical and film producer.

Torah—Means "The Law." Strictly applied, the term refers to the Pentateuch (The Five Books of Moses)—Genesis, Exodus, Leviticus, Numbers, and Deuteronomy—given to Moses and the children of Israel at Mt. Sinai. Broadly applied, the term at various times may be meant to include the Jewish Bible, Law, and Learning.

Tosafot—12th- to 14th-century France and Germany. A compilation of medieval commentaries and interpretation on the Talmud and Rashi (of whom many of those who wrote this material, Tosafists, were students and disciples) which runs parallel to the **Mishna** in context and is included in most Talmuds.

Tosefta—3rd- and 4th-century. Additional commentary to the **Mishna**.

Lionel Trilling—20th-century America. Writer, critic, philosopher, teacher. Taught at Columbia University, took the work of Matthew Arnold into sharper focus using psychology as a critic's tool. Highly regarded among influential intellectuals. Brought new awareness to authors whose work had been passed over and in whom public interest lay dormant.

Leon Trotsky—19th- and 20th-century Russia. Philosopher, Russian revolutionary, Communist leader, organizer of the Red Army. After the death of Lenin he formed an opposition party to the ruling Soviets. Assassinated in Mexico City on the orders of Stalin. Given name Lev Davidovich Bronstein.

Barbara Tuchman—20th-century America. Journalist, writer, historian. Winner of the Pulitzer Prize for her book *The Guns of August.*

tzaddik—Person of righteousness, deep faith, and piety.

Tzartkover Rebbe—19th- and 20th-century Eastern Europe. Hasidic rabbi who would fall into long periods when he would refuse to preach.

Tzupenester Rebbe—19th-century Eastern Europe. Hasidic rabbi.

Samuel Uceda—16th-century Israel. Preacher, commentator.

Samuel Ullman—19th- and 20th-century America. Civic leader in Alabama.

Louis Untermeyer—19th- and 20th-century America. Poet.

Abigail Van Buren—20th-century America. Writer, nationally syndicated advice columnist. Sister of **Ann Landers**. Born Pauline Friedman.

Barbara Walters—20th-century America. Television news figure, celebrity interviewer.

James Paul Warburg—19th- and 20th-century America. Businessman, banker.

Simone Weil—20th-century France. Writer, mystic.

Len Wein—20th-century America. Social commentator.

Chaim Weizmann—19th- and 20th-century England and Israel. Chemist of renown, Zionist, first president of the modern state of Israel.

Franz Werfel—19th- and 20th-century Austria, France, and America. Poet, playwright, novelist. Friend of **Franz Kafka**. Forced to flee from Germany in WWII. He reexamined his position as a Jew as he grew older and wrote: "Religion is the unending dialogue between humanity and God. Art is humanity's soliloquy."

Max Wiener—19th- and 20th-century Germany and America. Philosopher, teacher.

Elie Wiesel—20th-century Rumania and America. Writer, philosopher, Holocaust survivor. A continuing witness to the Holocaust through his literature and force of personality. Winner of the Nobel Peace Prize.

Walter Winchell—20th-century America. Print and broadcast journalist, columnist, social commentator, major 20th-century radio and print personality.

Louis Wirth—19th- and 20th-century America. Scholar, sociologist.

Wisdom of Ben Sira—2nd-century B.C.E. Israel. Comprised of teachings, ethical advice, and aphorisms. Also known as Ecclesiasticus. Attributed to Simeon ben Jesus ben Sira.

Isaac Mayer Wise—19th-century America. Rabbi, scholar. Founder and organizer of the American Reform Jewish Movement.

Stephen Samuel Wise—19th- and 20th-century Hungary and America. Rabbi, Zionist. With Louis D. Brandeis and Felix Frankfurter he helped structure the Balfour Declaration. Co-founder of the National Association for the Advancement of Colored People (NAACP). An early, but unheeded, warning voice on the plague of Nazism. He led support for the strike against the U.S. Steel Corporation in 1919. President of the American and World Jewish Congress, he left the important Congregation Emanuel in New York because they would not allow him a "free pulpit" to express his views without "board approval." Established the Free Synagogue with free pulpit and free pews without fixed dues. Helped found the Jewish Institute of Religion, which later merged with Hebrew Union College.

Shlomo Wolbe—20th-century Israel. Hasidic rabbi, scholar, ethicist.

Harry Austryn Wolfson—19th- and 20th-century America. Philosopher.

Herman Wouk—20th-century America. Novelist and playwright. Son of immigrants from Russia. He wrote for radio, then served in the navy during World War II as a line officer in the Pacific. Drawing on this experience wrote *The Caine Mutiny,* a Broadway play (later a film) that won the Pulitzer Prize. A learned Orthodox layman, he taught English at Yeshiva University. Much of his work speaks to or about the Jewish experience through Wouk's capacity as a gifted writer and concerned Jew.

Joseph Yaabetz—15th- and 16th-century Spain. Philosopher, theologian.

Yalkut Shimoni—13th-century Germany. Many times referred to as "the Yalkut" of Simeon of Frankfort, it is the most widely known and complete midrashic anthology encompassing the entire Bible. Scholars now attribute this work to Simeon ha-Darshan of whom little is known other than a reference to him as "chief of the preachers of Frankfurt." *Ha-Darshan* means "the preacher."

Yerachmiel of Parsischa—18th- and 19th-century Eastern Europe. Hasidic rabbi, known as the "Yud."

Yeshebab the Scribe—1st- and 2nd-century Israel. *Tanna,* scribe, martyr. A venerated colleague of **Rabbi Akiva** and pupil of Rabbi **Joshua ben Hanania,** he was executed at age ninety. Yeshebab (Yeshevav) was thought to have been in hiding with four other rabbis when he was captured during the rule of Hadrian. According to a Midrash, Yeshebab's last words to his followers were: "Support one another, love peace, love justice, perhaps there may be hope."

Yiddish—The common language of East European Jews, which finds much of its foundation in 16th-century Middle High German. A number of words have been adapted from the Slavic languages and English, and approximately a quarter of its vocabulary comes from Hebrew. Written Yiddish uses the Hebrew script. The source of the word *Yiddish* is the German "judisch," which means "Jewish."

Levi Yitzhok—See **Levi Isaac ben Meir of Berdichev.**

Joseph Zabara—circa 12th- and 13th-century Barcelona. Poet, physician, satirical writer. The name of his work *Sefer Shaashuim* means the "The Book of Delight." It is written in a rhyming Hebrew prose. Full name was Joseph ben Me'ir ibn Zabura.

Shenor Zalman—18th- and 19th-century Lithuania. Hasid.

Israel Zangwill—19th- and 20th-century England. Author, playwright, social philosopher. Friend of **Herzl** and **Nordau**. One of his most familiar lines is: "A chosen people is a choosing people." A major intellectual figure during his era.

Zohar—13th-century Spain. A text generally attributed to Moses de Leon. Considered the most important mystical work in the collection of Kabbalistic literature. The name means "splendor" or "radiance."

Meshullam Zusya—18th-century Ukraine. Hasidic rabbi.

TIME CHART OF JEWISH HISTORY AND SURROUNDING EVENTS, 2000 B.C.E.—MID-TWENTIETH CENTURY C.E.

B.C.E.

2000–1900	ISRAEL	Abraham
	EGYPT	The Middle Kingdom
1900–1800	ISRAEL	Isaac
	EGYPT	The Hyksos Kings
	BABYLON	The First Dynasty
1800–1700	ISRAEL	Jacob
	BABYLON	Hammurabi
	SYRIA	The Hittites
1700–1600	ISRAEL	Jacob's Family
	EGYPT	Joseph and the Children of Israel
1500–1400	EGYPT	Moses, the Exodus
1400–1300	ISRAEL	Joshua
1100–1000	ISRAEL	Samson, Samuel, Saul, David

	GREECE	Homer
1000–900	ISRAEL	Solomon; division of Israel
	ISRAEL	Northern Kingdom
	JUDAH	Southern Kingdom
900–800	ISRAEL	Prophets Elijah, Elisha
800–700	ISRAEL	Prophets Amos, Isaiah
		Northern Kingdom of Israel ends
600–500	ISRAEL	Destruction of First Temple by Nebuchadnezzar
		Death of the prophet Jeremiah
	BABYLON	Deportation to Babylon
	ISRAEL	Return from exile under Zerubbabel
	BABYLON	Large Jewish community remains in Babylon
	ISRAEL	Construction begins on Second Temple in Jerusalem
	CHINA	Confucius
	INDIA	Buddha
500–400	ISRAEL	Ezra
	PERSIA	Xerxes, Artaxerxes, Queen Esther
	GREECE	Socrates
400–300	ISRAEL	Alexander the Great, Simeon the Just
	GREECE	Alexander the Great, Plato, Aristotle

200–100	ISRAEL	Antiochus and Syrians forbid Judaism
		Sack of Jerusalem
		Revolt of the Maccabees
		The Temple rededicated
100–1 C.E.	ISRAEL	Hillel the Elder
		Pompey; Roman domination
	EGYPT	Cleopatra
		Large Jewish settlements
	ROME	Julius Caesar
		Augustus
		Jewish captives to Rome

C.E.

1–100 C.E.	ISRAEL	Jesus of Nazareth
		Rise of Christianity
		Destruction of the Second Temple
		Revolt against Rome
		Rabbi Johanan ben Zakkai
	EGYPT	Anti-Jewish riots; Philo
	ROME	Nero, Vespasian, Titus
	FRANCE	Jewish communities in Gaul
100–200	ISRAEL	Rabbi Akiba
		Bar-Kochba revolt; the Mishnah
		Rabbi Judah the Prince

	ROME	Hadrian
	S. RUSSIA	Jewish communities
	GERMANY	Jewish communities on Rhine
200–300	ISRAEL	The Jerusalem Talmud
		Rabbi Johanan
	BABYLON	Rav and Samuel
	ROME	Jews become Roman citizens
300–400	ISRAEL	Fixed calendar of Hillel II
	ROME	Constantine the Great
		Christianity becomes state religion
400–500	BABYLON	The Babylonian Talmud
	ROME	Fall of Western Roman Empire
	SPAIN	Visigoths
500–600	SPAIN	Catholicism becomes state religion
600–700	ARABIA	Mohammed
	ISRAEL	Arabs capture Jerusalem
	EGYPT	Arabs conquer Egypt
	SPAIN	Jewish religion forbidden
700–800	ROME	Holy Roman Empire
		Charlemagne
	SPAIN	Spain conquered by Arabs

1000–1100	ISRAEL	First Crusade
	SPAIN	Solomon ibn Gabirol
	GERMANY	Rhineland massacre of Jews
	FRANCE	Rashi
	ENGLAND	William the Conqueror
		Jewish settlement
1100–1200	ISRAEL	2nd and 3rd Crusades
		Saladin captures Jerusalem
	SPAIN	Judah Halevi
		Abraham ibn Ezra
		Maimonides leaves for Egypt
	GERMANY	2nd and 3rd Crusades
	ENGLAND	Massacre at York
		Richard the Lionheart
1200–1300	ISRAEL	Mongol invasion
	SPAIN	The Zohar, Ramban
	GERMANY	Rabbi Meir of Rothenburg
	FRANCE	Talmud burned
	ENGLAND	Expulsion of Jews
1300–1400	GERMANY	The Black Death
		Persecution of Jews

	FRANCE	Expulsion of Jews
	ENGLAND	Chaucer
1400–1500	ITALY	Law against the Talmud
		First Jewish printing presses
	SPAIN	Torquemada; expulsion of Jews
	PORTUGAL	Expulsion of Jews
	FRANCE	Jews expelled from Cologne
		Jews expelled from Lyons
	AMERICA	Columbus discovers America
1500–1600	ISRAEL	Kabbalists at Safed
		Isaac Luria, Joseph Caro: the Shulhan Aruk
	ITALY	Venice Ghetto
		1st edition of printed Talmud
		Talmud burned
		Papal states expel Jews
	GERMANY	Martin Luther, the Reformation
	FRANCE	Jews expelled from Marseilles
	ENGLAND	Shakespeare, Queen Elizabeth I
	HOLLAND	Marranos in Amsterdam
1600–1700	GERMANY	Thirty Years War
		Jews expelled from Hamburg

	ENGLAND	Oliver Cromwell
		Jewish resettlement
	POLAND	Chmielnik massacres
	HOLLAND	Spinoza
	TURKEY	False messiah Shabbatai Zvi
	S. AMERICA	Jews begin to settle
	N. AMERICA	Jews begin to settle
1700–1800	ISRAEL	Napoleon's campaign
	ITALY	Moses Hayyim Luzzatto
	GERMANY	Gluckel of Hameln
		Moses Mendelssohn
		Meyer Rothschild
	FRANCE	French Revolution
		Full citizenship for Jews
	ENGLAND	Industrial Revolution
	POLAND	Ba'al Shem Tov
		Hasidic movement
		Vilna Gaon
	N. AMERICA	The American Revolution
1800–1850	RUSSIA	Pale of Settlement
	GERMANY	Heinrich Heine

	ENGLAND	Jews fully emancipated
		Moses Montefiore, N. M. Rothschild
	POLAND	Polish revolutions
1851–1900	ISRAEL	Early Zionist settlements,
		Baron Rothschild, 1st Aliyah
	RUSSIA	Haskalah—the Enlightenment
		Pogroms, the May Laws
		Ahad Ha-Am, Bialik
	GERMANY	Karl Marx
		The German Empire
		Samson Raphael Hirsch
	FRANCE	Dreyfus Affair
	ENGLAND	Disraeli, Israel Zangwill
		Jew's College founded
	POLAND	The Bund
	N. AMERICA	Mass immigration from Russia
	SWITZERLAND	Theodor Herzl (1st Zionist Congress)
1900–1925	ISRAEL	Tel Aviv founded
		Arab riots
		Mandate to Great Britain
		Hebrew University opened

	RUSSIA	Kishinev pogrom
		Mass emigration
		Jews expelled from Kiev
		Russian Revolution
		Pogroms in Ukraine
	WORLD WAR I	Germany defeated
	FRANCE	Versailles Peace Treaty
	ENGLAND	Balfour Declaration
		Assumes Palestine Mandate
	POLAND	Strong anti-Jewish sentiment
	N. AMERICA	Jewish Theological Seminary
1926–1950	ISRAEL	Arab riots, Jewish Brigade
		Illegal immigration
		Modern state of Israel established 14 May 1948 / 5 Iyar 5708
		Chaim Weizmann, first president
		David Ben-Gurion, prime minister
		Ingathering of exiles
		Israel 59th U.N. member
		1 million Jews in Israel
	RUSSIA	Recognition of the state of Israel
		Imprisonment of Yiddish writers and anti-Jewish trials under Stalin

GERMANY	Rise of Hitler and Nazi movement
	The "Final Solution"
JAPAN	Attacks Pearl Harbor
ITALY	Mussolini
WORLD WAR II	Axis forces defeated
ENGLAND	Britain terminates Palestine Mandate
POLAND	Warsaw Ghetto Holocaust
N. AMERICA	The U.N. established
	U.N. decision on Palestine
	U.S. recognition of Israel

SELECTED BIBLIOGRAPHY OF BASIC TEXTS AND FURTHER SPIRITUAL READING

Bible & Bible Studies:

A. Ben-Isaiah, ed. *The Pentateuch & Rashi's Commentary*, 5 vols. New York: S.S. & R. Publishers, 1977.

Harvey J. Fields, *A Torah Commentary for Our Times*, 3 vols. New York: UAHC, 1993.

Louis Ginzberg, *Legends of the Bible*. Philadelphia: Jewish Publication Society, 1992.

J. Hertz, ed., *The Hertz Chumash*. New York: Soncino Press, 1960.

Raphael Hirsch, ed., *The Hirsch Chumash*. New York: Judaica Press, 1971.

Jewish Publication Society, *Tanakh, the Holy Scriptures*. Philadelphia: Jewish Publication Society, 1985.

Aryeh Kaplan, ed., *The Living Torah*. New York: Moznaim Press, 1981.

Koren and Fisch, eds., *The Jerusalem Bible*. New York: Feldheim Publishers, 1983.

Nehama Leibowitz, *Studies in the Weekly Sidra*, 7 Vols. New York: World Zionist Organization, 1993.

G. W. Plaut, ed., *The Torah: A Modern Commentary*. New York: UAHC, 1981.

Nahum M. Sarna, ed., *The JPS Torah Commentary*. 5 vols. Philadelphia: Jewish Publication Society, 1991.

Nosson Scherman, ed., *The Stone Edition of the Chumash*. New York: Mesorah Publishing Co., 1993.

Mishnah and Talmud:

Hayyim Nahman Bialik and Yehoshua Hana Ravnitsky, *The Book of Legends*. New York: Schocken Books, 1993.

Philip Blackman, ed., *The Mishnah,* 7 vols. New York: Judaica Press, 1964.

A. Cohen, *Everyman's Talmud*. New York: Schocken Books, 1975.

Herbert Danby, ed., *The Mishnah*. New York: Oxford University Press, 1958.

I. Epstein, ed., *The Soncino Talmud,* 18 Vols. New York: Soncino Press, 1960.

Hersh Goldwurm, ed., *Talmud Bavli: The Schottenstein Edition*. Selected Tractates (multivolume edition—incomplete). New York: Mesorah Publishing Co., 1989.

J. Hertz, *Pirke Aboth: Sayings of the Fathers*. West Orange, N.J.: Behrman House, 1945.

Adin Steinsaltz, *The Steinsaltz Talmud*. Reference Guide & Selected Tractates (multivolume edition—incomplete). New York: Random House, 1989.

Prayer Books:

Philip Birnbaum, *High Holiday Prayer Book—Rosh Hashana & Yom Kippur*. New York: Hebrew Publishing Co., 1960.

———. *Daily Prayer Book*. New York: Hebrew Publishing Co., 1949.

David De Sola Pool, *The Traditional Prayer Book for Sabbath & Festivals*. West Orange, N.J.: Behrman House, 1960.

Sidney Greenberg, and Jonathan D. Levine, eds., *Mahzor Hadash—Rosh Hashana & Yom Kippur*. Bridgeport: Media Judaica, 1977.

Jules Harlow, ed., *Mahzor for Rosh Hashana & Yom Kippur*. New York: Rabbinical Assembly, 1972.

———. ed., *Siddur Sim Shalom*. New York: Rabbinical Assembly, 1985.

J. Hertz, *Authorized Daily Prayer Book*. New York: Bloch Publishing Co., 1961.

Nosson Scherman, ed., *The Complete ArtScroll Siddur*. New York: Mesorah Publishing Co., 1985.

———. ed., *The Complete ArtScroll Machzor,* 5 vols.—Rosh Hashana, Yom Kippur, Succos, Pesach, Shavuos. New York: Mesorah Publishing Co., 1989.

Chaim Stern, ed., *Gates of Prayer*. New York: CCAR, 1975.

———. ed., *Gates of Repentance*. New York: CCAR, 1978.

———. ed., *On the Doorposts of Your House*. New York: CCAR, 1993.

Philosophy & Reference:

Philip Birnbaum, *Book of Jewish Concepts*. New York: Hebrew Publishing Co., 1975.

Ben Zion Bokser, *Abraham Isaac Kook*. New Jersey: Paulist Press, 1978.

Eugene Borowitz, *Liberal Judaism*. New York: UAHC, 1984.

Martin Buber, *Way of Man*. New York: Carol Publishing Group, 1990.

Hyman Goldin, ed., *Code of Jewish Law*. New York: Hebrew Publishing Co., 1963.

Abraham J. Heschel, *God in Search of Man*. New York: Farrar, Straus & Giroux, 1976.

Eliyahu Kitov, *The Book of Our Heritage*. New York: Philip Feldheim Publishers, 1978.

Samuel Levine, *You Take Jesus I'll Take God*. Los Angeles: Hamorah Press, 1980.

Gershom Scholem, *Kabbalah*. Jerusalem: Keter Publishing House, 1978.

J. B. Soloveitchik, *Halakhic Man*. Philadelphia: Jewish Publication Society, 1984.

Daniel B. Syme and Rifat Soncino, *Finding God*. New York: UAHC, 1993.

Joseph Telushkin, *Jewish Literacy*. New York: William Morrow & Co., 1991.

Isidore Twersky, *A Maimonides Reader*. West Orange, N.J.: Behrman House, 1973.

Trude Weis-Rosmarin, *Judaism and Christianity: The Differences*. New York: Jonathan David Co., 1965.

Geoffrey Wigoder, ed., *Encyclopaedia Judaica*. Jerusalem: Keter Publishing House, 1973.

————. ed., *New Standard Jewish Encyclopedia*. New York: Facts on File, 1992.

Life Cycle/Introduction to Judaism:

Anne Brener, *Mourning and Mitzvah*. Woodstock, Vt.: Jewish Lights, 1993.

Anita Diamant, *The New Jewish Wedding Book*. New York: Summit Books, 1985.

Hayim H. Donin, *To Be a Jew*. New York: Basic Books, 1972.

————. *To Pray as a Jew*. New York: Basic Books, 1980.

Samuel Dresner, *Jewish Dietary Laws*. New York: Rabbinical Assembly, 1983.

Karen L. Fox and Phyllis Z. Miller, *Seasons for Celebration*. New York: Putnam Publishing Group, 1992.

Philip Goodman, *Holiday Anthologies—Hannukah, Passover, Purim, Rosh Hashanah, Shavuot & Simchat Torah, Yom Kippur.* Philadelphia: Jewish Publication Society, 1974.

Blu Greenberg, *How to Run a Traditional Jewish Household.* New York: Simon & Schuster, 1993.

Irving Greenberg, *The Jewish Way.* New York: Summit Books, 1988.

Abraham J. Heschel, *The Sabbath.* New York: Farrar, Straus & Giroux, 1975.

Barry W. Holz, *Back to the Sources.* New York: Summit Books, 1984.

Morris Kertzer, *What Is a Jew?* New York: Collier Books, 1978.

Isaac Klein, *Guide to Jewish Religious Practice.* Hoboken, N.J.: KTAV Publishing House, 1979.

Peter Knobel, ed., *Gates of Seasons.* New York: CCAR, 1992.

Alfred J. Kolatch, *The Jewish Book of Why.* New York: Jonathan David Co., 1981.

Maurice Lamm, *Jewish Way in Death and Mourning.* New York: Jonathan David Co., 1972.

————. *Jewish Way in Love and Marriage.* New York: Jonathan David Co., 1992.

Dennis Prager, *Nine Questions People Ask About Judaism.* New York: Simon & Schuster, 1975.

Siegel and Strassfield, *The First Jewish Catalogue.* Philadelphia: Jewish Publication Society, 1973.

Milton Steinberg, *Basic Judaism.* New York: Harcourt Brace Jovanovich, 1982.

Michael Strassfeld, *The Jewish Holidays.* New York: HarperCollins, 1985.

Daniel B. Syme, *The Jewish Home.* New York: UAHC, 1988.

S. Wagachal, *A Practical Guide to Kashruth.* New York: Feldheim Publishers, 1991.

Ron Wolfson, *A Time to Mourn, a Time to Comfort.* New York and Los Angeles: Federation of Jewish Men's Clubs and University of Judaism, 1993.

Herman Wouk, *This Is My God.* New York: Simon & Schuster, 1986.

History:

H. H. Ben-Sasson, *A History of the Jewish People.* Cambridge: Harvard University Press, 1976.

Max Dimont, *Jews, God & History.* New York: Signet Books, 1964.

Arthur Hertzberg, ed., *The Zionist Idea.* New York: Macmillan, 1972.

Irving Howe, *World of Our Fathers*. New York: Schocken Books, 1989.

Paul Johnson, *A History of the Jews*. New York: HarperCollins, 1988.

Yigal Lossin, *Pillar of Fire*. Jerusalem: Keter Publishing House, 1982.

Paul Mendes-Flohr, *The Jew in the Modern World*. New York: Oxford University Press, 1980.

Dennis Prager and Joseph Telushkin, *Why the Jews?* New York: Simon & Schuster, 1985.

Howard M. Sachar, *A History of Israel, Vol. I*. New York: Alfred A. Knopf, 1979.

———. *A History of Israel, Vol. II*. New York: Oxford University Press, 1987.

———. *A History of the Jews in America*. New York: Vintage Books, 1992.

Robert M. Seltzer, *Jewish People, Jewish Thought*. New York: Macmillan, 1982.

Holocaust:

Michael Berenbaum, *The World Must Know*. Boston: Little, Brown & Co., 1993.

Lucy S. Dawidowicz, *The War Against the Jews*. New York: Bantam Books, 1986.

Yaffa Eliach, *Hasidic Tales of the Holocaust*. New York: Random House, 1988.

Anne Frank, *Diary of a Young Girl*. New York: Pocket Books, 1952.

Martin Gilbert, *Macmillan Atlas of the Holocaust*. New York: Da Capo, 1984.

Primo Levi, *Survival in Auschwitz*. New York: Collier Books, 1987.

Deborah Lipstadt, *Denying the Holocaust*. New York: The Free Press, 1993.

Art Spiegelman, *Maus*. New York: Pantheon Books, 1986.

———. *Maus II*. New York: Pantheon Books, 1992.

Hana Volavkova, *I Never Saw Another Butterfly*. New York: Pantheon Books, 1993.

Eli Wiesel, *Night*. New York: Bantam Books, 1982.

Leni Yahil, *The Holocaust*. New York: Oxford University Press, 1991.

Women's Studies:

Joyce Antler, *America & I*. Boston: Beacon Press, 1990.

Diana Bletter, *Invisible Thread: A Portrait of Jewish American Women*. Philadelphia: Jewish Publication Society, 1989.

Blu Greenberg, *On Women & Judaism: A View from Tradition*. Philadelphia, Jewish Publication Society, 1983.

Susannah Heschel, ed., *On Being a Jewish Feminist.* New York: Schocken Books, 1983.

Judith Plaskow, *Standing Again at Sinai.* New York: HarperSanFrancisco, 1990.

Letty C. Pogrebin, *Deborah, Golda & Me.* New York: Crown Publishing Group, 1991.

Sarah Shapiro, ed., *Our Lives: An Anthology of Jewish Women's Writings.* New York: Targum Press, 1991.

Ellen M. Umansky and Dianne Ashton, *Four Centuries of Jewish Women's Spirituality.* Boston: Beacon Press, 1992.

Child Care and Children's Literature:

Miriam Adahan, *Raising Children to Care.* New York: Feldheim Publishers, 1988.

Anita Diamant, *The New Jewish Baby Book.* Woodstock, Vt.: Jewish Lights, 1993.

Hayim H. Donin, *To Raise a Jewish Child.* New York: Basic Books, 1991.

Marc Gellman, *Does God Have a Big Toe?* New York: HarperCollins, 1993.

Melanie Greenberg, *Celebrations: Our Jewish Holidays.* Philadelphia: Jewish Publication Society, 1991.

Harold S. Kushner, *When Children Ask About God.* New York: Schocken Books, 1989.

Steven C. Reuben, *Raising Jewish Children in a Contemporary World.* Roseville: Prima Publishing, 1993.

Jeffrey K. Salkin, *Putting God on the Guest List: How to Reclaim the Spiritual Meaning of Your Child's Bar or Bat Mitzvah.* Woodstock, Vt.: Jewish Lights, 1993.

Sol Scharfstein, *A Reading and Prayer Primer.* Hoboken, N.J.: KTAV Publishing House, 1972.

Howard Schwartz, *The Diamond Tree: Jewish Tales from Around the World.* New York: HarperCollins, 1991.

Dennis Sheheen, *A Child's Picture Dictionary (English/Hebrew).* Tel Aviv: Adama Press, 1987.

Isaac B. Singer, *Stories for Children.* New York: Farrar, Straus & Giroux, 1962.

S. Weissman, *The Little Midrash Says,* 5 vols. New York: Bnei Yaakov Publications, 1986.

David J. Wolpe, *Teaching Your Children About God.* New York: Henry Holt and Co., 1993.

Literature & Poetry Anthologies:

Martin Buber, *Tales of the Hasidim*. New York: Schocken Press, 1987.

T. Carmi, ed., *The Penguin Book of Hebrew Verse*. New York: Penguin Books, 1981.

Irving Howe, ed., *The Penguin Book of Modern Yiddish Verse*. New York: Penguin Books, 1988.

Irving Howe and Eliezer Greenberg, eds., *A Treasury of Yiddish Stories*. New York: Penguin Books, 1990.

Peninnah Schram, *Jewish Stories One Generation Tells Another*. Northvale, N.J.: Jason Aronson, 1993.

Howard Schwartz, *Gabriel's Palace*. New York: Oxford University Press, 1993.

Ted Solotaroff and Nessa Rapoport, eds., *Writing Our Way Home*. New York: Schocken Books, 1992.

RARE JUDAICA BOOKSELLERS
IN NORTH AMERICA

Please note: This list does not purport to be a definitive list of Judaica book-sellers and is not meant to suggest that you won't find the books you may be looking for at another fine bookseller. This list's purpose is to serve as an ally in locating difficult-to-find Judaica in or near your community. All the books listed in the preceding bibliography were in print at time of publication.

New York:

J. Levine Company
5 West 30th Street
New York, NY 10001
212-695-6888

The Jewish Museum Bookstore
1109 Fifth Avenue
New York, NY 10028
212-860-1860

Westside Judaica
2404 Broadway
New York, NY 10024
212-362-7846

Boston:

Israel Book Shop, Inc.
410 Harvard Street
Brookline, MA 02146
617-566-7113

Pittsburgh:

Pinsker's
2028 Murray Ave.
Pittsburgh, PA 15217
412-421-3033

Los Angeles:

House of David
9020 W. Olympic Blvd.
Beverly Hills, CA 90212
310-276-9414

Northern California:

Bob and Bob
151 Forest Ave.
Palo Alto, CA 94301
415-329-9050

Washington, D.C., area:

Jewish Book Store of Greater
Washington
11250 Georgia Ave.
Wheaton, MD 20902
301-942-2237

Midwest:

Hamakor Judaica, Inc.
P.O.B. 48836
Niles, IL 60714
1-800-426-2567

Canada:

Negev Importing Company
3509 Bathurst Street
Toronto, Ontario M6A 2C5
Canada
416-781-9356

Sholom Books and Gifts
3712 Oak Street
Vancouver, British Columbia
V6H 2M3
Canada

INDEX

ABOUT THE AUTHOR

Noah benShea is an internationally bestselling author, poet, philosopher, and scholar. He has served on distinguished faculties, and his work has been included in publications of the Oxford University Press as well as the World Jewish Bible Society in Jerusalem. His timeless tales of Jacob the Baker are told and retold around the world.

In addition to his reflective life, he is currently an adviser to North American community and business leaders.

Born in Toronto, Noah benShea lives with his wife and two children in Santa Barbara, California, where he is working on a new book.